QUESTAR PUBLISHERS, INC.

SISTERS, OREGON

TODAY FOR ETERNITY

© 1991 by Darryl DelHousaye

cover design & illustration by Jerry Werner

PRINTED IN THE UNITED STATES OF AMERICA

International Standard Book Number: 0-945564-45-7

Scripture quotations are taken primarily from the *New American Standard Bible*,
© 1960, 1962, 1963, 1968, 1971, 1972, 1973 by the Lockman Foundation.
Additional Scripture quotations are from *The Holy Bible: New International Version*,
©1973, 1978, 1984 by the International Bible Society.

For information, write to:

QUESTAR PUBLISHERS, INC.
Post Office Box 1720
Sisters, Oregon 97759

The publisher believes so strongly in the value of these pages that we offer this Limited
Guarantee: If this devotional doesn't reinforce your spiritual strength, we'll refund your
purchase. (Any refund request should be accompanied by a sales receipt and must
include a written statement that the reader used the devotional daily for at least a two-
week period, and that the book did not fill the reader's devotional needs. Please send the
request to the address above.)

TODAY
FOR
ETERNITY

Darryl DelHousaye

A MAP FOR THE PURSUIT

Blessed are the poor in spirit
for theirs is the kingdom of heaven.
—Matthew 5:3

The Declaration of Independence tells us we have the right to life, liberty, and *the pursuit of happiness.* But where's the map for this pursuit? Where do we start?

The world goes after this thing called happiness without ever quite seeming to find it—though it's not because they aren't trying. (How many people do you know who are seeking a life of misery?)

In the opening verses of the Sermon on the Mount, the Lord turns the world's idea of happiness upside down. His message here is something most people just don't understand; yet in these words the map to the pursuit of happiness is right before our eyes.

You're never going to be happy unless you think right. You can't *do* right if you don't *think* right. So in this discourse—which is an ethic for living, a radical call to a distinctive righteousness—Jesus begins with our attitude. Why? Because the battle is not won in the arena of my actions. I can discipline my behavior yet still be a hypocrite. I can always do the things I do not feel nor think if I have good enough reason to do them. So my planned behavior tells *something* about me, but not much. Our reactions, however—our responses in life when we're bumped—that's the real battlefield. That's when you spill out what's really *in you.* And what is in you has everything to do with *the way you think*—your attitudes.

So I ask you: How *do* you think? What is *your* ethic for living, your mindset, your attitude? For here is the first step to being genuinely happy.

THE ONE ATTITUDE

BLESSED ARE...
the poor in spirit... those who mourn... the gentle...
those who hunger and thirst for righteousness...
the merciful... the pure in heart... the peacemakers...
those persecuted for the sake of righteousness.
—Matthew 5:3-10

"Happy New Year." We all want to be happy. And that's okay; there is nothing unspiritual about it. That's why our Lord addresses happiness in the Sermon on the Mount, right in the very core of all His teaching.

Jesus begins His longest recorded message by outlining eight character traits — the "Beatitudes" they're called, each phrase beginning, "Blessed are..." The Greek word translated "blessed" is *makarios*. It does not mean receiving a gift, or "getting" anything. The word speaks of a *happy condition*. "Oh, the happiness," Jesus was saying, "of those who are poor in spirit...of those who mourn...of the gentle and the merciful and the pure in heart!" For a person to be truly happy, Jesus says, these things will be true.

This is not a multiple choice test. It's not that you pick some and leave the ones you don't like. These are eight dimensions of *one* attitude — an entire, whole attitude that expresses the kind of kingdom people we are to be. It's to be our perception of what life is all about when we think about life.

Happiness is a byproduct. When we chase it, it eludes us. But when we find ourselves doing something else —learning and doing the will of God, living out His character, *being* what He calls and created us to be—happiness tends to smack us right in the face.

NOT OKAY

*And when He saw the multitudes, He went up on the mountain
...and opening His mouth He began to teach them...*
—Matthew 5:1-2

Popularity had fallen upon Jesus. There was a great temptation among the disciples at this time to think, *We picked a winner! We're on our way to being honored, we're going to be happy...* Jesus knew their hearts. He sat down, and began, "Blessed are the poor in spirit..."

Isn't this a strange formula for happiness? Poor in spirit? Mourning? Hungry and thirsty? Persecuted? Something seems wrong here. But then you read it, and think: *No, something's right here.* Compare Jesus Christ with Adolf Hitler. One said, "I am meek and lowly in heart"; the other said he would conquer the world. Which one found happiness?

What does *poor in spirit* mean? The Greek word speaks of abject poverty, possessing *nothing*, and able to produce nothing—left only to beg. This is the key to the entire kingdom ethic. Our Lord is saying this: "Oh, the happiness of those who are in abject poverty with respect to their spirit!"

This is not self-hate or personal deprecation. No, it is coming to grips with the truth of my spiritual condition: I am lost, and on my own can do nothing about relating with God, much less pleasing Him. On my own I am *not* okay! And if I'm not okay, I can never experience what happiness is all about.

As John Calvin wrote, the man poor in spirit "is reduced to nothing in himself—and relies on the mercy of God." How much are you *relying* on the mercy of God?

A KINGDOM STING

To this one I will look, to him who is humble and contrite of spirit.
—Isaiah 66:2

Being poor in spirit has absolutely nothing to do with material wealth—you could have millions of dollars and be perfectly poor in spirit. And it has nothing to do with being poor-spirited, in the sense of having no vitality or courage. Instead, it's a deep sense of need *within* one's spirit *for* one's spirit.

It is the deepest form of repentance, the essence of a repentant heart. It is what Isaiah wrote of: "For thus says the high and exalted One who lives forever, whose name is Holy: 'I dwell on a high and holy place, and also with the contrite *[the word means "crushed"]* and lowly of spirit…'" David says the same thing: "The Lord is near to the brokenhearted, and saves those who are crushed in spirit" (Psalm 34:18).

Do you hear what God is saying? "I am great, I am God—and those whom I notice are the ones who are crushed in abject poverty when it comes to their spirit." You cannot repent before God and you cannot *depend* on God unless you are poor in spirit…crushed …contrite in heart.

So how do I do it? Do I tell everybody I'm dirt, that I'm scum? No. The Word of God never calls you to lie. You have the worth of Jesus Christ; you are re- deemed with the blood of the Son. So you don't say you're nothing.

But you do admit you're nothing *without God.* It may sting for you to answer this…but are you living in absolute dependence on God's intervention in your life? To those who will do so, and who *think* this way, Jesus says, "Yours is the kingdom of heaven."

THE KEY TO COMFORT

Blessed are those who mourn,
for they shall be comforted.
—Matthew 5:4

You know you're poor in spirit when you find yourself mourning more often.

Again, Jesus is turning the world's concept of happiness upside down. He basically says, "How happy are the sad!" which doesn't make sense. But notice what He does *not* say: He doesn't say, "Blessed are those who *moan*." And He doesn't say the blessedness is *in* the mourning. No, *being comforted* is the reason for the happiness. The only way we can experience the comfort, however, is to know what it means to mourn.

Right now, think about anything that may be causing you sadness or grief: job pressures, family pressures, sickness, physical pain, a failure to meet your goals. And now, put them aside for a moment—for what Jesus is talking about in Matthew 5:4 is grief over something else, something many of us would not think of: grief over *sin*. It is Paul's grief when he cries out in Romans 7, "Wretched man that I am!" It is Job's brokenness when he finally answers God, "I repent in dust and ashes."

Nine different Greek words are used in the New Testament to express grief. Jesus uses the strongest of them all here in Matthew 5:4. It speaks of a deep, inner agony which cannot be hidden. People can see it in your eyes; they hear it in your cry.

Make the commitment today to learn about this grief, hard as it is. For Jesus says that in doing so you possess the key to true comfort—and true happiness.

DIRECTLY FROM GOD

...to comfort those who are in any affliction with the comfort with which we ourselves are comforted by God.
—2 Corinthians 1:4

Part of being happy is being able to offer something to someone else, and one of the greatest things to offer is effective, genuine comfort. But you have nothing to offer unless you know the comfort of God.

Genuine comfort does not come from optimism: "Smile, be happy." It does not come from positive thinking or possibility thinking. Genuine comfort comes directly from God, and—according to Jesus in Matthew 5—only from genuine mourning over sin. It's the comfort that comes directly from God when we honestly grieve over sin and all the pain it authors.

But how can I mourn over something that doesn't really grieve me that much? Sin at times feels good; how can I feel badly over it? *Am I supposed to fake it? Is that what God wants?* After all, the only time I really feel bad about sin is when I'm caught.

How can I be broken? How can I mourn?

Here's the answer: Only God can cause you to see sin for what it really is. Sin is evil to a holy God and His purity, and it's evil because of the misery it produces in the lives of everyone it touches. But only God can break your heart so you can really *see* that.

Here's the other side of the coin: Only *you* can ask God to cause you to see it (if you're interested enough to ask).

Do you grieve over your sin only after you're caught? Only after you suffer the consequences? Or have you learned to grieve over sin—both yours and others'—for no other reason than that it is sin?

HE WILL EXALT YOU

Be miserable and mourn and weep....
—James 4:9

Unwelcome though it is, sorrow is woven into the very fabric of all our lives. History, it is said, is the story of the tears of men. Sorrow is something we eventually *must* respond to, and if we don't know how, it can be devastating. It can produce anguish. It has ruined the lives of many.

On the other hand, it has *made* the lives of others, those who knew how to respond correctly.

When is sorrow destructive? When we reject the God of comfort—something we do very often. We want to be left alone in our pain, because it has turned into bitterness and anger. It separates us from the God of comfort, because we're angry at Him for permitting the pain. We feel we deserve better treatment.

And so our pain becomes destructive.

James shows us the right response: "Draw near to God," he writes, "and He will draw near to you." Then he tells us *how* to draw near: "Cleanse your hands, you sinners; purify your hearts...Be miserable and mourn and weep." This is the contrite spirit, the brokenness of heart that gets God's attention. Then He says to us, "When this is your thinking, I am closer than close."

James goes on: "Humble yourselves in the presence of the Lord, and *He will exalt You.*"

Yes, He will exalt you—for blessed are those who mourn! You *shall* be comforted. You *shall* experience the essence of happiness.

THE G-WORD

The sorrow that is according to the will of God produces
a repentance without regret, leading to salvation.
—2 Corinthians 7:10

Even my grieving over sin can be destructive if I
don't respond to it correctly. Paul speaks of a proper
sorrow over sin "that produces a repentance *without
regret*, leading to salvation." What's another word for
this regret (it starts with a "G") that's such a big word
in our society? *Guilt.* The right response to the sorrow
Jesus speaks of in Matthew 5:4 leads to salvation, not
guilt. Guilt, Paul says, leads to something else: "the
sorrow of the world produces *death*." Death is separation from God, and when I feel guilty, it can harden
my heart into bitterness toward the very God who
can comfort me. I get tired of feeling bad, tired of feeling condemned. Finally I find myself bitter against
the One who I think makes me feel that way (though
it's really myself, not God). I do not let sorrow do
what God wants it to do.

The mourning over sin that Jesus speaks of in
Matthew 5 produces *repentance* and *dependence*—not
guilt.

Compare Peter and Judas. Peter was filled with
sorrow and repentance; Judas was filled with sorrow
and guilt. One was changed and comforted; the other
was not. One was forgiven, and went on to fulfillment and fruitfulness; the other hung himself, and
was lost in hell.

What are you grieving over? Is it leading to regret
…guilt…bitterness…anger?

Stop getting angry with God over your sorrow. Instead, let it lead to repentance and dependence.

I WAS TOLD

Blessed are the gentle [the meek, the humble],
for they shall inherit the earth.
—*Matthew 5:5*

The formula Jesus uses here makes for real tension with what others have told us for a long, long time.

I was told that if you want something, you'd better go out and get it. I was told that the real, masculine man sees what he wants and grabs it. I was told: If you want to get on top, you'd better start climbing. I was told: You have rights, you live in America, you'd better protect your rights. I was told: Popularity is the key to everything; you'd better be wanted, you'd better accumulate enough things so that people want what you have, and then they'll treat you…like a god.

But I know I'm *not* a god. And maybe that's why it feels so empty and I'm still so miserable when I'm treated like a god after I've worked so hard for it.

Could it be that Jesus is *absolutely right?* That I'll be happy only when I stop grabbing? When I stop worrying that I'm going to miss out on something, in this life or the next? When I say…

God, I am poor in spirit, I depend on You for everything, I mourn over my sin; and therefore I'm concerned only about what's right in Your sight. I will use everything—my strength, my ability, my influence—to bring about whatever You wish. For I desire to be a gentle man, a gentle woman.

Is that *your* prayer?

If it is, go ahead—*tell* Him.

THE INHERITANCE NOW

Learn from Me, for I am gentle and humble in heart.
  —Matthew 11:29

Just how do the meek and the gentle inherit the earth? The word *inherit* in Matthew 5 means "to receive one's allotted portion." What is that portion?

There's a reference to the future here. Revelation 21 tells us that when Christ comes again, we shall reign with Him. Paul tells us, "The saints will judge the world" (1 Corinthians 6:2). But it also has something to do with inheriting the earth *now*.

Only once did Jesus use character qualities to directly describe Himself—when He says at the end of Matthew 11, "I am gentle and humble in heart." In this passage we find the key to what our inheritance is now.

"Come to Me," He says, "and I will give you rest." How? "Take My yoke upon you." And how do we do that? "Learn from Me." Learn what? "I am gentle and humble in heart." And what do we get? *"You shall find rest for your souls."* When Jesus applies our inheritance to life today, it comes out *rest*.

Happy people know how to rest—even when their spouse leaves them, or they lose their teenage daughter to a drunken driver, or everyone makes fun of them because they have a physical handicap. They still know how to rest in happiness.

You don't have to grab for yourself anymore. Because in following and living like Christ you're not going to miss out on anything important—now or later.

FEELING GOOD

Blessed are those who hunger and thirst for righteousness,
for they shall be satisfied.
—Matthew 5:6

I was taught that if I want to be happy, I have to be happy about *me;* that if I want to feel good, the only way is to feel good about *me*. So it was of utmost importance for me to come up with reasons to believe I was pretty good at something.

However, in Jesus' formula for happiness in the Beatitudes in Matthew 5, I don't see a whole lot of "I've got to feel good about me" stuff. According to Jesus, the key to my being happy apparently has nothing to do with contemplating my worth. My *worth* doesn't seem to be an issue with Him. In fact, the only time He talks about it directly in the Sermon on the Mount is when He says simply that I'm worth more than birds and sheep!

No, with Jesus, the issue is not how good I can feel about myself (so I can be happy), but how good I feel about *Someone else* who feels good about me—Someone else who has the perfect goodness I don't have.

"Oh, how happy," Jesus is saying, "are those who hunger and thirst for righteousness." Dr. Martyn Lloyd-Jones helps us understand the meaning of that verse by putting it negatively: "We are *not* to hunger and thirst after happiness... Put happiness in the place of righteousness, and you will never get it."

The most important thing in my life is not trying to feel good about me, but feeling good about the fact that *God* feels good about me. This is the knowledge that makes us want to do what is right in His sight.

GETTING AWAY WITH ANYTHING

The desire of the righteous is only good.
—Proverbs 11:23

The Sermon on the Mount is for kingdom people, those who understand that *Jesus is their Lord.*

How do you know if He's your Lord?

Jesus answers this Himself: "Why do you call Me, 'Lord, Lord,' *and do not do what I say?*"

Talk is talk; our walk is something else. Jesus is our Lord if we do what He says.

How important is it to you to *do what is right?* If you were alone in a place where no one knew you and you could get away with anything, what's the "anything" you would get away with?

The answer to that question has everything to do with what *you* are all about.

In the fourth Beatitude, Jesus says the most important thing in life is my passion to do what is right in the sight of God. But what if this is *not* how I feel? How do I develop an appetite for living out my God-given righteousness? This is how: You simply start choosing to *do* what is right in the sight of God; then you do it again; then you do it again. And you try to do it all the time, always building up your appetite for more righteousness.

Just get on with doing it, letting it become part of your nature. And the more you do it, the more you'll develop a passion to do it until finally it will be a consuming desire in your life. You'll hunger, you'll thirst for righteousness—to do everything God wants you to do, all the time. It will be as natural as breathing spiritual breath.

FROM THE HAND OF GOD

Blessed are the merciful, for they shall receive mercy.
—Matthew 5:7

Only those who are merciful qualify to receive mercy from the hand of God. "For judgment will be merciless to one who has shown no mercy; mercy triumphs over judgment" (James 2:13).

The issue here is not salvation. You don't earn salvation by being merciful. We are saved by God being merciful to us; and He has been merciful to us *so we can become merciful…*

Through Christ, God continues to show us His great mercy—His forgiveness and kindness: Jesus Christ is our advocate, and "He always lives to make intercession" for us (Hebrews 7:25). He continues to apply His sacrifice to forgive us, to lift off the blemish and restore the relationship, to cleanse us. He is our high priest "that we may receive mercy and may find grace to help in time of need" (4:15). This is the mercy that motivates us to show mercy to others. The greatest evidence of one who knows he has been forgiven, one who enjoys the kindness of God, is that he shows the same forgiveness and kindness to others.

That's the point of the prayer in Matthew 6:12—"Forgive us our debts, as we also have forgiven our debtors." When you receive mercy, you give mercy. And if you don't give it, it's because either you haven't received it…or you don't understand that you have. "He who is forgiven little," Jesus says, "loves little" (Luke 7:47).

How well do you understand what you've received from the hand of God?

THE PLEASURE PRINCIPLE

Be merciful, just as your Father is merciful.
—Luke 6:36

Mercy is hard to define because we don't see a lot of it around. The Pleasure Principle says that people seek naturally to avoid pain and to strive for pleasure. The standard for what is right or wrong is this: If it gives me pleasure, I'll do it; if it gives me pain, I won't (unless I'm convinced that ultimately it *will* give me pleasure). This kind of thinking has no tolerance for any true concept of mercy. The Pleasure Principle blocks mercy.

In the Bible, mercy proceeds from the ability to get inside another person, to see with his eyes, think with his mind, feel the things he is feeling. It's actually closer to the literal meaning of our word *sympathy,* which comes from Greek roots meaning "to suffer with" someone. But how can I learn to suffer with someone else if I can't get out of *me?* If I'm consumed with my pleasure and comfort, and resent every experience of pain...I will never have the capacity to suffer with another, or to comfort anyone.

If your goal in life is to never comfort another soul, then pursue pleasure, and stay bitter toward God about any suffering He brings your way. Never let suffering have its perfect work in your life (which is why God permits it).

But if you want to become more merciful—how do you do it? First of all, repent of the Pleasure Principle. Stop thinking that your goal in life is to get through it with the most pleasure possible.

UNMIXED, UNDIVIDED

Blessed are the pure in heart, for they shall see God.
—Matthew 5:8

This verse is often considered the watershed statement among all eight Beatitudes; the previous five flow to it, the next two will flow from it. After all, where else do you find the promise from Jesus Himself that someday some of us will have the opportunity to enter God's chambers and actually *see Him?*

The word here translated "pure" is *katharos,* a form of the word from which we get *catharsis*—to cleanse or purge yourself. The term originally was used to simply mean clean. Then it was used to describe grain which had been sifted and cleaned of all chaff. Then it was used to speak of an army purged of all discontented, cowardly, and unwilling soldiers. It was used of wine which was unmixed with water, and metal without a tinge of alloy. A pure heart is unmixed. A pure heart means a will, motives, intentions that are undivided.

A pure heart is not merely sincere. A person can be sincerely right or sincerely wrong. The issue is not how sincere you are, but, *What is your heart?* A pure heart is an unwavering will committed to obeying the Word of God. When it comes to following God, is your will undivided? Are the intentions and the motives within you unmixed?

"But I don't *feel* pure in heart," you say. Remind yourself to do what you believe, not what you feel. Remind yourself that the real you is your belief, not your emotions.

THE BOND OF PEACE

Blessed are the peacemakers,
for they shall be called sons of God.
—*Matthew 5:9*

This matter of "peace" between you and me—what's going on between us—is important to God. God created and designed life to be relational. To cut yourself off or to be cut off from others is to be cut off from life itself. Being alone takes you to misery.

We sometimes wonder why we get so miserable even though we have so much. The Bible talks about being blessed and happy..."but I don't always feel blessed, and I don't always feel happy." This verse hints why.

After Jesus' resurrection, the first words out of His mouth were these: "Peace be with you..." Paul says we're to be diligent to preserve "the bond of peace" between us (Ephesians 4:3). So why do we struggle so much with preserving this peace?

Some of us just don't know how to do it. Others don't realize how important it is, not only to us but to the Lord. And some of us have tried, and then been burned by the repercussions that followed our attempts. Peacemaking can be risky business.

Our efforts at resolving conflicts come down to this: *Why am I doing it?* Is it to make or keep a friend? Or to make a disciple of Jesus Christ?

When the conflict is there, you aren't helping your brother or sister at all by leaving it alone.

The blessing is on the peacemaker, not the peace-lover. The peace-lover runs from conflict and confrontations. The peacemaker meets it and resolves it, as much as he's able to do so.

HIS MOST VIOLATED WORDS

If your brother sins against you,
go and show him his fault, just between the two of you.
—Matthew 18:15

"Just between the two of you"—literally, "between you and him alone." It's no one else's business!

These are the most violated words of Jesus Christ, among those who call Him Lord. Why do we so often "go public" first when our brother sins against us?

Is it because we are hurt, so we call in the troops to feel sorry for us? (If so, then let's allow God—"the Father of mercies and God of all comfort"—to comfort us instead.)

Is it because we are angry, so we call in the troops to help us hurt the one who offended us? (If this is true, let's remember Romans 12:19—"Never take your own revenge, beloved, but leave room for the wrath of God, for it is written, 'Vengeance is Mine, I will repay, says the Lord.'")

Is it because we are fearful of rejection, so we call in the troops for reinforcements? (Then let's instead believe with David in Psalm 27:1, "The Lord is the defense of my life.")

Our relationships are always targeted by Satan. Why? Because to the world our unity is the verification of Christ. If Jesus prayed that His followers "may all be one...that the world may believe that Thou didst send Me"—then if you were Satan, what would you target?

Satan will never let our relationships flow naturally. That's why the "peace" must be preserved by the peacemakers...and why peacemakers are called "sons of God" (Matthew 5:9).

BECAUSE YOU'RE DIFFERENT

Blessed are those who have been persecuted for the sake of righteousness, for theirs is the kingdom of heaven.
—*Matthew 5:10*

Of all the Beatitudes, this is the greatest paradox. It sounds as if Jesus is saying, "Happy is the man who leans into a right hook." It's one thing to say life is tough and brings hardship; it's quite another to say, Happy is the man who gets the worst of it.

Isn't it interesting that this Beatitude follows "Happy are the peacemakers"? We're supposed to be bringing about peace; Jesus then turns around and says we'll get beat up for it, and adds, "Smile, you're blessed."

But no, all the other Beatitudes make sense when we really think about them, and this one will too. Jesus never blows smoke in your face. He never said He came to make life easy, but He did say He came to make life make sense.

Why is there persecution of those who want to live godly lives?

There's a collision course set in motion every time you get friendly with the world. "Do you not know," James warns us, "that friendship with the world is hostility toward God? Therefore, whoever wishes to be a friend of the world makes himself an enemy of God."

Jesus said, "Because you are not of the world ... therefore the world hates you. If they persecuted Me, they will also persecute you" (John 15:19-20). They hated Jesus, not because He was good, but because He was different. And if *you* are going to be different — you're on a collision course with the world.

FIGURING OUT LIFE

This also I have seen, that it is from the hand of God.
—Ecclesiastes 2:24

There's a tension in life—the fact that we can't always figure out how it works. At times life doesn't make sense. Why do evil men so often succeed? Why do the wrong people seem to run the world? Why do the innocent so often suffer and die, while the murdering rapist lives? Where are life's real pleasures?

In Ecclesiastes, the "thinking man's book," the wise, aged, disciplined Solomon has "searched to find just the right words" (12:10-11) about life: words "like goads," the iron tip on a pole—sharp words to prod us out of our haze, motivating us to *think right*, to escape the stupor of simply surviving. His words are "well-driven nails," words to hang something on or to fasten something permanently—words to stand the pressure of real life. And they are words "given by one Shepherd"—God Himself.

Going deeper in Ecclesiastes we learn that *God is wise* and has a plan in all of life even if we can't always figure it out—"He has made everything appropriate in its time" (3:11). *God is good*, and life is His good gift—"There is nothing better...than to rejoice and to do good in one's lifetime" (3:12). And *God is just*, and will reward good and judge the bad—"It will be well for those who fear God.... But it will not be well for the evil man" (8:12-13).

Life is like a vapor or breath, passing too quickly for you and me to figure out—but not for the eternal God who created it. Don't try to understand it all yourself. Ask God to teach you about it, to open your mind to things you might be afraid to think about.

THE PROFOUND SIMPLE

*Here is what I have seen to be good and fitting: to eat,
to drink and enjoy oneself in all one's labor in which he toils
under the sun during the few years of his life which God
has given him; for this is his reward.*
—Ecclesiastes 5:18

Life just doesn't get simpler. So you have a decision to make: Either drown in the confusion of the complex, or move on to what has been called "the profound simple." And what's that? It's taking another look at life and deciding what's really important, what really matters, what truly satisfies my desire to live. And then to get rid of whatever *isn't* important and *doesn't* matter.

How do you view yourself? As someone who's just trying to make it? Make it for what? To boxing day, when they put you six feet under?

"Do not be anxious for tomorrow," Jesus said, "for tomorrow will care for itself." In Ecclesiastes, Solomon drives home the preciousness of life today. Make it count, every moment! Don't let tomorrow rob you of life today. Too many of us live in the future or past, instead of the present. Don't spend your whole life missing life. Enjoy the good of creation now, for our lives pass quickly, like a vapor. Life is here; life is now. Go ahead and grieve over the suffering, but seize this moment of life, for it is God's precious gift.

What are you deferring until later—and why? What could you be enjoying *now* with your family, your friends, but are putting off for no sufficient reason? What good are you being distracted from carrying out? Why defer it until later? (What makes you think there will even be a later?) Why not do it *now*?

BIRTHMARKS

There is a time for everything...
a time to be born, and a time to die...
—Ecclesiastes 3:1-2

Life, someone has said, is one long struggle trying not to think about death. Still, reality hits us: People die—even people full of life, people who don't want to die. And there's the nagging question about our own demise: Does it have to be my *demise*?

The apostle John said he wrote his first epistle "so that our joy may be made complete" (1:4). What is joy? It is the absence of fear. Then what takes away my fear of dying? "There is no fear in *love*," John answers; "perfect love casts out fear" (4:18). So how can I really know God loves me that much?

John says, "I have written to you...that you may know you have eternal life" (5:13). The only way to have complete joy is to have absolute assurance of eternal salvation. Otherwise you'll always be fearful in this life because of your fear of judgment in the next. Do you have that absolute assurance?

God doesn't want anyone to rob His children of this assurance and joy. Throughout this epistle John deals with life's absolutes, the black and white. In his no-nonsense way, John shows us we can have absolute confidence in our eternal salvation. He gives us three birthmarks, three proofs of our spiritual birth: our belief in Jesus Christ; our response to it (love); and our practice of it (righteousness). Do you have these birthmarks? Ask yourself this: What do I really believe about Jesus the Christ? How do I view others around me? (Am I growing in love toward the people God loves?) And how do I feel about the sins I commit?

THE SIGNIFICANT SOMETHING

Therefore be careful how you walk, not as unwise men,
but as wise, making the most of your time,
because the days are evil.
—*Ephesians 5:15*

We have only so much time, so much energy and resources. Where do we invest? People are more important than things—but how do we invest in people? What mark can we leave on another that will somehow have significance?

We all invest in something; what's the *significant* something? What are the important things to God, the things He will honor when our time on earth is over?

There will be a judgment for believers—not a condemnation, for there is no condemnation for those who are in Christ. But there will be a judgment. "Each one of us shall give account of himself to God" (Romans 14:12). And what we'll be accountable for is the way we build upon the foundation that was laid for us, "which is Jesus Christ" (1 Corinthians 3:11). When we follow the wisdom and traditions of religious men or the church, we build upon another foundation, not Christ. Ours is not to entrust a human philosophy or code of personal ethics to others, but to share "Christ Jesus, who became to us *wisdom from God*" (1:30). Communicating and demonstrating this wisdom to others—"not in words taught by human wisdom, but in those taught by the Spirit"—is what building on the foundation of Christ is all about. Basically it means *to disciple* others; in Jesus' words, "teaching them all that I have commanded you" (Matthew 28:19-20).

Right now, how are you communicating the wisdom of God to those around you?

BUILD WITH THE BEST

As a wise master builder I laid a foundation...
But let each man be careful how he builds upon it.
—1 Corinthians 3:10

Upon the foundation of Jesus Christ we can build with either noncombustible material—"gold, silver, precious stones"—or combustible—"wood, hay, straw" (3:12). These materials represent not our talents or wealth or spiritual gifts, but rather *our works.* We aren't saved by works (Ephesians 2:8-9), nor are they the source of the Christian life—but they are the marks of the Christian life.

Gold, silver, and precious stones represent the things of great and lasting value which we build into the lives of others. Wood, hay, and straw represent things that are trivial; they're what I call the "busy stuff," things which time itself will burn up.

We are to build up others with the best material: to demonstrate and communicate to others in any way you can the wisdom of God—the truths of God, from milk to solid food—whether through your teaching, writing, example, or counsel, and whether formal or informal.

Is that all there is? Just get out there and teach those people? No; there's the matter of our motives. Paul says the Lord will "disclose the motives of men's hearts" (4:5). Paul tells the right motive in 2 Corinthians 5:9—"We have as our ambition...*to be pleasing to Him.*" Paul's motives focused on eternity: "Reaching forward to what lies ahead, I press on toward the goal for the prize of the upward call of God in Christ Jesus" (Philippians 3:13-14). Is this your motive, your goal, as well?

THE FIRE THAT REVEALS

*Each man's work will become evident; for the day
will show it, because it is to be revealed with fire.*
—1 Corinthians 3:13

There will be a day when we give an account, and
the test will be *by fire*.

Why fire? The picture is not of purifying fire, but
of testing, as you would test materials for building. It
is bringing out what there is of worth and what is
lasting, and consuming that which is insignificant.
The fire will be the flaming discernment of the Lord;
it brings to mind what John saw: "The Son of God,
who has eyes like a flame of fire" (Revelation 2:18).

For some, the outcome of our testing will be reward (1 Corinthians 3:14). The reward will include
hearing from the Lord, "Well done, good and faithful
servant," but it doesn't stop there. Paul says, "If we
endure, *we shall also reign with Him*" (2 Timothy 2:12).

For others, the outcome of the testing will be something else; "If any man's work is burned up, *he shall
suffer loss*" (1 Corinthians 3:15). Does he forfeit his salvation. No, "he himself shall be saved." If worse
comes to worse, if you've accomplished zip in this life
as a Christian—if all your labor smells like charcoal—
still you will be saved, "yet so as through fire." The
picture is of a man pulled out of his burning house
just before it is consumed. You will see reduced to
nothing the work you congratulated yourself for; you
will bring grief to the Master who had hoped you
would do well.

Therefore "watch yourself, that you might not lose
what we have accomplished, but that you may receive a full reward" (2 John 8).

DANGER: DESTRUCTION

Do you not know that you are a temple of God,
and that the Spirit of God dwells in you?
—1 Corinthians 3:16

This *you* is plural—"All you Christians." We're a temple of God in two ways: as individuals ("Your body is a temple of the Holy Spirit"—1 Corinthians 6:19); and as a community of believers ("You are fellow-citizens with the saints...being built together into a dwelling of God in the Spirit"—Ephesians 2:19-22). You are made sacred by the presence of God. God doesn't dwell in houses made with hands, but He does dwell in us.

"If any man destroys the temple of God," Paul continues, "God will destroy him." Paul is speaking of how the unbeliever treats the church, and the word for "destroy" also means "ruin." Is it possible for someone to destroy the church as a whole? No, but it is very possible for someone to ruin the local church. How? The context of 1 Corinthians shows how: division...strife...quarrels...pride. The testimony of a local church can be destroyed.

Do people see the wisdom of God in your fellowship? Do they see you living by a different standard of life, the standard of God's Word rather than the world's opinions? Do they see God's presence displayed? To the unbeliever who tries to ruin that testimony, God says, "I will destroy him." Why? "For the temple of God is holy" (1 Corinthians 3:17).

If God feels this way when unbelievers attempt to ruin the testimony of His church...what must He feel when His own holy ones attempt to do the same?

THE SOURCE OF THE FLOW

Will God indeed dwell on the earth?
—1 Kings 8:27

God's presence cannot be confined; the entire creation is always in His presence. But after God had chosen a people to be His witness to the world, He instructed them to build a tabernacle. "And the glory of the Lord filled the tabernacle" (Exodus 40:35). God later directed Solomon to build a temple, and "the glory of the Lord filled the house of the Lord" (1 Kings 8:11). *God's presence would dwell with them!*

Because of His people's idolatry, the temple became defiled. In Ezekiel 10:18, "the glory of the Lord departed from the threshold of the temple"; this temple later was destroyed by Nebuchadnezzar, for it had become just a building.

Centuries later Jesus returned to the rebuilt temple, but only to show that it too had been defiled: "He cast out all those who were buying and selling in the temple, and overturned the tables of the moneychangers" (Luke 21:12). This temple was destroyed in A.D. 70—it had again become merely a building.

Ezekiel tells us there will be another temple built, and the glory of God shall return to it (42:4). But we need not wait until then, because of what God says to us in Ezekiel 36:27—"I will put My Spirit within you." God is not distant from you; His presence dwells within you. Do you see yourself that way? Your life flows out of how you view yourself. People who are generally down on others are generally down on themselves. Out of the heart flows the way you treat yourself, and the way you treat brothers and sisters in Christ. So how do you view yourself?

THE SPIRITUAL HOUSE

You are a chosen race, a royal priesthood,
a holy nation, a people for God's own possession.
—1 Peter 2:9

Do you love the local church?

Do you love what is happening to you in the local church—the growth in your life, seeing God use His family to disciple you? Are you grateful that the local church is instructing you in the commandments of Jesus Christ, holding you accountable by asking you the hard questions, allowing you to spend time with Christians who love Christ and to observe their holy lives, and affirming you as you grow and become more like Jesus? This is the teaching of God's wisdom to one another.

Are you doing all you can to preserve the local church—especially its unity? Or are you destroying the church by chipping away at it (not at the building, but at the people)?

The longer we're with each other in the church, the more irritated we can become with each other. Familiarity breeds contempt. When we start looking for them, we can quickly find things we don't like in each other—even mannerisms ("I can't stand the way he rubs his nose").

Do you know who it is who can give us affection for one another? It is the Holy Spirit, and together, we are His temple. Do you view yourself as a part of it? "You also, like living stones, are being built up as a spiritual house for a holy priesthood" (1 Peter 2:5). Or do you "grieve the Holy Spirit of God" (Ephesians 4:30)?

How do you feel about the church?

IT'S ALL HIS

Let a man regard us as servants of Christ...
—1 Corinthians 4:1

"Jesus is Lord!" We know what that makes Him... but what does it make us? When we gave our lives to Jesus Christ we changed drastically from being a possessor to a possession.

We are to be regarded, Paul says, "as servants of Christ"—under His authority. Do you struggle with authority? Most people do. We resist submitting to anyone, not believing that God can and does work in our lives through the authority placed over us.

Paul takes it a step further; he says we are "stewards of the mysteries of God"—the wisdom, the truths He has revealed through His apostles and prophets about the provision of His Son to bring us back into a personal relationship with Him, and about how to live in that relationship. These are things men could never know on their own unless God revealed them.

Is this all we are to be stewards of—the spiritual truth we know? No, there's the stewardship of our gifts: "As each one has received a special gift, employ it in serving one another, as good stewards of the manifold grace of God" (1 Peter 4:10). And the stewardship of our resources—"Remember the Lord your God, for it is He who is giving you power to make wealth" (Deuteronomy 8:18).

We are stewards of everything we do not ourselves own—which means everything, period. A servant, a slave, possesses *nothing* of his master's. "The earth is the Lord's and all it contains" (Psalm 24:1).

MAKING THE TRANSFER

It is more blessed to give than to receive.
—Acts 20:35

With these words Paul was reminding the elders about what produces happiness. But if we're honest with ourselves, we ask: Why is self-sacrificial giving —whether of money, time, or energy—not really always a happy thing for us to do? It seems to grate against our nature. Some of us even get a bit offended when people talk about it. We have not learned the joy of giving, nor are we eager to learn it.

There is within the human heart a tough, fibrous root of fallen life whose nature is *always to possess*. The roots of our hearts have grown down into "things," and we dare not pull up one root lest we die. We have failed to understand the simple truth of stewardship. On this issue as on any other, the way we *think* about it determines what we *do* about it.

Have you transferred the ownership of your assets to the Lord? Not to some organization—that's cultic, and it's also bailing out of your responsibility to be a steward. You don't give it over to someone else, but to Jesus Christ.

If you have transferred the ownership to Christ, the words *my* and *mine* take on new meaning. Enjoy those assets you no longer possess. Maintain them, expand them, develop them, as did the rewarded servants in the parable of the talents in Matthew 25. Seek God's guidance on how He wants them to be administered.

And remember: Every time we give as the Master directs, we give a little bit more of our selfishness away.

ONLY ONE INTEREST

To me it is a very small thing that I should be examined by you,
or by any human court; in fact I do not even examine myself.
I am conscious of nothing against myself, yet I am not
by this acquitted; but the one who examines me is the Lord.
—1 Corinthians 4:3-4

How do you handle criticism? We have only one thing to determine about it: Is it of God? The means may not always be godly—but is God trying to get your attention?

The Greek philosopher Antisthenes said, "Only two people can tell you the truth about yourself: an enemy who has lost his temper and a friend who loves you dearly."

When we receive criticism, the issue many times is not *Who is my master?* but *Who is not?* Paul says, "I don't even examine myself." Reflection is good and healthy, but negative introspection can be dangerous. We can place a standard upon ourselves (and upon others!) that is perverted, based on our own terms of results, success, performance.

In this matter of criticism, remember who it is you serve. "Who are you to judge the servant of another? To his own master he stands or falls; and stand he will, for the Lord is able to make him stand" (Romans 14:4).

What should a master expect of a servant, a steward? Paul says, "It is required of stewards that one be found trustworthy" (1 Corinthians 4:2). Are you trustworthy? Are you faithful? Are you conscientiously giving out what has been committed to you?

We have one main interest, and that is the Master's interest.

THE WELCOMING APPLAUSE

Who then is the faithful and sensible steward...?
—Luke 12:42

The only thing required of a servant is faithfulness to his master. Only this is required by our Master—and yet we can't always judge it for ourselves.

In 1 Corinthians 4, Paul said he was not aware of any unfaithfulness in his stewardship, "yet I am not by this acquitted; the one who examines me is the Lord." A good conscience is important, but Paul knew he could still be wrong. We can deceive ourselves. That's why David prayed, "Search me, O God, and know my heart..." (Psalm 139:23-24). We are to admonish and correct one another, but one's faithfulness to his stewardship has to do with two things most of us will never see in each other. Paul says God will "bring to light the things hidden in the darkness" — those things no one knows about but you— "and disclose the motives of men's hearts"—the driving thoughts you had in mind while stewarding the grace given to you (1 Corinthians 4:3-4).

What a frightening thought, you say; but it's not supposed to be. Paul continues, "And then each man's praise will come to him from God" (4:5). *Praise*—this is applause, the acclaim of commendation.

You can't enter heaven through the back door. How loud will be the reception when you enter at the gate?

Will you hear this?— "Well done, good and faithful servant. You were faithful with few things; I will put you in charge of many things. Enter into the joy of your Master."

CONSTANT COMMUNICATION

...this is God's will for you in Christ Jesus.
—1 Thessalonians 5:18

Do you want to know the will of God for your life right now? Here it is: "Rejoice always; pray without ceasing; in everything give thanks; *for this is God's will for you in Christ Jesus*" (1 Thessalonians 5:16-18).

What is Paul talking about? Going around with your eyes always closed, bumping into trees? No, he's talking about *constant communication* with God.

Do you want proof that you totally depend on God? This is it: *constant, unceasing communication* between you and your Father in heaven.

Lord, what should I do? What should I say? Father, I don't know how to handle this situation; give me Your wisdom. Lord, this person's problems are so great, I don't know how to help...what would You have me answer?

Father, I'm starting to feel frustrated...and Your word says, "Be anxious for nothing." Okay, Lord. Help me now to obey.

Lord, I'm tired, I'm angry, I'm getting defensive. I can't take this. Father, I don't know how to respond; help me right now to say and do what Jesus would say and do. Let me forget about myself, Lord, and to just be Your servant.

And here's the miracle: As that anxiousness rises in your heart, and you then talk to God about it, you begin to experience (though sometimes it takes a while to notice) the peace that passes all understanding. And you're okay. People around you notice it— because you're responding as Jesus would.

Do you have it today?—that attitude of constant communication—consistently talking to the Lord... about *everything*.

REDEEMED AND DEFINED

...saints by calling, with all who in every place
call upon the name of our Lord Jesus Christ.
—1 Corinthians 1:2

Paul addressed the Corinthians as "saints," but they sounded more like "aints." Look at 1 Corinthians 6:8—"You yourselves cheat and do wrong, and you do this to your brothers." Though none of us is worthy of the title "saints," in the sight of God we wear it. Presidents do not always act presidentially, kings do not always act kingly, but they are still presidents and kings. And we are *saints,* even when we don't act saintly, which was the case with the Corinthians. Like many of us, they had a hard time not mimicking the corruption around them. They wanted to keep a foot in the world and another in the kingdom of God— which is the easiest way to get split up the middle. It brings stress, anxiety, struggle.

The parallels between us and the Corinthians are too many to ignore. Our temptations to compromise are so great that those among us with spiritually normal temperatures are treated as if they had fevers— as if they were radicals.

Our purity and distinctiveness is at issue. God has placed us in the midst of the world, among those who are not saints. Either our lives will change theirs, or theirs will change ours. Which will it be? Will we walk worthy of our calling, and be a strong and healthy confirmation of the gospel of Jesus Christ? We do *not* have to mimic the world.

God has redeemed us; He has also *defined* us. Will you walk worthy of the name you bear? Remember who you are.

A HIGHER STANDARD

I thank my God always ... for the grace of God
which was given you in Christ Jesus.
—*1 Corinthians 1:3*

The grace of God is more than just His favor toward you. It is undeserved, unrepayable kindness—free and unearned. Therefore three things are impossible to coexist with it:

Guilt cannot coexist with it. Guilt means not accepting the reality of God's forgiveness, because you will not believe in God's grace. His forgiveness takes away all guilt, all punishment, all sin. That is grace.

Debt cannot coexist with it. Grace is free. Grace is a gift, not a loan. To try to pay back God for it is an insult. How do you pay for that which is priceless without insulting its worth? We are completely indebted, but we have no debt. We owe God everything out of gratitude—but we owe Him nothing out of debt.

Merit cannot coexist with grace. Grace is not given to "good people." There is no room for boasting. We are not "better people" than others. It is all grace!

This is the fellowship, the partnership we have with Jesus *now*. Because of all He has done for us, we can live a higher standard of life. There is no reason for us not to live that standard—other than that *we will not!*

The only way we will be able to resist the corruption in the world around us, the only way to keep from compromise, is to *want* the testimony of Jesus Christ confirmed in our lives.

BABY BRETHREN

And I, brethren, could not speak to you as to spiritual men,
but as to men of flesh, as to babes in Christ.
—1 Corinthians 3:1

Paul calls these Corinthians "brethren"—he is admonishing fellow Christians here, as a brother. (We are not to judge each other as judges; we are *family*—and with that comes responsibility.) They were believers, not unbelievers, yet he could not call them spiritual men and women. They were in a third category. Paul calls them babies. A baby is a wonderful thing, but an adult who acts like a baby is a tragedy.

Though they had the Spirit, they were not walking by the Spirit (Galatians 5:16) or filled by the Spirit (Ephesians 5:18). They were grieving the Spirit (Ephesians 4:30), quenching the Spirit (1 Thessalonians 5:19). In their immaturity they could not understand what God says in the Scriptures.

It was not that they were unintelligent or ignorant. You can be able to outline the Bible and still be carnal. The *breadth* of knowledge is not the issue; the *depth* of knowledge is. Some say, "The Bible's too deep for me," but the problem is not lack of intelligence, but carnality.

These Corinthians were lacking in strength because they were unwilling to sense their weakness and their need for wisdom. They had not changed. They had not grown. The only wisdom they believed in was their own: "I will not submit to what I do not agree with." Sound familiar?

"I gave you milk to drink," Paul says, "not solid food; for you were not yet able to receive it" (1 Corinthians 3:2). Are *you* into solid food?

WISE UP

Since there is jealousy and strife among you,
are you not fleshly, and are you not walking like mere men?
—1 Corinthians 3:3

When Jesus prayed for our unity there was no doubt that this was the will of God. Then why are so many churches in such division? What force fights against the will of God for His people in this area? The force is the power of darkness, and the pawns are carnal Christians. The cure for division is the wising up of the believer.

Have you ever asked yourself, "Am I a hypocrite?" If so, the fact that you ask the question is pretty good evidence that you're not. But some do need to ask it. They need not always be doubting their salvation, but they just may need to be doubting their growth. You may no longer be an unbeliever, but are you carnal?

The symptom is not how you view smoking, drinking, and chewing, but how you view yourself and others. That's where you find the ugly head of carnality. If you want to see carnality at its greatest, watch how people view people; watch for division. Carnality is at the root of division every time. The proof of no spiritual growth is the existence of divisions.

The flesh is not eradicated when we are saved. We are no longer under its control, but its influence is still here with us. The flesh is "self"—I want what I want when I want it. The drive is to please and glorify myself, not God. I submit to no one but myself.

Have you come through the door of faith—but gone no further?

THE DEATH OF DIVISION

I planted, Apollos watered, but God was causing the growth.
—1 Corinthians 3:6

The Corinthians lined up behind their favorite man: "One says, 'I am of Paul,' and another, 'I am of Apollos'" (3:4). But Paul says he and their pastor Apollos were not the sources of anything, but only instruments used by God, "even as the Lord *gave opportunity* to each one" (3:5). Luck, it's been said, "is when ability meets opportunity"; but ability and opportunity are both given by God. No man can make a work of God grow. Human instruments are only tools, and all honor goes to the Master Designer. Jeremiah was a faithful, dedicated servant of God, yet he saw few results, and was ridiculed and persecuted along with the message he preached. Jonah, on the other hand, was petty and unwilling; yet through him God won all of Nineveh in one brief campaign. Our usefulness and effectiveness are purely by God's grace.

"Now he who plants and he who waters are one" (3:8). The oneness here is not primarily their relationship as brothers; rather, they are one *in their work.* It is the *same* work. They labor for the same Lord.

We may not agree with all those in our community who preach Christ, but we are one with them *in the work.* We labor among the same people, but we labor not for them, but for Him. That's why we're not to take shots at other churches, other pastors. This is His church, not ours, and within it "we are God's fellow-workers" (3:9).

Here is the death of division: laboring together *for Him.* Are you following men — or Him? Where do you get your guidance?

WHAT HAVE I SEEN?

*...and now being built up in Him,
and established in your faith...*
—*Colossians 2:7*

Let's face it: Salvation is something you really cannot verify until your death. Then how can you know for sure...now?

Because we are *eyewitnesses!* And how can that be? The apostles saw Christ alive after His crucifixion, but what have I witnessed? How do I have faith in someone I have never seen?

It has to do with what I'm trusting Him for. I am an eyewitness when I see God do something in my life.

Here are promises of God you can trust and see *here and now:* "By this we know that we have come to know Him, if we keep His commandments" (2:3). "We know we have passed out of death into life, because we love the brethren" (3:14). "Everyone who has this hope fixed on Him purifies himself, just as He is pure" (3:3). "If we confess our sins, He is faithful and righteous to forgive us our sins and to cleanse us from all unrighteousness" (1:9).

Obedience, love, purity, the knowledge of forgiveness—how do you see God working in your life? What have you witnessed?

John says, "We have seen and bear witness..." (1 John 1:2). To bear witness is *marturos* in Greek, the source of our word *martyr*. There may be some personal cost to personal faith. And you won't pay the price for what you're not really sure you believe. Personal investment, it's been said, is the difference between mere mental belief and a true personal faith.

SENSORY FAITH

What we have seen and heard,
we proclaim to you also.
—1 John 1:3

Faith—to be a personal faith—must be more than the faith of our fathers, more than faith in the faith of another. A sensory faith is when what I believe to be true *is true in my life.*

Personal doesn't mean you don't talk about it. *Personal* means it's real and important to you—and if it's important to you, you talk about it.

Have you heard someone say about your faith, "That may be good for you, but not for me"? If you agreed with that, it's only because *you don't know Him.* When you know Him, you realize faith in Him is something we *all* need—not just a select few who happen to be "religiously inclined."

We were all created by God to have a relationship with Him. That's why He made us capable of having close relationships. No animal communicates as we do. No other creature writes books and songs, can sit and share deep feelings, or is capable of experiencing the love and understanding which we can. God has made us unique beings for a reason: He already knows us, and He wants us to get to know Him *personally.*

What you believe about Jesus has everything to do with a sensory faith. John is saying, "Listen, I heard Him; with my own eyes I have seen Him." Jesus was as real as you or me. "I know it," John says, "because I've experienced it, and so I must proclaim it."

If faith is personal, it is because we know it to be true…and this is no time to be shy about it!

FOCUS YOUR MOTION

Man is like a mere breath,
his days a passing shadow.
—Psalm 144:4

A distracting restlessness often robs us of the joy God wants us to have in life. We tend to be in constant motion—yet where does it all take us?

If we never break the busy cycle of "constant motion"—we may miss the point of living.

"Vanity of vanities! All is vanity"—so opens Ecclesiastes, and this word *vanity* is the key to understanding the entire book. Its primary meaning is "vapor" or "breath." We see it used also by Job—"My days are but a breath" (7:16)—and by David—"Surely every man at his best is a mere breath" (Psalm 39:5).

This is a New Testament thought as well: "You are just a vapor that appears for a little while and then vanishes away" (James 4:14). Solomon is saying, "Vapor of vapors, the thinnest of all vapor—so is life." It passes so quickly that to try figuring it out is futility; it will appear senseless to one who sees it go by like a breath of air.

Solomon's intent in Ecclesiastes is *not* to say life is hopeless, but to help us understand how life "under the sun" is to be lived if you truly want to enjoy it. This book tells us that life is given by God as a gift, and that He has a plan for it all. But Solomon focuses first on the fact that the "distracting restlessness" within and around us keeps us from enjoying life.

Ask yourself, How can I focus my motion so that everything has a reason—and the reason is Jesus?

REASON FOR THE MOTION

The fear of the Lord is clean,
enduring forever.
—Psalm 19:9

"A generation goes and a generation comes, but the earth remains forever" (Ecclesiastes 1:4). It doesn't seem fair; man was made to rule the earth, yet it's the earth that hangs around while we're gone before you know it. Life is like that: *transient.*

"The sun rises and the sun sets; and hastening to its place it rises there again" (1:5). Life is like that: *repetitive.*

"On its circular courses the wind returns" (1:6). Blowing in circles, never seen, always changing…life is like that: *aimless.*

"The rivers flow into the sea, yet the sea is not full" (1:7). Life is like that: *futile.*

What is true of earth, sun, wind, and water is true of everything else. "The eye is not satisfied with seeing, nor is the ear filled with hearing" (1:8). No matter how much, how good, how long it is, we're left only with the desire for more; you never find yourself saying, "Well, that's enough for one lifetime."

But go back to Psalm 19 and look at the real reasons for motion in earth and sky and all of nature: "The heavens are telling *the glory of God…* their line has gone out through all the earth… in them He has placed a tent for the sun; it rejoices as a strong man to run his course…"

We share this same reason for the motion of life: "Glorify God in your body" (1 Corinthians 6:20); "Whether then you eat or drink or whatever you do, do all to the glory of God" (10:31).

MAKE A STATEMENT

Do your work heartily,
as for the Lord rather than for men.
—Colossians 3:23

Solomon reminds us that life is just a passing vapor, then asks in Ecclesiastes 1:3, "What advantage does a man have in all his work which he does under the sun?" (By life "under the sun," Solomon does *not* mean life as if there were no God, but simply all of mortal life on earth.)

The Hebrew word here for *advantage*, sometimes translated "profit," is a commercial term referring to "the value left over." After it's all over, what's in life for me? Will I receive a just return for my investment? Or is life cheating me? What's left after all that energy goes into life? What do we achieve for all our sweat and stress?

So asks the businessman trying to build an estate, only to have it reversed and lost ... the social activist changing the world, only to see it regress again ... the homemaker keeping a home intact, only to see it fall victim to the Second Law of Thermodynamics...the scientist unraveling the perplexities in the universe, only to see his discoveries used to pollute and damage the creation...the surgeon implanting a new heart, only to have the patient die.

To live for the glory of God is to *make a statement about God* in everything I do, just as the rest of creation makes a statement about God in everything it does.

How can I live here on earth so that in my job, my home, my appearance—in everything—I am able to say, "This I do because it tells you about Jesus"?

THE RIGHT CAUSE

There is nothing new under the sun.
—Ecclesiastes 1:9

"Nothing new..." That's what makes life boring, which makes us restless, distracting us from enjoying the gift of life God has given us.

But, you may say, *there are new things to make life exciting—new technologies that open up a whole new future.* No, answers Solomon: "Already it has existed for ages which were before us" (1:10). New technology in reality only speeds things up—meeting the same old needs and desires faster and perhaps more efficiently, but the needs and desires are still the same: to communicate, to heal, to influence, to destroy. Transcontinental communication is still an extension of the mouth; magnetic resonance imaging is an extension of the eyes; computers are an extension of the mind; intercontinental ballistic missiles are an extension of the fist.

There must be emotion behind my motion, a reason for my life. There must be a *cause*. There must be a reason for the motion. We were all created to have purpose; life is a restless, empty shell without it. But if you miss on your choice of causes—you'll miss what produces life out of restlessness. What's the right cause? What's the real reason for the motion?

Life which is transient, repetitive, and aimless becomes an adventure of living by *watching the glory of God in it.* "Whatever you do, do your work heartily, as for the Lord rather than for men" (Colossians 3:23). Is Jesus *periodic* in your life, or does He *permeate* your life? Does He affect what you do...in everything you do?

HISTORY LESSON

*That which has been is that which will be,
and that which has been done
is that which will be done.*
—Ecclesiastes 1:9

Hope in this life — for those who have no other life —means believing we're making progress, moving ahead, learning new things. Life will be different if we can just…if we can just…just *what?*

Herodotus and Thucydides, Greek historians of the fifth century B.C., said the major problems of their day included the threat of war, the breakdown of marriage and rise of divorce, the rebellion of youth and their preoccupation with fads, the corruption of politics and injustice in the courts, and the terrible condition of public roads. What has history taught us? Not much. "There is no remembrance of earlier things," Solomon says; "and also of the later things which will occur, there will be for them no remembrance among those who will come later still" (1:11).

We're passing on to the next generation only that which is marketable—but what of *integrity?* What of *wisdom, vision, courage?*

Instead of the transient, repetitive, aimless motion of futility, we find the permanent, fresh, focused motion of significance in living in Christ for the glory of God.

An assignment: Ask yourself, What am I going to leave for my children, grandchildren, and great-grandchildren—three generations to be affected by me? What can I do now that will be remembered—and be *truly significant?*

THE COMMON BOND

We have fellowship with one another.
—1 John 1:7

We play games with each other. We alienate each other because there's no one to identify with. No one else seems to have any needs. We all try to act like we're sinless. But James says, "Confess your sins to one another, and pray for one another" (5:16).

John says that "if we walk in the light"—exposing ourselves openly and honestly to it—"we have fellowship with one another" (1 John 1:7). Our walking in the light will have an effect on our relationships with each other. Our "fellowship" as Christians is the common bond we have with one another because of our common faith in Jesus.

But John also says, "Our fellowship is with the Father, and with His Son Jesus Christ" (1:3). Can that relationship be broken?

The truth is that you can never break fellowship with God. Paul says there is absolutely nothing that "shall be able to separate us from the love of God, which is in Christ Jesus our Lord" (Romans 8:39). At the time of my salvation I was forgiven for all my sins. "We have been sanctified through the offering of the body of Jesus Christ *once for all*" (Hebrews 10:10). On the cross Jesus "offered *one sacrifice* for sins *for all time*... For by one offering He has perfected for all time those who are being sanctified" (10:12-14).

But even after coming to Christ for salvation you can forfeit the joy of that relationship with God, in the same way you can lose the joy of the relationship with your husband or wife and still be married.

How is your joy with God today?

FREEDOM IN FORGIVENESS

After listening to the message of truth,
the gospel of your salvation—
having also believed, you were sealed in Him
with the Holy Spirit of promise.
—Ephesians 1:13

Why did God's Holy Spirit come to be within us? Titus 3:5 speaks of "the washing of regeneration and renewing by the Holy Spirit." God sent His Holy Spirit to dwell within us that we might come alive to the spiritual reality of having a walking relationship with God. Jesus calls Him our "Helper" and "the Spirit of truth," and says, "You know Him, because He abides with you, and will be in you" (John 14:16-17). A key to that abiding relationship, that fellowship with God, has to do with how we look at sin in our lives.

God's Spirit within us convicts us of our sin. The word is *convicts*, not *condemns*. Remember that God convicts; Satan condemns. From condemnation there is no release—only guilt. But from conviction there is freedom in forgiveness. With conviction from God there is also *God's provision*.

It's amazing how many of us are still guilt-ridden. Some are crushed by it. Others bathe in it, even *enjoying* a certain level of guilt because it gives them some sense of false humility, as if there were some masochistic goodness in punishing yourself for the past.

The only way our joy can ever be full is for us to deeply understand how much we are loved by God.

How deeply do you understand it today?

GETTING SPECIFIC

Search me, O God…. See if there be any hurtful way in me.
—Psalm 139:23-24

If we walk in the light, John says, "the blood of Jesus His Son cleanses us from all sin" (1 John 1:7). *But*, you say, *I thought my sins were already forgiven?* The issue becomes clearer in the next two verses.

In verse eight John writes, "If we say that we have *no sin*, we are deceiving ourselves, and the truth is not in us." Verse nine then begins, "If we confess our *sins*…" In the first sentence John is talking about denying *our sin nature*, our fallen nature, our bent toward pride and self-centeredness. If we say we have no capacity to sin, we are deluded. And who would say that? Just about everyone! Most folks have a hard time admitting they're sinners; after all, there's always someone else who's worse. Most religions deny sin. Even some believers teach the eradication of the sin nature: that you can reach a place where you *cannot* sin. That's dangerous thinking; we redefine sin and convince ourselves it isn't there when it is. Paul said, "I am of flesh, sold into bondage to sin" (Romans 7:14).

In verse nine John says, "If we confess *our sins*"—here he refers to the *specific* acts of ignorance and impurity; our attitude is not to bathe in the guilt of our sins, but to confess them. The Greek word for *confess* means "to speak together, to agree with, to say the same thing." John doesn't tell us to ask for forgiveness. No, you were forgiven when you came to Jesus Christ in repentance. But we agree with God that a specific act of sin was indeed sinful.

Is there any "agreeing with God" for you to do today about some specific sin?

PROOF IN THE PRACTICE

*If we say we have fellowship with Him
and yet walk in the darkness, we lie
and do not practice the truth.*
—1 John 1:6

Our *practice* is the proof of whether we have a relationship with God. What practice? It's described in the next verse: "If we *walk in the light* as He Himself is in the light..."

And how do we walk in the light?

Darkness is the absence of light. Since God is light, to walk in darkness is to walk as though there is no God. We may believe He exists—most of us do—and yet still be indifferent to what He has to say about our sin. We stop spending time with other believers who hold us accountable, the believers whom God uses as a channel for His light to you and me. We stop reading the Word. And we stop asking ourselves the honest, hard questions about truth and purity.

Are we just letting the light bounce off?

The way to walk in the light is to keep exposing ourselves to the light—through time spent with genuine believers, time spent in the Word, time spent in honest self-examination. "Let a man examine himself" (1 Corinthians 11:28).

To walk in the light is to walk in the Spirit. Paul says, "Walk by the Spirit, and you will not carry out the desire of the flesh. For the flesh sets its desire against the Spirit, and the Spirit against the flesh; for these are in opposition to one another, so that you may not do the things that you please" (Galatians 5:16-17).

TRUE AND PURE

This is the message we have heard from Him
and announce to you…
—1 John 1:5

John says he is giving us a message from the Lord Himself. His message is the basis to the whole matter of sin and holiness, of darkness and light: "God is light, and in Him there is no darkness at all."

God is not *"a light"* or *"the light"*; *He IS light.* In His essence, His nature, His character, He is light.

In Scripture, light means two things: truth and purity. Light is knowledge of truth, while darkness describes ignorance and blindness (Ephesians 4:18). Light is purity of behavior, while darkness describes deeds of evil (5:8-11). There is no mixture of light and darkness. Here is the basis of our fellowship with God: the fact that God is light—true and pure. If we are to enjoy a relationship with Him, it can't happen with ignorance and impurity.

One of the birthmarks of the believer, a proof of our fellowship with God, is how we respond to that light, what we say when we are exposed to the truth and purity of it.

The Gnostics in John's time were saying there is no such thing as sin. That's also being said today: What your body does is no big deal; lighten up, it's just a body—the real me is my spirit inside. That thinking is just as wrong today as in John's time.

Our nature is to defend our sin, or rationalize it, or ignore it—or be paralyzed by it. Confession is not whipping ourselves with guilt, but rather dealing in God's way with the sinfulness of our sin.

What is *your* view of your sin?

NO GREATER MOTIVATION

If we confess our sins, He is faithful and righteous to forgive us our sins and to cleanse us from all unrighteousness.
—1 John 1:9

What is this confession of sins all about? The Greek tense of the word translated *confess* speaks of continuing confession. It's all about our spiritual growth—sometimes called our sanctification. God is faithful and righteous "to forgive us our sins" and even "to *cleanse us* from all unrighteousness." God continues to forgive each of us our offenses, and by doing so He is *cleansing us from them.* How so?

There's no greater motivation for doing good than knowing we've been completely forgiven for doing bad. My guilt would push me to just give up and sin again; but my continual forgiveness pushes me to try again to please Him.

As I seriously look at my sins and let the light of God's Word expose them for what they are, I turn away from them, for I know of their evil. It comes down to learning to *discern*—becoming one of the mature ones "who because of practice have their senses trained to discern good and evil" (Hebrews 5:14).

But "if we say that we have not sinned"—if our response is to deny both our sin nature and our specific sins—"we make Him a liar, and His word is not in us" (1 John 1:10). We choke off our growth, and forfeit the joy of our fellowship with God.

There is a mystery in the confession of our sins. In that confession there is a release from them, from the guilt and from bondage to them. And because this is so important to our spiritual health, God commands us to do it.

MOVING AHEAD

I came that they might have life,
and might have it abundantly.
—*John 10:10*

Walking in the light is not a massing together of all the "don'ts" you can think of. The Christian life is *not* a lifestyle of prohibitions—I don't and I don't and I don't... The Christian life is what I *do*.

Jesus said He came that we might have life—not to take it away from us. The Christian walk is a *positive* thing, a moving ahead in life as God created it to be lived and enjoyed.

So why did God give commands and laws to be followed? Was it to cramp our style? No—from the beginning, after God gave the law to His people, He said, "O Israel, you should listen and be careful to do it, *that it might go well with you*" (Deuteronomy 6:3). The law was for Israel's well-being.

But, you may say, it always seemed such a hassle for God's people to carry out God's commands. The whole Old Testament is about people blowing it, and suffering the consequences for their failure.

And out of that very failure came the promise of a better covenant, a new covenant fulfilled in us through Jesus Christ: "After those days," God said through the prophet Jeremiah, "I will put My law *within them*, and on their heart I will write it" (31:33). "Moreover, I will give you a new heart and put a new spirit within you ...I will put My Spirit within you and cause you to walk in My statutes" (Ezekiel 36:26-27). The basis for walking with God is internal, not external.

Is your personal Christianity rooted in external laws...or internal grace?

THE DESIRE TO HONOR

By this we know we have come to know Him.
—1 John 2:3

This word *know* means "to come to know by experience." I can actually see and experience something that will give me the certainty that I have a personal, eternal relationship with Jesus Christ. And what is the evidence? *"We know we have come to know Him if we keep His commandments."*

Does this mean cold obedience, the military stuff? The word *keep* means "to watch over something of great worth to you." You guard it and honor it as something precious. Legalistic obedience, as most religions demand, is not what John is talking about here. It is more what Jesus spoke of in John 4:34—"My food is to do the will of Him who sent Me, and to accomplish His work."

Is John saying a Christian never sins? The disciples were not always obedient. Look at John himself: He wanted to blow up a Samaritan town, he asked presumptuously for one of the top seats in the kingdom, he fell asleep with the others in the garden…and yet hear what Jesus prayed for John and the others on the night before He was to die: "I manifested Thy name to the men whom Thou gavest Me…and they have kept Thy word."

Notice what Jesus *didn't* say that night: "Men, I'm leaving you, and if one of you blows it even once, you're dead meat." If that were true, I would never get out of bed for fear of messing up and losing it all.

A mark of knowing Christ in this life is this: To have a *continual desire* to honor what Jesus has said.

TRUE TO HIS CHARACTER

Whoever keeps His word,
in him the love of God has truly been perfected.
—1 John 2:5

When we have the deep-seated desire to please God and carry out His commands—*we* hurt when we hurt *Him*. Godly fear is the fear of bringing shame upon this One you love. God's love "has truly been perfected" in us—*established*, implanted in our hearts. Others can see it in our obedience of Him. We understand that we "ought to walk in the same manner as He walked" (2:6). We follow His pattern, His steps.

But "the one who says, 'I have come to know Him,' and does not keep His commandments, is a liar, and the truth is not in him" (2:4). This person is so caught up with the pride of what he knows that he has no knowledge, no relationship with Jesus. He *says* he knows—but talk is cheap.

The question for us is simple: Do I possess a passion to honor God's word? Yes or no? No one, not even Satan, can argue this point with us. And "by this we know that we are in Him" (2:5).

What if we want to keep His commands but don't know them all, and we're fearful we'll mess up? The answer is, If you stay true to His character, you'll stay true to His commands. Have you noticed how Jesus *thought about* what He did before He did it? And He thought about *God and His character*, not about a list of commands: "I always do the things that are pleasing to Him" (John 8:29).

Cultivate your desire to obey and honor what Jesus has said, and you'll grow in your knowing—in your friendship with Him.

ACKNOWLEDGE THE GIVER

I did not withhold my heart from any pleasure.
—Ecclesiastes 2:10

If the world avoids pain and pursues pleasure ... is pleasure from the devil? Why give the devil credit for what God has given us to enjoy? "Every good thing... and every perfect gift is from above, coming down from the Father of lights" (James 1:17). Paul said, "Everything created by God is good, and nothing is to be rejected, *if it is received with gratitude*, for it is sanctified by means of the word of God and prayer" (1 Timothy 4:4). Our problem with pleasure is that we grab for the gift without acknowledging the Giver... forgetting that only in acknowledging the Giver do we find the ultimate enjoyment of the gift.

Solomon records, "I said to myself, 'Come now, I will test you with pleasure. So enjoy yourself'" (Ecclesiastes 2:1). He denied himself no pleasure: esthetic pleasure for the eyes, ego pleasure for the pride, sensual pleasure for the flesh (2:2-10). The apostle John also talked about "the lust of the flesh and the lust of the eyes and the boastful pride of life" (1 John 2:16). All these, John said, were "from the world. And *the world is passing away*." Likewise, Solomon's conclusion was that he received a reward: immediate pleasure. But this, too, was only a vapor—"striving after wind" (Ecclesiastes 2:11). There was no lasting satisfaction.

"Delayed gratification" isn't popular these days; that's why we don't hear much about heaven. But by demanding immediate pleasure we sacrifice the ultimate gift of the enjoyment of life. Jesus said, "Seek first His kingdom and His righteousness; and all these things shall be added to you" (Matthew 6:33).

IRON OR WAX?

God is opposed to the proud,
but gives grace to the humble.
—James 4:6

As God continues to shape our lives, His sculpturing tool meets our hearts. There it touches either the iron of pride, or the malleable wax of humility.

We want to grow in our spiritual lives. We know we've got to change and we want to see change. We want to be "becoming in the faith." We want to see God paint our lives with His kindness, gentleness, strength, commitment, and sensitivity. We want to see 2 Corinthians 3:18 proving true for us: "We all... beholding as in a mirror the glory of the Lord, are being transformed into the same image from glory to glory."

But the attitude of pride brings all that change to a screeching halt. Pride is at the root of the defensiveness, anger, and frustration with which we stifle God's work within us. It's hard to admit we're wrong in anything. When our character flaws are mirrored back to us, it grinds against our nature.

What are we to do with our pride? Honest transparency is the very key to our change.

It was the apostle Peter who said, "Humble yourselves, therefore, under the mighty hand of God, that He may exalt you in due time" (1 Peter 5:6).

Are you honestly transparent? Or are you proud? How important are your rights over others? How consumed are you over your own personal needs? Is recognition for what you have done very important to you?

Are you iron, or are you wax?

ALL THINGS

*...in order that no one of you might become arrogant
in behalf of one against the other.*
—1 Corinthians 4:6

In his first letter to the Corinthians, Paul spoke about division in the church, specifically over teachers. The cause of the Corinthian factionalism—some proclaimed Paul, some Apollos, some Cephas—was basically pride. They were proud of their leaders. That doesn't sound bad; these leaders were godly, humble servants of the Lord. But problems began when instead of being grateful for these leaders in their lives, the Corinthians were proud of them, and thus divisive over them. There were those who were captivated by one teacher to the disparagement of another. Paul calls this attitude "arrogant" (4:6), or literally, "inflated"—puffed up with hot air like a balloon. When we exalt one man over another, we take credit *to ourselves* for the admiration we feel. We glory in being able to recognize and appreciate a superiority which apparently others fail to see. Thus we hold contempt not only for other leaders, but also for those who follow them.

Paul asks a question: "Who regards you as superior?" (4:7). Where are you getting your information about yourselves? He reminds them, "What do you have that you did not receive?" If we have had noble parents, if we have a good mind or an attractive appearance, or even great possessions or position—all these are from the hand of God.

Today, pray as David prayed: "Our God, we thank Thee, and praise Thy glorious name ... for all things come from Thee" (1 Chronicles 29:13-14).

CORINTHIAN PRIDE

What do you have that you did not receive?
But if you did receive it, why do you boast
as if you had not received it?
—1 Corinthians 4:7

If we possess only what God has given us, why should we boast as if we created or earned it ourselves? The answer is *pride*. The whole foundation of boasting is nothing more than a fabrication issuing from our pride.

Nothing is more deceptive than pride. The Corinthians considered themselves so spiritually endowed, it was as if they were already reigning in the future kingdom, living in triumph, having arrived at a spiritual high. Paul reminded them, however, that they had left someone out—"You have become kings *without us*" (4:8); Paul says he wishes the Corinthians indeed *were* reigning in the kingdom, since it would mean the kingdom was here and we would all be reigning: "I would indeed that you had become kings so that we also might reign with you."

Corinthian pride is an attitude of superiority: being convinced that my blessings were created or earned by myself. Thus there is no gratefulness—only boasting. There is no openness or transparency—only defensiveness, anger, frustration.

In contrast, personal humility means knowing that *all I have* has been given to me; I am not proud of it, but grateful for it, and that gratefulness moves me to not be consumed with my rights over others, my personal needs, or my recognition for what I have done.

Can you trace within yourself any residue of Corinthian pride?

SELF-REALITY PERCEPTION

I think God has exhibited us apostles last of all,
as men condemned to death.
—1 Corinthians 4:9

Learning humility has a lot to do with your perception.

Listen to Paul, as he contrasted his situation with the raw pride of the boastful Corinthians: *As teachers, we look foolish,* he was saying, *because we preach the clear gospel; you appear prudent and wise to men because you change the gospel to be more acceptable.*

As to appearance, we look weak because we do not go out in our own confidence (we know that in our weakness, God is strong); we do not have the lordly air that emanates from you Corinthians.

As to our reception, you are honored by men, popular; we are treated as scarcely worthy of notice, for our desire isn't to bring attention to ourselves.

The point: Men (like the apostles) who are condemned to die are not consumed over their rights as teachers and leaders; that is not their focus. Nor are they consumed over their appearance or reputation, or their needs, or the recognition of their ministry.

"We have become as the scum of the world, the dregs of all things" (4:13)—Did Paul have a self-image problem? No, he had a self-reality perception. It's easy to know whether a person has a servant's attitude by how he reacts when he's treated like one. How did Paul react? "When we are reviled, we bless; when we are persecuted, we endure; when we are slandered, we try to conciliate."

How do you react?

WHAT TIME IS IT?

There is an appointed time for everything.
And there is a time for every event under heaven...
—Ecclesiastes 3:1

The literal rendering here is:"To all a set time, and a time for every purpose under the heavens." There is a purpose, a delight, a pleasure, a good reason behind anything and everything that comes into your life. The point is illustrated in the verses that follow, a poem considered one of the finest pieces of literature ever written: "A time to be born and a time to die, a time to plant and a time to uproot, a time to kill and a time to heal, a time to tear down and a time to build, a time to weep and a time to laugh..." and on through a total of fourteen pairs—the double intensification of the Hebrew number of completion, seven. It is intended to be a representative list of all aspects of living, as if Solomon cut away a section of life for our review and reflection.

And the point: There's a time for every kind of activity and event in my life. There are no "oops" in life. This is life—mourning and dancing, silence and speaking, war and peace—and there are appointed times in your life for all of it. Not all of these may appear beautiful in themselves, but when they are seen as parts of the whole work of God, of God's plan, then we understand: "He has made everything appropriate in its time, " or in the King James translation, "everything *beautiful* in its time" (3:11).

The wise man is one who wants to know *what time it is*. "And if any of you lacks wisdom, let him ask of God, who gives to all men generously and without reproach, and it will be given to him" (James 1:5)

KINGDOM TENSION

Behold, the kingdom of God is in your midst.
—Luke 17:21

The Pharisees asked Jesus when the kingdom of God would come. He answered, "The kingdom of God is not coming with signs to be observed; nor will they say, 'Look, here it is!' or, 'There it is!' For behold, the kingdom of God is *in your midst.*"

In a mysterious way Jesus has instituted the kingdom of God and introduced people into it, though the kingdom itself is yet future. The kingdom on this earth will not happen, as explained in Revelation 19, until Jesus returns and establishes it. It's then that Satan will be bound for a thousand years; the calf will lie down with the lion, and your little children can play with snakes (which you don't want them to do just now). That's the kingdom, and it's not here yet.

But there *is* an aspect of the kingdom that *is* here—and Jesus says it is *in your midst.* What is it? It's *us.* We are a unique people—aliens, pilgrims, saints—because we are ruled by a King who is not on this planet. We are ruled by One who sits at the right hand of the throne of God in heaven, and we pray, "Thy will be done on this earth as it already is in heaven." We are a heavenly people because we have a heavenly King, and we submit to Him.

And to His kingdom people, Jesus promises persecution: "If they persecuted Me, they will persecute you" (John 15:20). There will be tension, conflict—even within your family. Jesus said He came not always to bring peace, but to bring a sword to your household if need be. Living the kingdom ethic is something very sacred—and something very serious.

READY AND WAITING

...to the church of God...to those who have been sanctified in
Christ Jesus, saints by calling.
—1 Corinthians 1:2

The word *hypocrite* chills our souls. Are we hypocrites when we act saintly ... or hypocrites when we do not? Paul says we are "saints by calling," and to be anything else is to distort the truth about you. We are sanctified—but would you admit to being a saint? (The saints we usually think of are all dead.)

The word *calling* here might be better understood as "summoned." You have been summoned by God, and because of that summons you are now a saint—*hagios*, a set-apart one, a holy one. You are marked out by God as being *different*. That's why you are part of God's church: Set apart from the world unto God both as individuals and as a community—as saints, and as a church. You are *sanctified*; Jesus did it for you, and you will never be the same because of it. We should be living holy lives, but holy living does not make us holy; we *are* a holy people.

We are also a *waiting* people, "eagerly awaiting the revelation of our Lord Jesus Christ" (1 Corinthians 1:7), anticipating the day when either He comes, or we go. Death is not a fearful thing to us.

Meanwhile, God promises that He will confirm us "blameless in the day of our Lord Jesus Christ" (1:8). When we enter heaven it is not with our sins flashed before us for all to see; no, Christ will affirm before the throne of God that we are blameless for all eternity. We are not innocent of sin, but declared forgiven —forever!

EVERYTHING NEEDED

His divine power has granted to us everything
pertaining to life and godliness.
—2 Peter 1:3

To live as saints, God's grace has given us everything we need—though maybe not everything we always want. "In everything you were enriched," Paul told the Corinthian Christians, and then mentioned three areas in which this was so: speech, knowledge, and gifts (1 Corinthians 1:5-7).

God gives every believer the capacity to *speak* for Him. The issue is not eloquence, impressive vocabulary, or captivating personality. God gives us the ability to speak for Him as *He* wants us to speak. The only problem is getting our mouths in gear, and even Paul prayed for help in that area (Ephesians 6:19). Ask God to give you the freedom to speak whatever He wants spoken. Then begin to say *that which you know is true.* Will you tell it to someone this week?

We're also given everything we need to *know* to speak for God. He's given us all the revelation we need. Paul says we've received "the Spirit who is from God, that we might *know* the things freely given to us by God" (1 Corinthians 2:12). The more you know what He wants known, the easier it is to speak it. Are you reading your Bible? If not, why not?

God has also provided all the *gifts* you need to grow—not in yourself, but in the believers around you. The Holy Spirit uses other believers in your life for your spiritual growth. Are you making yourself open to it?

DEATH PENALTY

Just as a father has compassion on his children,
so the Lord has compassion on those who fear Him.
—Psalm 103:13

What happens to God's compassion when we blow it? In an interesting paradox, John says, "I am writing these things to you that you may not sin. And if anyone sins…" (1 John 2:1). I write so you won't sin, he says—*but if you do*, let's talk about it. Notice that he doesn't say, "that you may think about cutting down on your sinning." God's desire for us is clear in Scripture: "You shall be holy, for I am holy" (1 Peter 1:16). When I sin, I know what *I* am to do: confess it (1 John 1:9). But what does the holy God do when I sin?

In Jesus Christ, the holiness of God and the love of God come together concerning our sins. Jesus is our Advocate, our *Paraclete*—"one called to your side," your Defender, the One who pleads your case on your behalf. Jesus pleads our case first because God is holy and we're not, and second because Satan accuses us "before God day and night" (Revelation 12:10).

Does Jesus plead our innocence? No, He doesn't lie. We are sinners; we have sinned against our heavenly Father, shaming His name. For that we deserve to be cast out of any relationship with Him. We deserve death. But Jesus shows the Father the scars in His hands, and claims our legal acquittal. He has paid our death penalty Himself, on the cross. This is not love pleading with justice, but justice pleading with love. God desires to show grace and mercy if given a holy and just basis to do so. And that basis is the righteousness of Christ. Because of what Jesus did—and does now!—we stand acquitted, justified.

ONE SIN AT A TIME

...that you may not sin...
—1 John 2:1

Don't sin. Can you think of any simpler directive for how to enjoy the relationship you have with God?

But how do I *not* sin? What would motivate me not to?

As we confess our sins, we grow to hate sin as God hates it—because we understand *why* He hates it. We see the evil for what it is, the pain it brings to us and to those around us.

One of the birthmarks of a believer is that we take our sin seriously. We don't ignore it, defend it, justify it, rationalize it, or enjoy it. The Christian is the first to take responsibility for sin, and *confess it*. We have become "children of God" (Romans 8:14-16), and nothing can separate us from that relationship (8:38-39); but we can forfeit the joy of it by our acts of sin. We can stop our spiritual growth. That's what 1 John 1:9 is all about: maintaining our *spiritual growth* as we get more and more serious about our sin, because we grow to love more and more the joy of our relationship with God. The joy of my walk with God is too important to me to blow it with any sin.

To *not sin,* where do you begin? *Deal with it one sin at a time.* Shorten the length of time it takes you to take responsibility for it. Take time to examine the evilness of it so you'll see better why God calls it sin.

And each morning, take ten minutes to reflect on Psalm 139:23-24—"Search me, O God, and know my heart; try me and know my anxious thoughts; see if there be any hurtful way in me, and lead me in the everlasting way.'

BUMPING THE LINE

That which I purpose, do I purpose according
to the flesh, that with me there should be
yes, yes and no, no at the same time?
—2 Corinthians 1:17

The pursuit of holiness before God has a lot to do with the pursuit of godliness before man. As people of God we are called to be above reproach. We are called to be people of integrity.

There are times we are misunderstood and accused of wrong which we never did. At other times we bring it upon ourselves because we keep bumping up against the line of integrity.

Paul knew what it was like to be misunderstood. But it wasn't because he was bumping against anything. Paul had to explain: He'd had a perfect plan for visiting the Corinthians again (which they had expected)—but God changed it. There's nothing wrong with planning. There are times God lets us carry out our plans; there are also times He lets us crawl out of them. Paul could adequately explain his actions to the Corinthians—and before God: "I call God as witness to my soul" (1:23).

A man or woman who lives a self-centered existence is necessarily undependable. Their yes or no depends on the whim of the moment, on what would be best for them right then. They will at any moment change their minds and plans to suit their own interest. But for the Christian, it comes down to your word: "Let your yes be yes, and your no, no" (James 5:12). What about the purity of your word? When something comes out of your mouth…is it filtered by your concern for the reputation of Jesus Christ?

INTEGRITY TEST

If you falter in times of trouble,
how small is your strength!
—Proverbs 24:10

In times of adversity we tend to get a good look at ourselves—what we're really like. Then again, Solomon says in Proverbs 27:21, "Man is tested by the praise accorded him." It's not only the bad times, but also the good times that test our character, our integrity.

Picture in your mind the people you know who are people of integrity. If I asked your best friends to do the same thing...would they think of you?

As Paul instructed young Timothy in the requirements for the office of overseer, the first quality he mentioned was "above reproach." The Greek word in 1 Timothy 3:2 means, "not to be taken hold upon"—his life is such that there isn't any handle which others could take and injure his reputation.

For most people who have a problem with the Christian message, it's because of their problems with Christians. When people doubt your life, they begin to doubt your message.

It has something to do with this thing called "integrity." Integrity means wholeness, being in an "unbroken condition," of sound moral character. It comes down to purity in your word and motives. Do you lie? Do you deceive others? Are you honest about who you are and what you want?

It's not so much what you tell us about others; that's honesty. Integrity has to do with what you tell us about *you*. Is it always true?

A RELIABLE CONSCIENCE

For our proud confidence is this,
the testimony of our conscience…
—2 Corinthians 1:12

Paul said his conscience could testify that he had conducted himself "in holiness and godly sincerity." What is this "conscience"?

Conscience has been explained as the ability to detach yourself *from* yourself, to view your character honestly. The danger comes when you can no longer trust what your conscience says…when you have ignored it so long that it's ground down to nothing. Paul spoke of those who were "seared in their own conscience as with a branding iron" (1 Timothy 4:2).

Paul never seared his conscience. He could call upon it as a truthful witness for or against himself. By his conscience he could tell the Corinthians he had conducted himself "in holiness"—he did what he believed God wanted him to do—and "in godly sincerity"—his motives in doing it were right as well.

This is the first priority of integrity: that what I do and the motives behind what I do are pure, pleasing to Him, right in the sight of God. And this is not, Paul said, "in fleshly wisdom, but in the grace of God" (1:12). Man's wisdom is to take care of numero uno; if you have to bend a little honesty to do it, go ahead. Some of us call this kind of wisdom "good business sense." James calls it "demonic" (3:15).

Paul relied on something else than human wisdom: God's grace. "I'll do what God says, and leave the success of it to God's grace."

Can you say this too?

PICK UP AN ORPHAN

I have no greater joy than this,
to hear of my children walking in the truth.
—3 John 4

We speak of "making babies," but *we* don't really make them—we're vessels God uses to create a child. So it is in spiritual parenting: We don't make Christians, but we can be vessels used by God in the creation and growth of His child. In both the physical and spiritual realms you can parent a child whose birth you didn't witness, for there's more to being a parent than giving birth; a real parent takes continuing responsibility for parenthood.

In the church there are too many fatherless and motherless babes around, people led to Christ but now left to grow on their own—orphans in Christ. If you don't consider yourself a spiritual babe—how about becoming a parent? Pick up a few of those orphans waiting around.

As a spiritual parent to the Corinthians, Paul could be harsh in rebuking their sins (1 Corinthians 4:8-10). But he tells why: He loved them as a father loved his own children. "I do not write these things to shame you" (4:14). *Shame* means to strip someone of respect, to humiliate—"you're worthless, hopeless; you'll never change." But no one is worthless or hopeless or incapable of change. In Christ we're beloved children of God, bearing the worth God placed on each of us. Paul said he wrote, not to bring shame, "but to admonish you as my beloved children." He could not bear to see them stray from the truth and come to ruin.

This is a parent's love, and in that love we remind a spiritual child constantly of what God has said.

THE SEED OF ARROGANCE

Some have become arrogant,
as though I were not coming to you.
—1 Corinthians 4:18

The Corinthians had become arrogant—inflated. They thought they could do whatever they pleased—for who would hold them accountable? Lack of accountability is the seed of arrogance. Paul told them, "But I will come to you soon, if the Lord wills, and I shall find out, not the words of those who are arrogant, but their power. For the kingdom of God does not consist in words, but in power" (4:19-20). Paul promised to find out where these men are coming from, for a person's true spiritual character is not determined by the impressiveness of his words, but by the power of his life. As Jesus said, "You will know them by their fruits" (Matthew 7:20).

Discipline means holding our children (both physical children and spiritual) accountable for the consequences of their actions, and being as firm as we have to be to do that. Paul asked the Corinthians, "What do you desire? Shall I come with a rod or with love and a spirit of gentleness?" (1 Corinthians 4:21). As a loving father to them, Paul said he could deal with them with either the stick or gentleness. He was flexible; the choice was theirs.

"But discipline is so unloving," you may say. If you believe that, you're at odds with God's opinion: "Whom the Lord loves, He reproves" (Proverbs 3:12); "He who spares his rod hates his son, but he who loves him disciplines him diligently" (13:14).

Who are *you* being accountable to? And are you giving loving discipline to those accountable to you?

YOUR MODEL: PRESSING ON

I press on toward the goal for the prize
of the upward call of God in Christ Jesus.
—Philippians 3:14

As a father to the Corinthians, Paul said, "I exhort you therefore, be imitators of me" (1 Corinthians 4:16). He added, "Be imitators of me, just as I also am of Christ" (11:1). How different this is from what Jesus said of the scribes and Pharisees—"Do not do according to their deeds; for they say things and do not do them" (Matthew 23:3). When children see a discrepancy between what they hear from their parents and what they see in their parents, generation gaps are created. Paul said, "For this reason I have sent to you Timothy" (1 Corinthians 4:17). Paul sent Timothy so they could see Timothy's example, which was after Paul's example, which was after Christ's example. And the examples have been passed down over the centuries: models of humility, self-forgetfulness, consecration to the Lord, courage in the faith.

Example is key. Our spiritual children must be *shown how* to live; they can't merely follow a definition in a book. But I know what you're thinking: "Who am I for someone to follow?"

Remember that Paul knew himself to be "the worst of sinners" (1 Timothy 1:16); "I know that nothing good dwells in me" (Romans 7:18). Paul's attitude was this: "Not that I...have already become perfect, but I press on...forgetting what lies behind and reaching forward to what lies ahead" (Philippians 3:12-13). He added, "The things you have learned and received and heard and seen in me, practice these things" (4:9). *The model is the pressing on.*

BE A REMINDER

Restore such a one in a spirit of gentleness.
—Galatians 6:1

Correcting a child (either a physical child or a spiritual child) can be sticky business. You build up—or you tear down. You either curb the will or crush the spirit. That's why Paul would write, "Fathers, do not exasperate your children, that they may not lose heart" (Colossians 3:21). There is a right *attitude* in admonishment as well as right action. Admonishment speaks literally of placing "something to mind," in a sense of warning. We remind someone of a danger because we value that person. I have been admonished and rebuked before, and it has helped me grow. I have also been shamed in the name of an admonishment, and have felt my spirit crushed. (You know what I'm talking about.) Sometimes we shame people because we think there's no other way to get them to change. But remember: (1) *We* do not change people—God does; (2) *Hope*, not hopelessness, is what brings about a desire to change.

We're not to crush the spirits of others, but to remind them of what God has said, to bring their will into submission to God's Word. Our tool is not our own opinions, but the Word of God—which is "profitable for teaching, for reproof, for correction, for training in righteousness" (2 Timothy 3:16).

Paul sent Timothy to the Corinthians to "remind" them (1 Corinthians 3:17) of what Paul had taught. Many of our errors are not due to deliberate rebellion (though some are), but to the fact that we conveniently forget how God must be in the center of things. We all need to be constantly reminded.

PAINFUL LOVING

It is actually reported
that there is immorality among you.
—1 Corinthians 5:1

So often when the church disciplines its own, the accused is seen as the abused, and the church is looked upon as the abuser, the bad guy. But is genuine love blind to sin?

When we speak of being part of the family of God, we're not merely throwing out platitudes to warm the soul. We are serious about what we say. Jesus Christ has designed it that way. God loves us…*through* us… all of us. Yet some of that loving is painful, because there are times we must *deal with* sin. We want to deal with it so we can continue to grow into what God wants us to be, *for sin holds us back.*

Merely to declare something sin is not enough. If I know I've blown it—what can I do about it? How do I handle the deep struggles I have, but which I feel I can't tell anyone about without being condemned?

In the situation of sexual immorality which Paul addressed in 1 Corinthians 5, there was sin in the camp. But what was more shocking to Paul than the sin itself was the church's toleration of it: "You have become arrogant, and have not mourned" (5:2). They had become defensive, believing themselves above accusation. They had no deep sadness over the destructiveness of the sin; it was no big issue to them, though Paul had already written to them once before about it (5:9).

Immorality is sin and must be faced head-on—yet not with a collision, but with a spirit of love, healing, and forgiveness.

CLEAR IT OUT

A little leaven leavens the whole lump of dough.
—1 Corinthians 5:6

Paul called on the church to acknowledge sin's seriousness. The action he called for ("to deliver such a one to Satan"—to be thrust out from the care of Christian fellowship) was an exercise of discipline, not to punish or condemn, but to awaken an unrepentant believer to the seriousness of sin. The Corinthians should then have "mourned" (1 Corinthians 5:2); the action was to be carried out in sorrow, not with prideful disgust or cruelty. The hurt ones were not to become angry, but to remain *hurt* and *concerned*.

It's been said that our security against sin lies in our still being shocked at it. Sin is a spiritual malignancy, and will not stay isolated. Unless removed it will spread, its infection scarring everyone. The picture Paul uses is of leaven, which in a small measure makes the whole lump of dough rise. Evil permeates the whole; that's what blatant, unrepented sin does. It is the nature of sin to ferment, corrupt, and spread.

"Clean out the old leaven," Paul says. Before the feast of Passover, when the Jews celebrated their deliverance from the bondage of slavery, they would light a candle and search their house ceremonially for leaven. It was a picture of cleaning themselves of evil. Paul says, "Let us therefore celebrate the feast, not with old leaven, nor with the leaven of malice and wickedness, but with the unleavened bread of sincerity and truth." He was saying we should continually celebrate our deliverance from sin's bondage by clearing out the leaven of sin in our lives.

Is there any clearing out to be done in your life?

OUR SECRETS

Admonish the unruly, encourage the fainthearted, help the weak.
—1 Thessalonians 5:14

We need to know what's going on in the *thinking* behind our sin, to deal with it in an understanding way. At times, we sin because we seek to meet a legitimate need in an illegitimate way. As in the case Paul speaks about in 1 Corinthians 5, this often ends up in sexual perversion.

Why do we move to perversion so easily? We have a basic need for intimacy, to have close relationships and to feel good about ourselves. Just mentioning the word *intimacy* makes some of us feel self-conscious, for it deals with the private areas of our lives. We have our secrets, the very doorways to intimacy.

Some have a struggle with flesh magazines for the same reason others go after the gossip columns—we crave to get at the secrets of others. We think we can *find some kind of intimacy* with another, even if it's only on a piece of paper. When we don't really find it, we go after *more* secret things...and more...and then we have sexual perversion. It becomes almost an abuser syndrome. We do such incredible damage to ourselves as we seek for intimacy—and tragically, we do such incredible damage to others as well.

In private counseling and support groups, and in worship and Bible study together, the body of Christ provides the *spiritual intimacy* needed to give the believer real hope in dealing with sin. The church is there *for you*—Jesus designed it that way. Let your intimacy be first with Him. He knows, and He wants to free you from sin. Tell Him your secrets, and let Him use the family of God to help you.

A HANDLE ON THE DESIGN

Do not be conformed to this world,
but be transformed by the renewing of your mind,
that you may prove what the will of God is,
that which is good and acceptable and perfect.
—*Romans 12:2*

Many times we miss that "good and acceptable and perfect" will of God because we're too busy trying to get conformed to each other.

The special work of the Spirit of God is not unity in conformity—that's something that can be counterfeited at every turn in the world. No, the uniqueness of the Spirit's creativity is *unity in diversity*. When we don't understand this diverse uniqueness, we begin to fail each other. We forget that *the basis of our unity in Christ's body begins not with our similarity, but with our diversity*. Once we get a good handle on that simple statement, we begin to permit God's design for our diversity in unity to unfold. We understand God's design for spiritual gifts, the very reason spiritual gifts were brought into existence. God's Holy Spirit is within every believer to create a communion between us and a ministry *through*, us *to* us. The Spirit's ministry *through* each of us—and *to* each of us—gives design to spiritual gifts.

But when we conform to each other, and try to be just like each other, we *compare* and *compete*. The result? Jealousy over our individual spiritual gifts, or else paralysis of our gifts by way of discouragement. We fail each other many times because *we're just not there* with our special gift to help.

Ask yourself today: Do you see your unique place within the body of Christ?

BE A PART

For by one Spirit we were all baptized into one body.
—*1 Corinthians 12:13*

It's been said that pride is never satisfied, self-pity never content. In reality there's no distinction between the two. When we downplay our part, where do you think our excuses come from? *Who am I?...I have nothing to offer...My gifts can't be that significant...My gifts aren't like yours...* Disclaiming responsibility does not remove responsibility. Refusing to function as part of the body does not make us any less a part of it.

This baptism of the Holy Spirit "into the body" is the same as being "made to drink of the one Spirit" (1 Corinthians 12:13)—it is when you receive the Spirit of God. At that time you are placed into the body of Christ and into communion with all other members of it. This happens the moment you place your faith in Christ, receiving forgiveness of your sin. Every genuine believer in Jesus Christ has the Holy Spirit. For "if anyone does not have the Spirit of Christ, he does not belong to Him" (Romans 8:9). The Holy Spirit is in every Christian, and carries out His design for the function of the body, the very interdependence we have on each other.

To be discontent and discouraged about your gifts and your part means you're lacking in more than just common sense. You're lacking in common trust in the wisdom of the Spirit of God, who has "arranged the parts in the body, every one of them, *just as He wanted them to be*" (12:18). A Christian not participating as part of the body is a living contradiction. He denies the right of God to use him in the life of others.

If you're part of the body... *be* part of the body.

NOT A MACHINE

*From Him the whole body…grows and builds itself up
in love, as each part does its work.*
—Ephesians 4:16

The human body is still the most amazing creation of God. It is marvelously complex, baffling to the scientific mind, yet it is unified with unparalleled harmony and interdependence. It cannot be subdivided into several bodies. It is a unit. If it is divided, the part that is cut off ceases to function; it dies, and the rest of the body loses some of its effectiveness. The body is so much more than the sum of its parts.

The spark of life in the human body still remains a mystery to man, but the spark of life in the body of Christ is not a mystery: It is the Holy Spirit of God.

The Holy Spirit knows that the human body is the best "eye-opener," the best explanation of how the church, the body of Christ, was designed to function. We are not an organization, but an organic unity. The only reason some churches fall back on organization (that's where they hire everyone to do the ministry, and you just attend) is because the organism is too weak to function. We could hire professionals to do it all, and have our churches all running like a clean machine. But Paul did not say, "We are the machine of Christ." No, we are His *body* — a spiritual organism.

I cringe at the words *clergy* and *laity*. They breed an irresponsibility in the body: "Let the professionals do it." What are those "professionals" to do? Paul says God provided spiritually gifted leaders "for the equipping of the saints for the works of service" — for training all of us to do the ministry.

BEHIND OUR FREE WILL

This also I have seen,
that it is from the hand of God.
—Ecclesiastes 2:24

Have you heard of "the providence of God"? This is it: "There is an appointed time for everything" (3:1). The man who has learned the secret of enjoying life as a gift from God, who knows there's a plan for his life, will not be anxious over the length of it. He's not afraid of the plan. He knows there is "a time to be born, and a time to die" (Ecclesiastes 3:2). He knows that the times and seasons are beyond his control. For now he can say, "I have seen the task which God has given the sons of men with which to occupy themselves" (3:10).

He knows that behind our free will stands the will of God which orders all the events in our lives with a view to a plan for eternity. "The steps of a man are established by the Lord; and He delights in his way" (Psalm 37:23).

The words of Jeremiah 29:11 take the sting out of life: "'For I know the plans I have for you,' declares the Lord, 'plans to prosper you and not to harm you, plans to give you hope and a future.'"

Life is a gift from God to be enjoyed, yet the enjoyment of it comes only as we see it as a reward from His hand. "To rejoice and to do good in one's lifetime, moreover, that every man who eats and drinks sees good in all his labor—it is the gift of God" (Ecclesiastes 3:12-13). Pleasure is our reward for good labor, and even the ability to enjoy it comes from Him.

Despite what some Christians look like (what do *you* look like?), God has not called us to misery.

WHY A CROSS?

This Man...you nailed to a cross
by the hands of godless men,
and put Him to death.
—Acts 2:23

Did you ever wonder why Jesus had to die on a cross? If the penalty for sin was death, why not death by some more humane method? Sacrificial lambs died simply and quickly from a cut to the throat; they weren't nailed to little two-foot crosses. So why was there a cross for the sacrificial Lamb of God?

At the Lord's Supper we take the bread, and we recall His words: "This is My body which was *broken* for you; take, eat, and *remember*." Remember what? Remember the meaning of the brokenness. He did not just *die* for our sins. He suffered. He was tortured.

But why?

I'll tell you: He died this way so that we might see the rawness of sin. The rawness of sin took the loveliest, most innocent life on this planet, and threw it against the cross.

The purpose of the cross is to open our eyes to sin and all its horror; to look beyond the sugar-coating of sin, and see our vicious pride and selfishness for what they really are. For there is a violence within each and every one of us which is frightening.

Has the cross opened your eyes?

Thank God for the cross of Jesus Christ!

MAN OF MERCY

And seeing the multitudes,
He felt compassion for them…
        —Matthew 9:36

Why did Jesus take on flesh?

Indeed it was to die for our sin. As our high priest He offered the sacrifice for sin—Himself.

But Hebrews 2:17-18 tells us something else as well: "He had to be made like His brothers in all things, that He might become a merciful and faithful high priest…" He became flesh like us so He could become our high priest. Because He became flesh, "He is able to come to the aid of those who are tempted."

He can come to our aid because "we do not have a high priest who cannot *sympathize with our weaknesses*, but one who has been tempted in all things as we are, yet without sin" (Hebrews 4:15). He suffered with us, that He might experience what we experience. He knew what it was like to be hungry, thirsty, tired, hurt, disappointed, sinned against, angry, grieved, troubled, aching.

Jesus felt everything we feel, and more. Why? That He might be *merciful*—that He might be able to *sympathize* with us. That He might come to our aid. He came in the flesh to *suffer*, so that He might be able to offer forgiveness and kindness, the two dimensions of the biblical concept of mercy.

The most sensitive people I know of are those who have gone through much suffering. They *know* suffering. They have *felt* suffering.

Do you need to become *more human*—human in the way Jesus was?

NO OTHER OPTION

He Himself is the propitiation for our sins; and not for ours
only, but also for those of the whole world.
—1 John 2:1-2

Jesus Christ Himself—no one else—is the propitiation for our sins. But doesn't the sincere Moslem or Buddhist or Hindu worship the same God as the Christian, but under a different name? In other words, is Jesus Christ really the only way to God?

Neither sincerity nor intensity of faith can create truth. Believing something doesn't make it true; refusing to believe something doesn't make it false. As Christians we are not being bigoted or prejudiced or presumptuous when we say Christ is the only way to God. We have no other option—because Jesus Christ Himself said it: "I am the way, and the truth, and the life; no one comes to the Father, but through Me" (John 14:6). One may choose to believe whatever he wishes, but we have no right to redefine what Jesus said to appease ourselves. If we are going to be faithful to Jesus, we must take our stand on what He said, not on what we want Him to have said. If He is God the Son, what He said was true.

Jesus, Himself, is the propitiation for our sins. He is the satisfaction of all the claims of divine justice and holiness. In the moral and spiritual realm, the penalty is inherent in the violation of God's law. Death is the only way God could communicate the seriousness of sin! Sin results in the eternal death of the sinner. There is only one way to have a relationship with God—and it's by His provision, not ours. That provision is only by the death of Christ—for your sins, for my sins, and "also for those of the whole world."

A TIME TO SPEAK

...those who bring good news, who proclaim peace,
who bring good tidings, who proclaim salvation...
—Isaiah 52:7

We are witnesses, not attorneys. The only question is: Are we faithful witnesses?

We share what we know to be true—no more, no less. The Spirit of the God of peace takes it from there. He reconciles man to God. That's salvation!

Solomon wrote about "a time to be silent, and a time to speak" (Ecclesiastes 3:1). There are times you say something, and there are times you say nothing. Paul said, "Let no unwholesome word proceed from your mouth, but only such a word as is good for edification *according to the need of the moment*, that it may give grace to those who hear" (Ephesians 4:29). What good word is needed now? What word gives grace?

They called Jesus "the Word"—*logos* in Greek. It means "the full expression of the thought." Jesus, the Logos, is both Creator of the world and Communicator of God the Father. "In the beginning was the Word...all things came into being through Him" (John 1:1-3). They called Him "the Word of life. " (1 John 1:1). What is life? It is the opposite of death. To be dead is to not be able to respond to what is real around you. You can be physically dead, emotionally dead, spiritually dead. We're born into the world with life in only those first two dimensions, and not the third, though God created us to be three-dimensional. Only Jesus can introduce us to three-dimensional living.

Are you a faithful witness to the news? Jesus said, "I am the way, and the truth, and the life"!

PEACE, YES

Peace I leave with you; My peace I give to you;
not as the world gives, do I give to you.
—John 14:27

What is peace? There's the world's "peace of escape"—run from trouble and pain, escape from anything you fear. But the sum of life is not the absence
of bad things, but rather the confident rest we can
have, whether we face good times or bad.

In Isaiah 26:3 is this promise from God: "The steadfast of mind Thou wilt keep in perfect peace, because
he trusts in Thee." Paul wrote, "For as many as may
be the promises of God, in Him they are *yes*" (2
Corinthians 1:20). What is this "yes"? It is Jesus
Christ, the answer to God's promises in the Old Testament. Jesus is God's answer to God's plan for us—
and that, Paul says, is why we preach Jesus Christ
(1:19).

Paul goes on: "He who *establishes* us with you in
Christ and *anointed* us is God, who also *sealed* us..."
(1:21-22). There's nothing ambiguous about any of
this: God has established us—confirming our salvation. He has anointed us—chosen us to carry out His
plan. And He has sealed us—with His Holy Spirit.

If there is anything you ought to have peace about,
it's your eternal destiny. With this there is no room
for guesswork. *Why is it so important to know?* Study
Ephesians 6, and you'll see that our spiritual armor
has *so much to do* with what we believe to be true.

Trust God for this today: His intent is that you
have your doubts removed, and that you enjoy His
gift instead—peace in Jesus Christ.

REMEMBER...AND RELIVE

*Jesus...took bread; and when He had given thanks, He broke it,
and said, "This is My body, which is for you; do this in
remembrance of Me." In the same way He took the cup also...
saying,"This cup is the new covenant in My blood; do this,
as often as you drink it, in remembrance of Me."*
—*1 Corinthians 11:24-25*

No passage in the whole of the New Testament is
of greater interest than this one, for these could be the
first recorded words of Jesus. Paul did not receive
them from the gospel accounts, for conservative
scholars agree that this first letter to the Corinthians
was written before any of the gospels.

Here the bread was the symbol of His body, which
would be broken that we might have eternal life.
Bread was the symbol of new life, and Jesus was
showing that what would happen to His body would
give us new life.

"Do this in remembrance of Me," He said. In the
Jewish mind, to *remember* meant more than simply
bringing something to mind; it meant to mentally re-
capture as much as was possible of the *reality* and *significance* of it; to relive it. His command for us is to relive with Him what happened—His life, His agony,
His suffering, His death. It happened "once and for
all" (Hebrews 10:10-12), but we relive it for our own
benefit—we remember who we are, and we remember why we are one.

The cup, Jesus said, "is the new covenant in My
blood." The new covenant *cost* Him something; it cost
Him His blood, His life. At the table of this sacrament
we are commanded to *remember* what He did. How
well are you remembering?

ONE BREAD, ONE BODY

We all partake of the one bread.
1 Corinthians 10:17

Self-centeredness has a way of manifesting itself in
...*self-centeredness*. The folks in Corinth were doing
some things well—but others were a disaster. The primary disaster was the way they "took, ate, and forgot
to remember." In the matter of the Lord's Supper,
Paul told them, "I do not praise you, because you
come together not for the better but for the worse" (1
Corinthians 11:17). Instead of receiving spiritual benefit from the Lord's Supper, they were worse off for
coming. Their way of doing it contradicted the whole
purpose behind it, the reason the Lord Himself commanded it. Paul said, "In the first place, when you
come together...I hear that divisions exist among
you." The Greek word here for "divisions" is *schis-
mata*, literally "tearing apart." These Corinthians apparently could not agree on anything. Instead of serving each other, they'd rather be divided—one of the
first and surest signs of spiritual sickness.

Paul made it clear that our unity is the major point
of the Lord's Supper: "Since there is one bread, we
who are many are one body; for we all partake of the
one bread" (10:17). "You're not eating the Lord's Supper," he told the Corinthians; "you're eating your
own supper." Bitterness, selfishness, and divisive
spirits mock the table at which our Lord commanded
us to remember His sacrifice. For when we truly remember how we got to this table—what it was that
He did for us—this has a profound effect on how we
feel about each other.

Is there any division you need to work now to heal?

EXAMINE YOURSELF

...forgiving each other...as God in Christ also has forgiven you.
—*Ephesians 4:32*

In the Lord's Supper we are taken again and again to the foot of the cross. And there, remembering what He did for us, we're able to continue forgiving each other. That's why the word from Jesus is, "Remember"! It's a command; the question isn't whether or not we're to partake of the Lord's Supper, but rather, *in what manner do we partake?*

Paul issues a warning (when you care for others and don't want to see them suffer, you warn them): "Whoever eats the bread or drinks the cup of the Lord in an unworthy manner shall be guilty of the body and the blood of the Lord" (1 Corinthians 11:27). The "unworthy" refers not to us, but to how we partake. The point is not whether some of us are unworthy to partake; who is worthy of anything outside of Jesus Christ? Rather, to partake of the Lord's Supper and not be prepared for it is to mock the table, to dishonor the sacrament, scoffing at the significance of the death of Jesus Christ.

We are "guilty of the body and blood of the Lord" when we come with bitterness or hatred for another believer. We are guilty in that we mock our own forgiveness—for a *forgiven* person tends to be a *forgiving* person (Matthew 6:12).

"Let a man examine himself," Paul said (1 Corinthians 11:28). This is so hard. Even looking into a mirror can be troubling. Self-deception is just as real as life itself. Taking an honest look at ourselves is neither natural nor comfortable. Nevertheless...

Examine yourself. Are you prepared to partake?

HARD QUESTIONS

Let the word of Christ richly dwell within you.
—Colossians 3:16

No one loves to be wrong, and even fewer want to take the responsibility for being wrong. We want to be right! Everything within us cries out for that self-justification.

That's why we need two things: *the Word of God* ("living and active and sharper than any two-edged sword, and piercing...able to judge the thoughts and intentions of the heart"—Hebrews 4:12); and *each other* ("with all wisdom admonishing one another"—Colossians 3:16).

Ask yourself the hard questions—or let someone else ask them of you. Ask hard questions like these: Do I love my brothers and sisters in Christ? If they have repented, have I forgiven them? ("Above all, keep fervent in your love for one another, because love covers a multitude of sins"—1 Peter 4:8.)

Are you looking into God's Word—and putting into practice what you see there? For whoever is not "a forgetful hearer but an effectual doer, this man shall be blessed in what he does" (James 1:25).

Is any part of this prayer right for you today?

Lord, break my strong will, my self-protectiveness, my argumentativeness, my quickness to make decisions ahead of others and to always think I'm right, my desire to have my opinion always considered. I'm sure I'm often obnoxious, Lord — maybe even embarrassing to You. Forgive me, and convert my fervent spirit into one that is fervent simply in loving You and Your people, fervent in Your joy, fervent in Your peace. Lord, break me ... and thank You for doing it.

THE DIVINE DESIGN

*The Lord is…not wishing for any to perish
but for all to come to repentance.*
—2 Peter 2:9

God so loved the world… If it's true, how does He let
all those people know?

You and I are created and redeemed *to love*—that
we might glorify God by doing it.

"Beloved, let us love one another, for love is from
God" (1 John 4:7). Love is *from God*. The source of all
worth, of anything of worth, is in God. It is God who
created everything, and it is God who sets the value
on what He has created. When you take away God
from anything…you take away its inherent worth.

"Everyone who loves is born of God, and knows
God" (4:7). Those who know God know the worth of
what God has created. "The one who does not love
does not know God" (4:8). Those who do not know
God do not know the worth.

"For God is love" (4:8). This is not something God
does; it's something He *is.* Love is an attribute of God;
as God is holy, so God is love. There is something in
God which moves Him to give worth to what He
makes. God values what He creates, no matter how it
turns out—as compared to us, who value what we
make only if it turns out the way we want.

What pain and misery is there around you? What
have you done lately with the influence or power you
have to relieve it?

We are a people who care! This is part of God's
plan, His divine design: to use us in carrying out His
love, so others will know.

IF GOD IS LOVE...

By this the love of God was manifested in us...
—1 John 4:9

But if God is love ...why does He let what He values go through so much pain? Why is there so much suffering in this world? —It is sin that has produced such pain, and God did not introduce sin into this world.

But God still permits it; so isn't He responsible for it? —Absolutely not! God permitted sin to be introduced into our world because He created us as freewill beings, which demands choice. No choice, no free will.

Then why doesn't He take away the pain of our choices? —If He took away the natural results of our choices for sin, we would be doomed to hell; we would never realize the consequences of sin—in this life or the next.

Why doesn't He at least do something about it?

He has! "God has sent His only begotten Son into the world so that we might live through Him" (1 John 4:9). He sent His "only-One-of-His-kind" Son (you and I can become God's children, but we are never part of the Trinity; we're not gods). The Father gave the Son—Jesus Christ. That's proof of His love for us. God was saying, "I care" (these days, most don't). God was saying, "I care about value, and you have value!" God's care *initiated* ("not that we loved God, but that He loved us..."); His care *acted* ("and sent..."); His care *communicated by self-sacrifice* ("His Son..."); His care *touched real needs* ("to be the propitiation for our sins"—4:10). That's what love looks like. That's what care does.

The real question is not where is God's love in all the pain around us...but where's ours?

THE STRANGE ABSENCE

Beloved, if God so loved us,
we also ought to love one another.
—1 John 4:11

We know: "We know that we abide in Him and He in us, because He has given us of His Spirit" (4:13). But "no one has beheld God at any time" (4:12); no one can see God the Father; so how will *others know?*

Others will know God cares for them by *our believing* and by *our loving*. Whoever believes will experience the love of God personally. "Whoever confesses that Jesus is the Son of God, God abides in him, and he in God" (4:15). Because of His touch on my life, I have no problem knowing I am loved and cared for by God, and that I have great worth.

Those who know they are loved and cared for are not the fearful ones; for "there is no fear in love; but perfect love casts out fear" (4:18). There is no fear of judgment; we have "confidence in the day of judgment" (4:17). Why? "Because as He is, so also are we in this world"—as Jesus was the beloved Son of God, so we are beloved children of God (3:1). People will know of the love of God when they see us believing in that love, when they see the joy in our lives—the strange absence of fear.

And so "His love is perfected in us" (4:12)—in and through us. At our own cost we seek the good of others, that they may come to know their worth in God's eyes.

We all know we should be touching others, caring for others. Why don't we? What about our fear of them? "There is no fear in love, but perfect love casts out fear."

KNOWING THE WORST

The unrighteous shall not inherit the kingdom of God.
—*1 Corinthians 6:9*

"There are sins...and there are *sins*." Do you believe that? In our "sanctified prejudice" we tend to "rank" sins according to "sinfulness"; we're actually ranking them by their offensiveness. But offensiveness to whom? To God, or to us?

God is serious about sin because He is serious about forgiveness. We, His people, must be just as serious about both.

Our personal response to sin doesn't determine its sinfulness. Some sins are downright disgusting to us; we wouldn't be caught dead doing them. As for others, we just wouldn't want to be caught. But they're all offensive to God. They're all unrighteousness—which means living in an unright relationship with God. People's sins are symptoms of their unrighteousness, of their hearts bent against pleasing God.

No man is worse for knowing the worst about himself. If an X-ray reveals a serious break in one of your bones, do you blame the X-ray? Do you break the thermometer if it shows you with a fever of 105? Would you blame a doctor for informing you of a life-threatening situation? In the same way, when God talks about sin, it's the diagnosis of the very disease He wants to cure. *God condemns sin because He redeems from sin!* We can't receive His forgiveness by redefining sin; don't let anyone deceive you into thinking that something the Bible calls sin is normal, and not necessarily wrong. God says He condemns it—but only because He can redeem you from it. Are you willing to hear all that He says?

WE'RE ALL EX-SOMETHING

*You were washed...you were sanctified...you were justified
in the name of the Lord Jesus Christ,
and in the Spirit of our God.*
—1 Corinthians 6:11

Do you believe this verse is true for all of us?

In the two verses above it, Paul spells out the major types of moral sin which characterize an ungodly society: "Neither fornicators, nor idolaters, nor adulterers, nor effeminate, nor homosexuals, nor thieves, nor the covetous, nor drunkards, nor revilers, nor swindlers, shall inherit the kingdom of God." Then he adds: "And such were some of you."

In the church, we are all ex-something — ex-thieves, ex-adulterers, ex-homosexuals, ex-idolaters, ex-whatever. But we have all been *washed*—cleansed, forgiven—"by the washing of regeneration and renewing by the Holy Spirit" (Titus 3:5). We have been *sanctified*—we're a possession of God, set apart to be used by God because we've been made spiritually alive. And thus we are *justified*—declared to be in a right relationship with God.

We, the body of Christ, are a redeemed community celebrating each other's salvation, *no matter what each one of us has been redeemed from.*

Now, as part of the redeemed church, are you calling sin *sin*—a disease that will never cease if it is not diagnosed for what it is? Are you giving unconditional love—including freedom from the fear of rejection—to all who are redeemed? No matter what their sin, He will free them from it, just as He has freed you from yours. And are you regularly involved in fellowship as part of the church family?

BODILY DEMONSTRATION

Glorify God in your body.
—1 Corinthians 6:20

Why talk here about our bodies? Isn't this time for *spiritual* things? But Paul says spiritual worship is "to present your *bodies* a living and holy sacrifice, acceptable to God." When he prays for believers, he says, "May your spirit and soul and *body* be preserved complete, without blame at the coming of our Lord Jesus Christ" (1 Thessalonians 5:23).

As Christians we are given freedom with our bodies, but a freedom intended to help us remain free, not to fall back into bondage. The fact is, our faith does not make us free to sin; it makes us free *not to have to sin*. That's why freedom must breed responsibility.

"All things are lawful for me," Paul says in 1 Corinthians 6:12. Once you are a child of God, there is nothing that can forfeit your salvation. "I can do anything I well please," you could say; "it's my life and my body!" That's the point. You can be as irresponsible as you want, but not if you want to remain free. "All things are lawful" was probably a common statement in the "liberated society" of the Roman world. But a liberated society is not necessarily a free society.

Be free—and *stay free*—with your body! "You are not your own," Paul says; "for you have been bought with a price" (1 Corinthians 6:19-20). The price was a Person—the Person of God's Son. He redeemed not just our spirits and souls, but our bodies as well. My responsibility, therefore, is to glorify God with my body—to use it to demonstrate who He is.

STAYING FREE

All things are lawful for me, but not all things
are profitable. All things are lawful for me,
but I will not be mastered by anything.
—1 Corinthians 6:12

Freedom means you have some choices to make, between right and wrong. What makes something right? In this verse Paul gives us an answer by giving us two guidelines: Is it profitable, and does it preserve my freedom?

Is it profitable? Does it contribute to my good? Literally, does it bring me wholeness and strength? The question goes beyond just me, however. Paul says later, "All things are lawful, but not all things edify" (10:23). Does it edify—build up—those around me?

Does it preserve my freedom? Some things can be pleasurable, but (as many have come to know the hard way) can later become very binding, and all-consuming. On the other hand, personal discipline—self-control, controlling our selves—leads to a tremendous sense of freedom. Where can a train go without staying on the tracks?

Body passions can be enslaving. A good example is the passion for food, a real struggle for many. The more it's indulged, the more it controls the indulger. It's the same with any of the passions. That's why Paul says, "I buffet my body" (9:27). He wanted to keep his body from enslaving him, robbing him of his freedom in Christ.

The point: I am free, and now I am responsible with that freedom to stay free—to do what is right, what will profit me in wholeness and strength, and preserve my freedom to be whole and strong within.

DON'T BLOW YOUR BLESSING

These things happened as an example for us.
—1 Corinthians 10:6

Are you using your blessings to serve God better…
or demanding Him to serve *you* better with more
blessings? (Maybe that question stings a bit…)

In 1 Corinthians 10 Paul reminds us of how the
people of Israel blew their blessing. When they came
out of Egypt they were blessed with miraculous deliverance from bondage, a godly leader to guide
them, and a Rock to sustain and protect them (10:1-4).
"Nevertheless, with most of them God was not well-
pleased; for they were laid low in the wilderness"
(10:5). Why? What did they do? They "craved evil
things" (10:6). In the next four verses Paul outlines
what they did: idolatry, sexual immorality, testing
God, and grumbling. The consequences were severe:
the death of 23,000 in one day, destruction by ser-
pents, destruction by the destroying angel (10:8-10).
Why such a stern response from God?

Paul answers it: "These things happened to them
as an example, and they were written *for our instruction*" (10:11). It was to get Israel's attention—and
ours. The significance of the past is realized only as it
affects the present. It's for our "instruction"—a word
that speaks of warning. We can see the consequences
of evil, and know better. We can know that sin brings
consequences (a reality that comes as such a shock
today).

You've been blessed by God to be a blessing to others—not to abuse and use that blessing for yourself.
Don't blow your blessing.

DO IT HIS WAY

They were laid low in the wilderness.
—1 Corinthians 10:5

In 1 Corinthians 10, Paul outlines for us Israel's evil desires and the consequences—so we can *learn* what will disqualify us from being a blessing to others:

Idolatry—When Israel persuaded Aaron to make the golden calf, they weren't denying what God had done for them; but they wanted to worship Him *their* way. Be careful of self-made worship—*my* religion—the "I did it my way" stuff.

Sexual immorality—They messed around with the Moabite women. God sent a plague, and 23,000 Israelites died in a single day.

Testing God—To test God is to demand more than God has given you. Israel didn't like the bread and water God had provided; they wanted more spice, more variety. They spoke against Moses and the God-appointed leadership, and it cost them dearly. God sent snakes all over the place. Push God, and you'll get bit.

Complaining—Numbers 16 tells us how 14,700 died after "the sons of Israel grumbled" because of God's judgment upon the leaders of the Korahite rebellion against Moses and Aaron. They were angry over divine justice; in other words, they were mad at God's sovereign will. It's okay to ask God why (see James 1:5)—but it's something else to set your will against His because you don't like it. It's useless to be offended by God because He isn't weaker, and doesn't do what you want Him to. Remember how much stronger and wiser than you He is. If you choose to mock Him and take Him on—you'll lose.

PROVING SOMETHING GOOD

No temptation has overtaken you but such as is common to man;
and God is faithful, who will not allow you
to be tempted beyond what you are able, but with
the temptation will provide the way of escape also,
that you may be able to endure it.
—1 Corinthians 10:13

This word *temptation* speaks of a test to prove something—something *good* about *you*. Most of the time we don't really realize how strong our faith is until it's tested.

This verse doesn't say God *does* the testing; "God cannot be tempted by evil, and He Himself does not tempt any one" (James 1:13). Rather, God *allows* the temptation. He controls it, however, for He will not permit it to be beyond what He knows you can handle.

Our trials are not as unique as we like to believe they are, but are "such as is common to man." These are human trials that humans always have to deal with.

And what is this "way of escape"? Is it a way out? Yes, but the way out is *through* it. Paul says God helps us to "be able to endure it"; the escape is escape from sin. We go through the trial sometimes by fleeing— "Flee from youthful lusts" (2 Timothy 2:22). At other times it has to do with whether you'll keep trusting God in your circumstances.

The trial just may be our death. But even then He will sustain us through it. We'll have the grace we need to *keep trusting Him* for His presence with us.

In the trial you're facing today...trust God to help you prove something good—your faith.

HIS GREATEST WORK

If Christ has not been raised,
then our preaching is in vain, your faith also is vain.
—1 Corinthians 15:14

If Christianity isn't based on truth, it shouldn't be too difficult to destroy. All you have to do is knock out its foundation. The Bible itself even tells you how.

But there's proof that what Jesus said about Himself was true. Jesus said, "The works I do in My Father's name, these *bear witness* of Me." The greatest work was His resurrection from the dead. That's why His resurrection is at the core of the gospel ever since it was first proclaimed (Acts 2:24).

Paul says Christian preaching and faith are in vain —meaningless, empty, only air—if Christ was not raised. Destroy the truth of the resurrection and you have destroyed the faith! And you will not only have destroyed it; you will also have exposed the real evil of it all. Paul says we are "found to be false witnesses of God" if we preach the resurrection when there was no resurrection. The gospel is not good news if it's all a lie. And look at the fool you've been! "If Christ has not been raised, your faith is worthless" (15:17). Your faith would be aimless, leading to nothing, having no object of truth.

Our faith cannot be "in faith." Sincerity isn't the issue. Faith must have an object, and its object must have reality to give credibility to the faith. The Christian faith is true because it is faith *in truth*. The Christian faith is not an enigma of history, but a fact of reality—the truth upon which all of Christianity stands. Because of it, you and I have not a religion, *but a personal relationship with the living Lord.*

HIS GREATEST PROOF

He was raised on the third day…
He appeared to Cephas, then to the twelve.
—1 Corinthians 15:4-5

Throughout history the testimony of responsible, honest eyewitnesses has been considered one of the most reliable forms of evidence in a court of law. However incredible it may seem in terms of what we know (or think we know) about the finality of human death, the greatest proof of the resurrection of Christ rests in eyewitness accounts of those who saw Him die, then saw Him alive again.

His resurrection is powerfully authenticated by the willingness of these witnesses to die rather than repudiate their testimony. Men might lie when it suited their convenience; but would they sacrifice their very lives for what they knew to be a hoax?

Their true witness has been handed down from generation to generation, sealed in their own blood: *Peter*, crucified upside down; *Thomas*, speared to death; *James the Less*, beheaded; *Bartholomew*, beaten and crucified; *Matthew*, pierced through by a halberd; *Andrew, Philip, Simon the Zealot, Jude*, all crucified.

Historian Kenneth Scott Latourette tells how "the conviction of the resurrection of Jesus" lifted the disciples out of despair and into "the perpetuation of a movement." Latourette adds that had it not been for the disciples' "profound belief" in His resurrection, "the death of Jesus and even Jesus Himself would probably have been all but forgotten." If the perpetuation of the Christian movement in your community depended on the testimony of *your* convictions, *your* faith—would Jesus soon be all but forgotten there?

NO OTHER EXPLANATION

God raised Him up again, putting an end to the agony of death,
since it was impossible for Him to be held in its power.
—Acts 2:24

The earliest attempt to explain away the resurrection of Christ was to accuse the disciples of stealing the body. Even into the second century it is recorded that Jewish authorities went throughout the Mediterranean world to counter Christian claims, armed only with the argument that someone somehow stole the body of Jesus.

But two big problems arise with that explanation: method and motive. How could the disciples have done it? The new tomb was in all probability cut out of limestone, its only entrance covered by a stone calculated to weigh nearly two tons, sealed by a Roman seal, and protected by a special Roman military guard who forfeited their lives if they failed at their post. The body within the tomb they guarded was prepared "in the burial custom of the Jews" (John 19), wrapped and bound in linen strips and a hundred pounds of spices—which along with the body added up to perhaps 270 pounds of dead weight. How could a band of frightened fishermen pull it off?

And *why* would they even try? What would be the motive to die a martyr's death for a scheme that brought them nothing but suffering, persecution, and ostracism?

Concerning Christ's crucifixion and resurrection, Oxford University history professor Thomas Arnold says no other fact in history "is proved by better and fuller evidence of every sort." It's an undeniable fact of history—and it declares His words to be true.

TO CRACK THE GLOBE

Suddenly a light from heaven flashed around him…
he fell to the ground, and heard a voice saying to him, "Saul,
Saul, why are you persecuting Me?"
—Acts 9:3-4

Paul says the resurrected Christ appeared to Him "last of all, as if to one untimely born" (1 Corinthians 15:8). In Greek, this term "untimely born" denotes the birth of a child in a violent, premature way. In becoming a Christian, Paul was torn, as by a violent operation, from the Judaism to which he was clinging with all the fibers of his heart and will.

Why this Damascus Road experience with Paul? I believe it's because the gospel wasn't getting out. The disciples were reaching the Jews, but weren't cracking the globe of the Gentiles. So the Lord chose Paul, calling him, "a chosen instrument of Mine, to bear My name before the Gentiles…"(Acts 9:15). He took Paul right out of his persecution of the Christians—suddenly, violently—and made him one of them.

Paul would never forget this act of grace. He joined the other martyrs of the faith, sealing his testimony when he was beheaded in Rome. He gave his life *because he had seen the risen Savior.*

The gospel as preached by the disciples and Paul was then handed down at the cost of many more lives, so you and I would not be left without a witness to the gospel of Jesus Christ. Why is the gospel "good news"? You're a sinner—you and God both know it; His Son Jesus was judged in your place, and that's why He died; then He rose to prove to you that He was who He said He was. *The gospel*—hear it, believe it, receive it…and live it out today with joy.

RESURRECTION PROMISE

I am the resurrection and the life.
—John 11:25

With so many faiths in the world, so many religions—how do you know your faith in Christ is true? And how could you ever say someone of another faith is wrong?

The religions of the world are all based on the lives and teachings of their founders...but the Christian faith rests only upon this: the *death and resurrection* of a Savior. This is not a philosophy of living or a discipline of thinking; this is *history*. It's the true story of a Person who claimed to be God the Son, who visited this earth to provide a way back into a relationship with God the Father.

A follower of Buddha wrote, "When Buddha died it was with that utter passing away in which nothing whatever remains." Mohammed died at Medina in Arabia on June 8, 632, at the age of sixty-one; his tomb there is visited by masses of Muslims who come to mourn his death. But the church of Jesus Christ, in honor of His rising from the dead on the first Easter, gathers every Sunday to celebrate the victory of her Lord over death, and the hope we therefore have. For He promises, "I am the resurrection and the life; *he who believes in Me shall live, even if he dies.*"

The gospel is the great fact of history, and every man or woman must come to some conclusion about it. *It has nothing to do with religion;* it has everything to do with a Person.

Was Jesus the Christ, the Son of God? What is the testimony of *your* heart...*your* mouth...*your* life?

WHAT DO YOU BELIEVE?

Now I make known to you, brethren, the gospel…
—1 Corinthians 15:1

After the risen Christ was seen alive by the disciples, He appeared "to more than five hundred brethren at one time," many of whom were still alive to testify of it when Paul wrote these words some twenty-five years later (1 Corinthians 15:6). Paul says Jesus then appeared "to James" (15:7), who was the half-brother of Jesus. What would you think if *your* brother was claiming to be God? In John 7:5 we learn that Jesus' brothers at first did not believe in Him. But history tells us that after seeing the resurrected Jesus, James became the leader of the church in Jerusalem. Later he was beaten to death with a fuller's club because he would not recant what he had *seen* and *believed* about Jesus Christ.

How you feel about the church or religion is one thing; but what do you truly believe about Jesus?

Paul goes to the heart of the issue by defining the gospel: "I delivered to you as of first importance what I also received, that Christ died for our sins according to the Scriptures, and that He was raised on the third day according to the Scriptures" (1 Corinthians 15:3-4). *Gospel* means "good message," or "good news." The great news is that *God did it*. Did what? Let Jesus tell you: "Thus it is written, that the Christ should suffer and rise again from the dead the third day; and that *repentance for forgiveness of sins* should be proclaimed in His name to all the nations…" (Luke 24:46-47).

What do you believe about Jesus Christ? And what are you doing about it?

NO PITY NEEDED

If Christ has not been raised … you are still in your sins.
—1 Corinthians 15:17

What does the resurrection have to do with our sins?

The resurrection confirms that Jesus' sacrificial death is accepted by the Father. Peter says God "raised up Jesus" and exalted Him "to His right hand." For what reason? "…to grant repentance… and forgiveness of sins" (Acts 5:30-31). In Romans 4:25, Paul says Jesus "was raised because of our justification."

The resurrection also secures our continual forgiveness, as explained in Hebrews 7:24-25—"Because He abides forever…He is able to save forever those who draw near to God through Him, since He always lives to make intercession for them."

If Christ's resurrection didn't happen, Paul says, we are all still under the holy wrath of God for our sin. Our expectation of eternal life in heaven is misguided and empty. As Paul says, "we are of all men most to be pitied"; we have passed over the pleasures of this life for a deceitful mirage.

It's not a mirage, however. *"BUT NOW,"* Paul says emphatically, "Christ *has been raised* from the dead, the first fruits of those who are asleep." Jesus Christ was the first to be raised in a body of glory, never to die again. All those who believe in Him will be next. The resurrection of Christ was the guarantee and sign of our own resurrections.

That empty tomb left ripples in history—and they'll someday grow into a tidal wave.

WHAT ARE YOU WAITING FOR?

I will come again, and receive you to Myself;
that where I am, there you may be also.
—John 14:3

Many in recent decades have been intrigued with the possibility of an afterlife. But the issue is more than "Is there life after death?" What *kind* of life is there after death? What is beyond, if there is a beyond? How do we know life after death will indeed be life, and not death?

An area of research has been developed called "thanatology"—the study of death and dying. The Greek word *thanatos* speaks of death as "separation," and it's the word used in Romans 6:23—"The wages of sin is *death,* but the free gift of God is eternal life in Christ Jesus our Lord." Here and elsewhere the Bible mentions two kinds of "life beyond": Eternal life is eternal residence in the kingdom of God, and eternal death is to be *separated* from that kingdom forever.

Do you have hope after death? Or does your life grow bitter with the wait? We all have many disappointments in life, especially with people; but if your hope is in the coming of Christ and in being with Him forever, you can patiently forgive them. Your eyes are on something more important than what people do to you now.

Take from a man his wealth, and you hinder him; take from him his purpose, and you slow him down. But take from man his hope and you stop him. He can go on without wealth and even without purpose; but he will not go on without hope.

What is our hope?

Jesus said, "I will come again."

THE CURSE REVERSED

Through one man sin entered into the world,
and death through sin; so death spread to all men,
because all sinned.
—Romans 5:12

Have you ever wondered why people have to die? We die because we are all descendants of the "one man"—Adam—in Romans 5:12, and are thus identified with him. We bear the consequences of his original rebellion against God.

But that's not fair, you say. *Why should we suffer for what he did?* We don't; we suffer for what *we* do. *"All we* like sheep have gone astray. *Each of us* has turned to his own way" (Isaiah 53:6). We are just like Adam, and in his situation would have done the same thing.

And what was his death? On the day Adam and Eve sinned, their spirit died—the part of them that could commune with God—and that began the process of death in their bodies.

So it is with all of us today. "In Adam all die" (1 Corinthians 15:22). But the verse continues: "…so also in Christ shall all be made alive." Jesus Christ reversed the curse. In Him shall all be made alive.

Does that mean everyone goes to heaven? No; look at the verse again: All who are in Adam die; all who are in Christ shall be made alive. Is everyone a descendant of Adam? Yes. Is everyone a descendant of Christ? No. Only those who have "received Him… those who believe in His name" are given "the right to become children of God" (John 1:12).

This, therefore, is your right, your privilege, your freedom: to become God's child—and *to live now* as God's child.

THE END IS THE BEGINNING

Then comes the end...
—1 Corinthians 15:24

What end? Jesus referred to "the end of the age" (Matthew 28:20). He will someday establish His eternal kingdom, but a few things must happen first. He must "abolish all rule and all authority and power" (1 Corinthians 15:24). This is better known as the "tribulation" taught in the book of Revelation, the time when the heat is turned up to bring to the surface the true character of all men. Jesus will judge and conquer every contending power, every "will" set against God's will. "He must reign until He has put all His enemies under His feet" (15:25). Then Paul says, "The last enemy that will be abolished is death" (15:26). Christ has already broken death's power over us (Hebrews 2:14-15); but on that coming day He will abolish death forever: "There shall no longer be any death" (Revelation 21:4). There will be no sin, and therefore no wages for sin, no death. All things will be restored as they were originally designed and created by God to be. In the end, it will be as it was "in the beginning."

Victor Hugo wrote this: "For half a century I have been writing my thoughts in prose and in verse, but I feel I have not said the thousandth part of what is in me. When I go down to the grave I can say like many others, 'I have finished my day's work.' But I cannot say, 'I have finished my life.' My day's work will begin the next morning. The tomb is not a blind alley; it is a thoroughfare. It closes on the twilight; it opens on the dawn."

Are you looking forward to the dawn?

MOTIVATION

Father, I desire that they also, whom Thou hast given Me,
may be with Me where I am...that they may behold My glory.
—John 17:24

Paul warns us in Galatians 6:9 about losing heart. He wouldn't have given us the warning unless he knew there would be times when we struggled, times when we wondered, *Why keep going in the faith?*

Motivation is a key to just about anything we do or don't do. So when it comes to serving Christ—why spend your life doing it? Why pursue purity? Without good answers, we'll be hard-pressed to keep going.

In 2 Corinthians 11, Paul told of being beaten, imprisoned, stoned, shipwrecked; "I have been in labor and hardship, through many sleepless nights, in hunger and thirst, often without food, in cold and exposure." What made him willing to go back for more? He admits that no "human motive" (1 Corinthians 15:32) could keep him going. It wasn't money, power, or reputation, for he left all that behind when he became a Christian. What could motivate him—and us —to endure, to keep on faithfully serving the Lord?

The answer is knowing we'll see Jesus "face to face" (13:12). To hear from His very lips at that time, "Well done, good and faithful servant," is the most powerful longing that could ever grip our hearts. It isn't commitment to doing right, but commitment to a Person; it's a Person we seek to please, not a philosophy to appease. It's not a formula for fun, but a Person we care about enough to actually die for.

Don't ever forget: Jesus is alive, risen from the dead...and we shall see Him face to face. Continue to practice His living presence.

THE RAPTURE

We shall all be changed, in a moment, in the twinkling of an eye,
at the last trumpet; for the trumpet will sound,
and the dead will be raised imperishable.
—1 Corinthians 15:51-52

"Behold," Paul says, "I tell you a mystery"—the Greek word is *musterion,* something revealed by God for the very first time. And what is it? It is what many call the Rapture, and it's one of the most fascinating truths in the Bible. There's no question it will happen, and no one who knows the Lord will miss the ride. Those who have already died and whose souls are "at home with the Lord" (2 Corinthians 5:8) will go first, their souls being reunited with their bodies.

It will happen quickly: "in a moment, in the twinkling of an eye." It will be an instant re-creation of new bodies with new flesh; the Lord will "transform the body of our humble state into conformity with the body of His glory" (Philippians 3:21).

When will this Rapture take place, especially in regard to the "tribulation" period described in the book of Revelation? On this issue we find great debate. Why? Because it's an issue that can be greatly debated. There are three major views, each with valid scriptural support. All agree, however, that there *will* be a Rapture of the church. Once we've waited long enough, we'll all know exactly when it happened; this is not an issue believers need to be arguing over, and we can agree to disagree on this one. Arrogance has no place here.

Jesus Himself said it: "Behold, *I am coming quickly,* and My reward is with Me..." (Revelation 22:12).

GOD WILL NOT FORGET

As is the heavenly, so also are those who are heavenly.
—1 Corinthians 15:48

Paul tells of four great changes (in 1 Corinthians 15:42-44) taking place at the time of our resurrection: Our bodies will change from "perishable" to "imperishable"; from "dishonor" to "glory"; from "weakness" to "power"; and from "a natural body" to "a spiritual body." Each of us starts life in a natural body created out of dust; Paul reminds us that we bear the image of the first man, Adam, who was "from the earth, earthy" (15:47-49). But our new spiritual bodies will be from heaven, and are thus called "heavenly." The substance from which they are formed is from heaven, and is like nothing on this earth. The process of decay that began on earth the moment we were born will be no more. The passions and drives that dishonor us will be gone. We will be able to more perfectly reflect the image of Jesus Christ.

With this hope in view, Paul tells us to be "always abounding in the work of the Lord" (15:58). What is "the work of the Lord"? Two things: either evangelism—bringing people to Christ—or discipleship—affirming them in their growth, instructing them, being models to them, holding them accountable for their walk and their deep desire to be like Christ.

You'll get a glorified body in eternity—but are you being a good steward with *the body God has already given you*? Right now, are you using your skills, wealth, time and energy to abound in the work of the Lord? If so, know this: "God is not unjust so as to forget your work and the love which you have shown toward His name" (Hebrews 6:10).

ON WITH THE OVERFLOW

O death, where is your victory?
O death, where is your sting?
—1 Corinthians 15:55

To the world, death has a sting like a scorpion's, and crushes like a conquering victor. As Socrates cried out, "Where shall I fly to avoid this irrevocable doom passed on all mankind?" A more recent philosopher penned, "Death is one bad joke on us all."

Not so for the Christian! "The sting of death is sin," Paul explains, "and the power of sin is the law"; in other words, the law makes us accountable for our sin for it tells us what sin is, and that its wage is death, eternal separation from God. *"BUT,"* Paul says, victory over sin and death is ours *"through our Lord Jesus Christ"* (15:57).

Therefore, he continues, let these three things be true in our lives: *"Be steadfast..."* Be firmly planted in your faith. How often do you get discouraged? How much can you take before you want to bail out? *"Be... immovable..."* Let there be no more discussion on whether you'll serve His will or not. *"Be...always abounding in the work of the Lord..."* Keep overflowing in your service to God—even as you get older, and have already served Him well. The closer you get to the end, the more real it ought to be. Why? Because "your toil is not in vain in the Lord," Paul says. There is no such thing as wasted pain, wasted energy. In your life today, how are you abounding in God's work? What are you doing to influence people for the kingdom of God? Are you teaching? Are you counseling? Are you sharing with someone regularly? Are you giving money to ministries you believe in?

LET GOD BE GOD

He has also set eternity in their heart.
—Ecclesiastes 3:11

We see only part of God's plan, for in this life we are mortal, finite in our existence. Yet we desire to see more. We have an inborn inquisitiveness to learn how everything in our experience can be integrated to make a beautiful whole. That's why life remains an enigma…until men learn to fear God. "God has so worked that men should fear Him" (Ecclesiastes 3:14).

"Do not be *afraid*," Moses said at Mount Sinai, "for God has come … in order that *the fear of Him* may remain with you" (Exodus 20:20). "Stop being terrorized," he was saying, "but fear…" This is fear without terror—it means honor, respect, and reverence. This is *our* part in God's eternal plan. The nearest word in the New Testament for it is "faith." This is what life is all about. You can have your questions, your confusion, your doubts — but never use them as a reason for not fearing your God. The issue is not *agreement.* You keep His commandments, obeying what He says, whether you agree or not. And this obedience produces enjoyment of the "whole"; this is what it means to be human. God's plan is established. It all fits: He makes the past fit with the future. Everything in my past—my hurts and tears, my joys and victories, my failures and embarrassments—it all fits to make me uniquely me according to the plan of God.

Life has a plan…*if we let God be God.* Moses wrote, "The secret things belong the Lord our God" (Deuteronomy 29:29). I don't have to be able to explain everything; but as I fear God and watch, His plan for my life unfolds before my eyes.

DIRT POTS

I have been crucified with Christ...and the life which I now live
in the flesh I live by faith in the Son of God.
—Galatians 2:20

When Paul calls our bodies "earthen vessels" (in 2
Corinthians 4:7), that's no compliment he's throwing
at us. Rather, it's a gracious way of calling us pots
made of burnt clay—easily broken, and not worth
much. It's amazing how much attention we place on
the pot. We shape it, rub it, polish it, fill in the cracks.
We make it smell good, look good, be good. But the
fact is, it's still an earthen pot. When God told Adam,
"You came from dust and to dust you shall return,"
He was not being poetic, but factual.

But a pot—even a dirt pot—was created to carry
something. Just as an ordinary vial is transformed by
the value of the precious perfume it contains, so it is in
the mystery of the new covenant: The holy, precious
treasure of the presence of God is kept in a dust vessel.
Why would God do that? Paul gives the reason: "that
the surpassing greatness of the power may be of God
and not from ourselves" (4:7). That is, so the greatness
of God's power would be seen clearly in *what it can do*
with dust.

Paul says it's amazing what happens to these pots
when they hang around life long enough. They get
"afflicted in every way...perplexed...persecuted...
struck down" (4:8-9). But we're "not destroyed" (4:9).
Life may knock you down, but not out. Why? It has
nothing to do with the pot, but with what's inside it:
We're "always carrying about in the body the dying
of Jesus, that the life of Jesus also may be manifested
in our body" (4:10).

MYSTERY OF MYSTERIES

For to me, to live is Christ, and to die is gain.
—Philippians 1:21

The mystery of mysteries to me is the fact that God created these bodies out of dust to be able to contain a spirit which in turn could contain the Spirit of God Himself. "We have this treasure in earthen vessels," Paul says, "that the surpassing greatness of the power may be of God" (2 Corinthians 4:7). What is this "treasure"? Isn't it the presence of God within us, showing His power by changing us from what we were? Paul points out the resilience of these earthen vessels filled by God's presence (1 Corinthians 4:7-8):

"We are afflicted in every way, but not crushed"—We are pressured by the normal irritations of life, and start to feel compressed — but we aren't rendered useless. *"...perplexed, but not despairing"*—We get confused, uncertain, not knowing what to do (isn't it good to know that even the apostle Paul could get like this?), but we don't give up hope. *"...persecuted, but not forsaken"*—The intended offenses come against us, everything from cold shoulders and snide remarks to deliberate hindrances, personal and bodily attacks, torture, or death; yet we know we aren't left alone. *"...struck down, but not destroyed"*—We face catastrophes, sudden blows, shattering and stunning hardships such as cancer, fatal accidents, heart attacks; but we aren't taken out.

We suffer, as Jesus suffered—and the life of Christ is seen more clearly in our suffering than at any other time. Others see the reality of Christ in me as they see me suffer. Suffering has so much to do with it...so how serious are you about the lordship of Christ?

EVEN MORE ALIVE

We look not at the things which are seen,
but at the things which are not seen.
—2 Corinthians 4:18

If you were given the assignment to choose the five most important things you do or have in your life, what would they be? The things that are most meaningful and important to us will consume us—that's the very nature of "things." To be consumed by them may not be all bad. As a matter of fact, it may well be a sign of spiritual maturity in you. The question is: What things are consuming us?

Things tend to fall in one of two categories: the visible and the invisible. We tend to fill our lives with the visible things because they're so "real." But as we grow we change, and change has to do with what we value. As we mature, our concerns move to the invisible. Spiritual maturity means our values move from the insignificant to the significant. The things that are invisible replace the things that are visible, which pass away.

"Though the outer man is decaying," Paul says, "yet our inner man is being renewed day by day" (4:16). The physical body is aging and wearing out, but what's inside the pot is not. Inside is the "new creation" (5:17). This is the "new self…being renewed to a true knowledge according to the image of the One who created him" (Colossians 1:10). *Renewed* means "made even more alive." As the visible begins to die, the invisible becomes more real and alive to you.

You can test the spirit of your faith by asking yourself this: What visible things, when taken away, would cause me to bail out of my faith?

SEEING THE INVISIBLE

For momentary, light affliction is producing for us an eternal
weight of glory far beyond all comparisons.
—2 Corinthians 4:17

Paul is *not* saying here, "Oh well, it all balances out in the end—a little suffering, a little glory." He *is* saying that your suffering in the arena of the visible is *producing* the glory of the invisible in you—and it actually *causes* the invisible to be seen: "while we look not at the things which are seen, but at the things which are not seen" (4:18). We actually *look* at what is invisible, for only these things are lasting and *real:* "The things which are seen are temporal, but the things which are not seen are eternal" (4:18). The visible things eventually wear out, break down, die, disappear. But the invisible things are eternal—and eternal does not mean *intangible.* What things around you are invisible and yet tangible and permanent? What is more real to you—the body of another, or that person's spirit? Which one is permanent?

What are the invisible things you're being drawn to as you mature in your faith?

Speaking is the effect and proof of your faith. Paul says, "Having the same spirit of faith, according to what is written, 'I believed, therefore I spoke,' we also believe, therefore also we speak" (2 Corinthians 4:13). This "spirit of faith" refers to the deep convictions of what you believe to be true. I don't believe because it's "cool" to believe; in fact, if you want to know what I really believe, ask me when it's not cool to believe; see what I say when my world is falling apart.

What are you saying now?

SELF-PORTRAITS

When they measure themselves by themselves,
and compare themselves with themselves,
they are without understanding.
—2 Corinthians 10:12

Self-deceit is based upon *self-conceit*, and not upon the facts God says about you. Some among the Corinthians ended up condemning themselves because they established themselves as a standard: "Be what I am, do what I do," they were saying, "and you'll have worth." They were so insecure that anyone doing it differently (such as Paul) was seen as a threat. But he tells them they're "without understanding." They have a false picture of themselves; they're deceived; they're wrong.

Of all the people I know who would lie to me, you may be saying, *I'm not one of them.* Or are you?

Do we lie and feed misbeliefs to ourselves *about* ourselves? How do I begin recognizing and having confidence in the truth about who I am, and the truth about what I'm doing—without having to second-guess everything?

As he responded to criticism from the Corinthians, Paul told them, "You are looking at things as they are outwardly" (2 Corinthians 10:7). They were letting external things determine worth and praise. But our picture of ourselves will always be fuzzy if we look to externals for strokes.

Paul said, "I say to every man among you not to think more highly of himself than he ought to think; but to think so as to have sound judgment" (Romans 12:3).

Does your self-portrait need focusing?

TESTED AND RECOMMENDED

We are not bold to class or compare ourselves
with some of those who commend themselves.
—2 Corinthians 10:12

Paul refused to let another man's gifts or ministry be the standard by which he judged himself. Paul said the proof of his labor, "within the measure of the sphere which God apportioned to us," was the *fruit* of it. And his expectation was that "we shall be, within our sphere, enlarged even more by you" (10:13-15). To be "enlarged" meant to be encouraged by them, affirmed.

In your own life and ministry, is there affirmation for what you're doing? Either something is happening, or it isn't. Either there is the fruit of people increasing in their faith, or there isn't. The issue is, How is God using me in the lives of others?

"He who boasts, let him boast in the Lord," Paul said (10:17). Is God being glorified by what I am doing? As I let my light shine before men, do I see happening around me what Jesus said in Matthew 5:16—"that they may see your good works, *and glorify your Father who is in heaven*"? How can I be sure it's happening?

By asking one more question: Can the Lord commend me? Paul said, "For not he who commends himself is approved, but whom the Lord commends" (2 Corinthians 10:18). This word approved means "approved by testing." Has the Lord tested and approved me? Would Jesus recommend me to someone else to be of some use to them? What is it I have to offer, that He would do so?

WHAT TO TELL YOURSELF

For not he who commends himself is approved,
but whom the Lord commends.
—2 Corinthians 10:18

Maybe you're a bit shaken in confidence about where you are in your life right now—as a husband or wife, as a parent, as a Christian...or maybe just as a human being you feel a bit like a dirt bag. What has shaken you up? An apparent failure? Criticism? Tiredness, and a sense of hopelessness that it isn't going to get any better? Let me replace some common misbeliefs—lies we tell ourselves—with some statements of truth which we *should* be telling ourselves:

(1) It isn't necessary for me to be liked by everyone. (2) I don't have to earn anyone's approval or acceptance. (3) I'm a child of God. I'm deeply loved by Him, and I've been forgiven by Him; therefore I am acceptable—and I accept myself. (4) If somebody doesn't like me, I can live with it. I don't have to work feverishly to get him to change his mind. (5) Jesus died on the cross for me so I can be free from the myth that other people decide my worth and success.

Now that we've established that it's not other people who determine our effectiveness or worth... where are you in life? Do you believe you're doing what God wants you to be doing? Whether its encouraging, serving, supporting, teaching, praying, counseling, or whatever—are you doing it? How do you feel about what you're doing? How does God feel about what you're doing? Is He being glorified? Do you see Him affirming you by giving evidence that the lives of others are being affected by what you're doing?

FOLDED AND PUT AWAY

For we know that if the earthly tent which is our house
is torn down, we have a building from God,
a house not made with hands, eternal in the heavens.
—2 Corinthians 5:1

Paul the tentmaker speaks in this passage of two different habitations and the thoroughfare between them. One is our earthly tent, which is someday "torn down," dismantled and folded and put away. It's the life we've worked hard to make, the visible things that take so much work from our hands to acquire, to maintain, to protect. But this life, this habitation, is like a sentence that ends not with a period, but with a comma. What follows is the next habitation: a house, a permanent building from God, not made with hands, eternal in the heavens. By faith the tent-dweller Abraham searched for this place "whose architect and builder is God" (Hebrews 11:10).

What most distinguishes the first habitation from the second is that in this earthly existence, "we groan" (2 Corinthians 5:2). We're "burdened" (5:4). We long to enter heaven which is prepared and waiting for us. Meanwhile, we endure affliction. There is no satisfaction in pain for the Christian. It hurts us like it hurts anyone. Jesus came into this habitation and felt the pain with the rest of us; He cried at times. But now He has gone to prepare a place for us, and God meanwhile "gave to us the Spirit as a pledge" (5:5), the first installment of what is coming in full blessing, the great down payment on heaven. But Paul reminds us: "We walk by faith, not by sight" (5:7). We walk by faith because we're not there yet; this tent isn't home. But home is coming soon…on the other side of the comma.

POWERFUL PROOF

*Therefore you are to be perfect,
as your heavenly Father is perfect.*
—Matthew 5:48

The Sermon on the Mount in Matthew 5-7 is addressed to those who follow Jesus Christ as their Lord. For unbelievers this is simply a senseless idealism. But for the believer it is very serious realism.

In this discourse Jesus lays down unattainable standards that are physically impossible for any human being to fulfill. On your own you cannot consistently obey what He says here. And that's why the kingdom people must obey these commands, this ethic of living, *by the power of the Spirit of God within them.*

Jesus commands us to do *what no man, no woman can do.* "Do it," He says. And so we do it—and we see the power of God in our lives by *doing the very things He's told us to do.* When we prayerfully depend on His Spirit to help us do what Jesus would do in our everyday encounters with life, this is the mystery we see: He does *through* us what He Himself would do in the same situation.

That's why it's a supernatural walk. That's why this is the very core of the teaching of our Lord.

Here is the guarantee of the Holy Spirit's presence within you. The greatest proof that you're different than you were before you were a Christian is your Spirit-given ability to live out in absolute obedience the very words of Jesus in the Sermon on the Mount.

And if you should choose not to try to live them out—you'll never know for sure that you could.

What proof is there in your life today of the power of God at work?

I KNOW MY TRANSGRESSIONS

Against Thee, Thee only, have I sinned,
and done what is evil in Thy sight.
—Psalm 51

David knew sorrow. He grieved over loneliness, rejection, discouragement. He mourned the loss of an infant child. He mourned the rebellion and deaths of two grown sons. Yet nothing broke his heart more than his own sin. Hear him in Psalm 51, after his sin with Bathsheba, as he comes to the Lord, ready to talk:

"Be gracious to me, O God," he cries; "according to the greatness of Thy compassion blot out my transgressions. Wash me thoroughly from my iniquity, and cleanse me from my sin. For I know my transgressions, and my sin is ever before me..."

After this confession, he adds these words to his prayer: "Thou does not delight in sacrifice, otherwise I would give it." *I could do penance,* he is saying to God. *I could do religious deeds, I could try to work off my sorrow and prove to You I'm okay.* But David knows that God desires something else: "The sacrifices of God are a broken spirit; *a broken and contrite heart,* O God, Thou wilt not despise."

David is like other godly men and women down through time who all seem to have this in common: the struggle and grief over their sinfulness. And what do we do? We immature ones try to make them feel better: "Don't be so hard on yourself," we tell them. "Don't go on a guilt trip." But no, they're not being hard on themselves. They see the truth. Spiritual maturity on this earth is not sinlessness (sinlessness is reserved for heaven). They see the sin, and they have learned the right response to it.

THE SIN OF MY PEOPLE

He saw the city and wept over it.
—Luke 19:41

Twice in the Bible we read clear statements that Jesus wept. One is in Luke 19, when He looks out upon Jerusalem and weeps over the sins of His people. The other is in John 11, after the death of Lazarus. Though He will be raising Lazarus in a few minutes, still He weeps, for He sees the consequences—the pain—of sin and death all around.

We are to mourn over sin, and not just our own. We are to grieve at the reality of sin around us.

God is serious about this. In one of Ezekiel's visions, the Lord commands an angelic being to go "through the midst of Jerusalem, and put a mark on the foreheads of the men who sign and groan over all the abominations which are being committed in its midst" (9:5). Daniel tells us that he was "praying and confessing my sin *and the sin of my people*" (9:20). And the psalmist writes, "My eyes shed streams of water..." Why? He has looked around: "because *they* do not keep Thy law" (119:136).

We'll confess our own sins, all right—but others' too? That's *their* problem, we say. Perhaps we even joke about them. John MacArthur has pointed out that much of the church today has a defective sense of sin. So we have a defective sense of humor, and we find ourselves laughing at the very things we ought to be crying over.

As you look around today, what makes you laugh? And what makes you weep—and pray?

THE POWER DRIVE

Blessed are the gentle [the meek, the humble],
for they shall inherit the earth.
—*Matthew 5:5*

What kind of formula is this for happiness?

The right one. This is not an opinion, because Jesus never uttered opinions. He never guessed; He *knew.* And those who will trust that Jesus knows life (because He's the Creator of life) will prove that He understands what He's talking about.

Frederick Nietzsche, of "God is dead" fame, argued that the hunger for power is the essence of our humanity, the basic human drive. Consequently he referred to those who believed in Jesus Christ as a "herd of inferior creatures." Why? Because Christ asked people to surrender to God and to reject any selfish attempts to control others. That was anathema to Nietzsche.

The remarkable thing was that Nietzsche was absolutely right. He knew that the gentleness Jesus taught precluded all power games; that the craving of power could not be reconciled with the Christian lifestyle; that Christ asked us to submit only to Him, and to be content only with Him. He understood the Christian faith better than most Christians. According to Nietzsche, Christ was asking us to live contrary to a basic human drive for power. In short, to be coercive and to be Christian at the same time is absolutely impossible.

What is it that God wants you to do now, and you haven't done it, for whatever reason? Make a commitment right now to do it—as an exercise in gentleness.

WE WOULD BE GODS

Jesus, knowing…that He had come forth from God…
began to wash the disciples' feet.
—John 13:3-5

The craving for power is at the heart of what the Bible calls sin. Satan promised Eve, *"You will be like God, knowing good and evil."* We, too, would be gods, served and treated as gods—even by God Himself. (When you pray, do you want *your* will to be done? Do you want to manipulate God? *God, treat me as a god, and do what I want.* Or do we pray because we want what God wants?)

What are you grabbing for? What's so important to you that you have to protect and pretend and be careful? Are you grabbing for reputation? Is it so important that people know exactly the wonderful person you are, so that they treat you…like a god?

Are you grabbing for honor? Do you want people to think you're spiritual, godly, pure? Do you want them to honor you as they would honor … a god?

Are you grabbing for power, for that position, that influence, so you can control people, that they might serve you as they would serve…a god?

What is gentleness? What is humility? What is meekness? It's realizing you're not a god, and you're not to be treated as a god. God the Son—who *is* to be treated as God—came to this earth, became a man, and showed us what human beings were wired to be: servants of the Most High. We are not wired to constantly shield ourselves, protect ourselves; it will rob us of any sense of happiness, *ever*.

Therefore we must be gentle people.

NOT WORTH THE EFFORT

Christ Jesus...emptied Himself,
taking the form of a bond-servant,
and being made in the likeness of men.
—Philippians 2:5-7

There's something here Jesus is trying to tell us: Men, human beings, were never wired to be treated as gods. Christ shows us here what humanity is all about. All those made "in the likeness of men" are to become bond-servants of God.

We are not wired to be gods, and it's a tremendous burden to try to be treated like one when we aren't. It's a burden that robs us of any chance for real happiness.

Think of the burden of pride and pretense. The labor of self-love is exhausting. Think for yourself how much sorrow has come from someone speaking evil of you. When you set yourself up as a god to whom you must be loyal, there will always be those who delight to offer affront to your idol.

The heart's fierce effort to protect itself from every judgment, to shield its tender honor from the painful opinions of friend or enemy, will never let you have rest. The burden of cringing under every criticism, flinching under every slight, tossing and turning during sleepless nights because somebody was preferred above you—there is no satisfaction in this.

The gentle man does not at all care who is greater than he is, for he has long ago decided that the esteem of the world is not worth the effort.

THE WHOLE THING

Blessed are those who hunger and thirst for righteousness,
for they shall be satisfied
—Matthew 5:6

You may know of someone who swears a little, gambles a bit, loses his temper now and then—and yet, if someone was in trouble, he would be the first to give his last penny or the very coat off his back. This is good, but it is only partial good. *We* may be satisfied with it, but it is not the person whom Jesus says is blessed—the person who hungers and thirsts for righteousness.

Jesus describes someone whose passion is for *total* righteousness. The word in the original Greek signifies not "some righteousness" or "partial righteousness," but the whole thing. Jesus is saying, "Oh, how happy is the one who hungers and thirsts for *total righteousness all the time.*" How happy are those who feel the most important thing in life is to always be in a right relationship with God, and to live out that relationship rightly! This longing is the believer's birthmark, a sign of the genuineness of one's faith. Righteousness is the believer's supreme desire.

It's a desire that brings satisfaction. "For He has satisfied the thirsty soul, and the hungry soul He has filled with what is good" (Psalm 107:9). "They who seek the Lord shall not be in want of any good thing" (Psalm 34:10).

It is one thing to be "haunted by goodness," having that little sting of guilt that says, "Maybe I ought to do something right once in a while." It's quite another to have a passion for doing what is right.

APPETITE FOR RIGHTEOUSNESS

My soul thirsts for God, for the living God.
—Psalm 42:2

If we have a healthy and truthful self-esteem, we know that God is God—and that we are not. We grieve over the sinfulness of sin in ourselves and in anyone else. And instead of demanding to be treated and served as a god, we know we're here to serve God and carry out His will.

This is the thinking that leads to happiness, because it leads to the fourth Beatitude: "Oh, how happy are those who hunger and thirst for righteousness."

What *is* this appetite for righteousness, for goodness? And how do we develop it?

Few of us know what it's like to be really hungry or thirsty. But in ancient Palestine a working man was never far from hunger. And on his journeys, a hot south wind would at times bring a sandstorm, and there was nothing to do but wrap his head and turn his back to the wind, and wait—while the sand filled his nostrils and throat until he thought he would suffocate. That's what thirst meant to him.

The question Jesus poses is this: How much do you want goodness? How much is it on your mind? Do we want righteousness as much as a starving man wants food, or a thirsting man craves water?

You can read Psalm 42:1—"As the deer pants for the water brooks, so my soul pants for Thee , O God" —but can you relate to it? Can you say, *"Yes, that's me"*?

COURAGE, AND MORE

… in your knowledge, self-control,
and in your self-control, perseverance…
—2 Peter 1:6

How great is your courage?

What does it take to get you to disobey what you know is right in the sight of God? A little criticism? A drop in your popularity? Losing a paycheck? However much you can handle before you go against what you know God wants you to do—that's the amount of courage you have.

What is self-control? If you know what's right, and want to do what's right, and then *choose to do what's right*—that's self-control.

What is perseverance? It is doing what is right even when it's hurtful and hard. No matter how difficult, you keep on doing it…until it's part of you. It becomes your nature, a habit.

What is righteousness? In Hebrews 5:13-14, "the word of righteousness" is described as "solid food." The teaching of righteousness is meat, and it's for the mature: "Solid food is for the mature, who *because of practice have their senses trained to discern good and evil.*" By practice, the mature have *knowledge:* This is right, this is wrong.

Doing what is right in the sight of God does not mean being perfect. I feel sorry for perfectionists, because they can never really be happy; I've never met a perfectionist who did not feel in some way a failure. As a matter of fact, perfectionism basically denies progress. God doesn't demand our perfection; He does ask us to hunger for righteousness, and—by courage—to grow in *doing it.*

RICOCHET PRINCIPLE

Blessed are the merciful, for they shall receive mercy.
—Matthew 5:7

At the time Jesus spoke those words, mercy wasn't on the world's top ten list of virtues. A popular Roman philosopher called mercy "the disease of the soul." Rome glorified strength and power, and saw mercy as the supreme sign of weakness. A Roman father could decide whether his newborn child would live or die. The infant was brought to him, and if the father raised his thumb, the child lived; if the father's thumb turned down, the child would be immediately drowned. Any society that despises mercy (think about how we treat the unborn today) will eventually glorify brutality.

In Jesus' words in Matthew 5:7, some see a ricochet principle: You scratch my back, I'll scratch yours. What goes around, comes around. Treat others right and they'll treat you right.

Is Jesus saying here that I can use mercy as a way to *get* mercy from others?

There's a problem with that interpretation: It doesn't always work. No one was more merciful and caring than Jesus Himself — and they crucified Him.

No, Jesus is not teaching that mercy to men and women will bring mercy *from* men and women. He is teaching that mercy to them will bring us mercy from God. There *is* a ricochet principle, but it's between *God* and *you*. David affirmed it in his prayer in Psalm 18: "With the kind Thou dost show Thyself kind."

REAL TEARS

And be kind to one another, tenderhearted, forgiving each other,
just as God in Christ also has forgiven you.
—Ephesians 4:32

The Greek word translated *tenderhearted* in this verse was used to describe one with "healthy intestines." Let yourself feel things from deep within. It's okay to cry if it's from the gut!

Get outside your own feelings, and start seeing what others see, thinking the way they think. Get into their skin. Put yourself in a place to feel their suffering. Stop isolating yourself from pain. Instead of running from it, learn and be affected by it.

Begin to look for suffering. It might be a good idea to spend time walking around in hospitals—especially the pediatrics floor. Watch the little children and see their suffering. Don't be afraid. Look at it.

Behind each suffering person, there's a story. Each one is a living novel. Listen to them. Learn from their suffering.

When you see disaster reports on television, don't turn it off. Instead of being upset by "all the bad news" (yes, it's bad news—*suffering* news), ask God to let it break your heart so you might feel some of the suffering. Feel what those involved must feel. Feel it in your intestines.

Stop getting bitter toward God when you're going through pain. Let suffering have its perfect work.

And then, when you see someone else suffering... you won't have to pretend sensitivity. You won't have to fake the tears. Your heart can break as quickly as anyone's.

WHERE YOU ARE WHO YOU ARE

Who may ascend into the hill of the Lord?
And who may stand in His holy place?
He who has clean hands and a pure heart…
     —Psalm 24:3-4

Jesus says it's "the pure in heart" who will see God (Matthew 5:8). But our hearts are pretty messed up in impurity and hypocrisy, as Jesus points out: *"Out of the heart* come evil thoughts, murders, adulteries, fornications, thefts, false witness, slanders" (Matthew 15:19). "The heart is more deceitful than all else," says the Lord in Jeremiah 17:9, "and is desperately sick; who can understand it?" Only God can purify a heart.

The heart is one's inner person, the center of personality, of intentions and will. Your heart is what makes you uniquely you. Your heart is who you are. That's why Solomon warns, "Watch over your heart with all diligence, for from it flow the springs of life."

God took the kingdom of Israel away from King Saul because of Saul's heart problems. And God gave it to David, not because he was younger, smarter, or stronger, but because the Lord "sought out for Himself a man after His own heart."

Today, if you will, speak to God the way David speaks in the Psalms: "Search me, O God, and know my heart" (139:23); "Create in me a pure heart, O God" (51:10); "Let the meditation of my heart be acceptable in Thy sight, O Lord" (19:14); "My heart is steadfast, O God, my heart is steadfast" (Psalm 57:7).

Paul tells us to present our bodies to God as a living sacrifice. Have you ever dedicated *your heart* to Him? Now would be a great time to do it.

GOD'S LINE OF WORK

...being diligent to preserve the unity of the Spirit
in the bond of peace.
—Ephesians 4:3

Peacemakers, Jesus said, "shall be called sons of God." Peacemakers, those who work to resolve conflicts, will be recognized as being Godlike, doing Godlike work—God's work. The man or woman who is a maker of peace is in the same line of work God is in.

The book of Romans closes with, "Now the God of peace be with you all" (15:33). The book of 2 Corinthians ends with, "The God of love and peace shall be with you" (13:11). The book of 1 Thessalonians ends with, "May the God of peace Himself sanctify you entirely" (5:23). And the book of Hebrews closes with, "May the God of peace...equip you in every good thing to do His will" (13:20-21). God is the *God of peace*, and those who know Him know what He's about: peacemaking.

Reconciliation is peacemaking. And reconciliation is the work God has given us: "God ... reconciled us to Himself through Christ, and gave us the ministry of reconciliation.... He has committed to us the word of reconciliation. Therefore, we are ambassadors for Christ" (2 Corinthians 5:18-20).

The first peace is peace with God—salvation. But the ministry of reconciliation doesn't stop there. *For Christ's sake*, our peace is also with one another. Jesus prayed for our unity, in order "that the world may believe that Thou didst send Me" (John 17:21).

Today, in which of your relationships is there need for peace, for reconciliation?

THIS MOMENT IN ETERNITY

Blessed are those who have been persecuted
for the sake of righteousness, for theirs
is the kingdom of heaven.
—Matthew 5:10

Notice that the word is *righteousness*, not *rudeness*. Some of us get beat up in the world because we act like jerks. But to be persecuted for the sake of righteousness is to suffer for doing what is right in the sight of God. It's to allow yourself to be persecuted rather than compromising what you believe.

Do you like getting harassed? I don't. I want people to like me, respect me, speak well of me. But Jesus said, "Woe to you when all men speak well of you" (Luke 6:26).

The righteous will be rewarded for their persecution. "Rejoice," Jesus said, "and be glad, for great is your reward in heaven" (Matthew 5:12). This is the leap for joy when the good guys get the victory. The persecuted righteous will have a great reward in heaven, and it doesn't bother Jesus to mention it.

The clash between the world and Christ is only a moment in the drama of eternity. To have a share in such a moment is not a penalty, but a glory.

It's only under pressure that we know what we believe. That's why Jesus says that through persecution we come to know that the kingdom of heaven is ours. We'll be there because we know our faith is genuine, tested, proven.

When you have to suffer for your faith, it's the doorway to the closest possible companionship with Christ and with those who belong to Him.

TRUE SIGHT FOLLOWS TRUST

We have as our ambition…to be pleasing to Him.
—2 Corinthians 5:9

Ambition here is a noble word. It means "to love as a point of honor." As a point of honor, we love being pleasing to God. For we know we shall stand before Him with the question before us: How did I honor Him? "For we must all appear before the judgment seat of Christ, that each one may be recompensed for his deeds in the body, according to what he has done, whether good or bad" (2 Corinthians 5:10). This is more than just "being there"—it means "standing publicly" before the raised platform on which is the judge's chair, from which he pronounces judgment. We shall be responsible for both the good and the good-for-nothing things we did while on this earth— the things that pleased Him, and the things that didn't.

He's expecting you. Jesus *wants* us with Him, and we *shall be* with Him. "We shall see Him as He is. And everyone who has this hope fixed on Him purifies Himself, just as He is pure" (Hebrews 3:3). While we wait in hope, we purify ourselves; we aim to please Him. While we wait, "we are of good courage" (2 Corinthians 5:8); we will not bail out of this life and out from under the weight it carries, because we know what's down the road; we live now "by faith and not by sight" (5:7). To be honest, if given a choice, we would "prefer rather to be absent from the body and to be at home with the Lord" (5:8). We'd rather have sight now, seeing Jesus face to face; but our faith is confident. Our faith is in *what we shall see*, not in what isn't there! True sight always follows trust.

THE WOUNDED WISE

Reprove a wise man, and he will love you.
—*Proverbs 9:8*

You learn a lot about a person by how he responds (or reacts) to correction. He can appear foolish: "Fools despise wisdom and instruction" (1:7)—or increasingly wise: "Give instruction to a wise man, and he will be still wiser" (9:9).

A true, loving friend will risk a friendship in speaking the truth for the good of another: "Faithful are the wounds of a friend" (27:6); "Iron sharpens iron, so one man sharpens another" (27:17). But what a fearful thing to do if there's a good chance you'll get your head torn off!

The wise know that God uses other people to be tools in their lives, shaping His holiness in them, enhancing their usability in the hands of God. The wise respond to reproof with the sorrow that produces repentance (2 Corinthians 7:9-10). The wise know that the reason God is so direct about sin is that He is so direct about forgiveness (1 John 1:9).

When was the last time you were reproved by one of your friends? If it hasn't happened lately—why hasn't it? Is it because they're afraid of you? Is it because of your foolishness?

Who does God use in your life to challenge and correct and exhort you? Go to that person once a year to give him permission to ask you the hard questions about your life.

Are you still angry at someone who corrected you in the past? If so—what is it time for you to do? (Look at Matthew 5:23-24 and Matthew 18:15.)

A PATTERN FOR REPROOF

You are in our hearts to die together and to live together.
—2 Corinthians 7:3

Paul sent a strong letter of reproof to the Corinthians, and possibly made another visit to them rebuking them for their sin. Later in 2 Corinthians 7 we see their response, but first Paul reminds them of his motive. "Make room for us in your hearts ... I do not speak to condemn you; for I have said before that you are in our hearts... Great is my confidence in you, great is my boasting on your behalf... I am overflowing with joy in all our affliction" (7:2-4).

Respond to us, Paul is saying, don't react; for I'm committed to your success. I want you to be all that God wants you to be. We have both died together to our old life, and are living together a new life to please Him. I am so proud of you and what God is accomplishing in your lives that I can't sit back and see you throw it all out. Even when I get beat up, it's my thoughts of you that comfort and encourage me.

Paul suffered with them, knowing his reproof would hurt. But he knew there were times when you have to inflict a little pain in order to relieve a lot of pain. "You were made sorrowful," he said, "in order that you might not suffer loss" (7:9). That loss would be to lose their usefulness to God in the lives of others.

Paul didn't waste time arguing about whose fault it was. That wasn't the issue. "I wrote to you ... not for the sake of the offender, nor for the sake of the one offended, but that your earnestness on our behalf might be made known to you in the sight of God" (7:12). The real issue, then, is the "earnestness" of the response in the sight of God.

MONEY

Though He was rich, yet for your sake He became poor.
—2 Corinthians 8:9

Money? you ask. *Shouldn't we be discussing spiritual things?* Did you know more is said in the New Testament about money than about heaven and hell combined? Or that of the thirty-eight parables Jesus gave, sixteen dealt with money?

But, you say, *I get offended when the church talks about my money.* Well, let's get ready to get offended together. Besides, we're not talking about *your* money; we're talking about His.

Do you believe Psalm 24:1?—"The earth is the Lord's and all it contains." As David prayed, "Both riches and honor come from Thee" (1 Chronicles 29:12). Paul reminded the Colossians that in Christ "all things were created...all things have been created through Him and *for* Him" (1:16).

Money, giving, and stewardship involve *all* of who and what you are.

Sometimes we need models—you can't imitate a definition. In giving, Paul gave the Corinthians the example of the Macedonians (in 2 Corinthians 8:1-6) ...and then the example of Someone else: "For you know the grace of our Lord Jesus Christ, that though He was rich, yet for your sake He became poor, that you through His poverty might become rich" (8:9). Jesus "emptied Himself" (Philippians 2:7). When you love, you give...and it comes down to being something tangible as to how and what you give. Jesus gave *Himself.*

Jesus said, "No one of you can be My disciple who does not give up all his own possessions" (Luke 14:33).

IN EVERYTHING

We wish to make known to you the grace of God
which has been given in the churches of Macedonia.
—*2 Corinthians 8:1*

We say we trust God. In what? "In everything," we answer. But how do we know that—unless we've actually gone through everything and trusted Him?

Because of tremendous persecution against the Jewish believers in Jerusalem, there was painful poverty in the church there. Their fellow Jews had cut them off. Gentiles wouldn't give them work unless they bowed to the local union god. And so, the Jerusalem Christians were in straits. Paul was taking up a collection among gentile Christians elsewhere to take back to Jerusalem as a "love gift" (the "collection for the saints" in 1 Corinthians 16:1).

But the Corinthian believers were slacking off in their giving for this, so Paul admonished them with the example of the Macedonian churches: "In a great ordeal of affliction their abundance of joy and their deep poverty overflowed in the wealth of their liberality" (2 Corinthians 8:2). This, Paul said, was "the grace of God" to the Macedonians (8:1); it wasn't something natural, but something supernatural happening within them, for they were in poverty. Their "great ordeal" was a testing of their trust in God. They were demonstrating their faith. Though economics were tight and budgets squeaking, their giving overflowed in liberality...and not with fear, but with abundant joy! They had made up their minds what was right to do, and they did it despite their circumstances.

They were committed to being a part of God's grace to others. Is that your commitment too?

EXPECTING A LOT

Enter into the joy of your master.
—Matthew 25:21,23

In the parable of the talents, the master entrusted different amounts to different workers. This parable applies to us living in this age now, and these "talents" speak of our time, influence, abilities, resources, creativity—all the things entrusted to us. At the end of the parable, the master demanded to know what each of the servants had done with what he had given them. Likewise, all of us will give an account.

"He who received the one talent went away and dug in the ground, and hid his master's money" (Matthew 25:18). This servant didn't do anything wild or vile, but he acted irresponsibly with what had been entrusted to Him. He preserved what he had, but didn't do anything positive by investing it wisely.

The master sure expects a lot—that was on the lazy servant's mind as he gave account to his master. Our Master does expect a lot from us—and that's a great compliment, because He *knows we can do it*. What can be more motivating than that?

Notice also that the reward for those who were good stewards with their talents was not a trip to Hawaii—it was more responsibility: "You were faithful with a few things; I will put you in charge of many things" (25:21,23). The reward for being responsible is more responsibility. The reward for good work is more work. Heaven will be more work than here (I'm glad; I wasn't really excited about playing harps for eternity).

The parable's major point: We're held responsible for how we invest all the resources we've been given.

GOOD INVESTMENTS

Lay up for yourselves treasures in heaven.
—Matthew 6:20

Foolish giving does not glorify God. The needs are too great for us to be wasting resources. Where are the good investments?

God has given you some of His funds to be channeled through you into ministries for His kingdom. How do you know where to give?

There is foolishness out there begging for your money. Satan would love to take money earmarked by God for the work of His kingdom and divert those funds into waste. There are shysters out there; and there are also good people who don't know how to use God's funds effectively for the kingdom.

Since we're held accountable for how we use all the resources we've been given, I want all the help I can get for significantly investing God's money. In 2 Corinthians 8:16-24, Paul illustrates for us four qualifications of a worthy ministry to support—four good questions to ask before you invest God's resources in "ministry":

(1) Do I see a servant's heart in this ministry?
(2) Is there clear proof this ministry exists only to honor God by presenting Jesus Christ and His Word?
(3) Is this ministry's reputation above reproach?
(4) Is this a "one-man deal," or is there a spirit of cooperation with other people, and with what God is doing in other ministries?

Have you asked those questions of each ministry you support? Where are *your* spiritual investments?

BRINGING ATTENTION

They will glorify God for your obedience.
—*2 Corinthians 9:13*

Our sense of having great worth has a lot to do with whether we're *doing* something of great worth. Some people never think deeper than a thimble; otherwise they end up on the road of pessimism. You can delude yourself into believing you're accomplishing great things; but if you're not, why live a deception?

Look at something significant in 2 Corinthians 9:12; Paul speaks of the act of giving: "The ministry of this service is not only fully supplying the needs of the saints, but is also *overflowing through many thanksgivings to God*" (2 Corinthians 9:12). This is more than collecting money. It's wrong to think our giving is only to help poor folks out of a jam; that might make us feel warm and fuzzy, but it's not Paul's point. Giving produces an *overflow of thanksgiving to God.*

The point is this: Money can be converted into something significant...something as significant as people giving praise and thanksgiving to God.

Paul says, "Because of the proof given by this ministry, they will glorify God" (9:13). The proof, the test of any gift is this: Does it cause others to glorify God, or does it glorify someone or something else (such as yourself)? The highest aim of any of us is this single purpose: to glorify God. The point is to bring attention to *Him,* who *He* is, what *He* has done. It's one thing to believe God loves people; it's another to put our money where our belief is, and treat people with that worth—Paul is speaking of the act of giving, investing in the lives of others. This demonstrates that they're important enough for us to invest in them.

STAND FIRM

Stand firm against the schemes of the devil.
—Ephesians 6:11

We don't wrestle "against flesh and blood, but against the rulers...the powers...the world forces of this darkness...the spiritual forces of wickedness in the heavenly places" (Ephesians 6:12). Where does the struggle lie? The "schemes of the devil" (6:11) fall into two attacks: deception, and affliction, both designed to attack your faith in Jesus Christ. Satan wants either to confuse you about what you believe is true, or through suffering get you to doubt everything—"How can I trust a God who lets this happen?" The battle ground of affliction is in our emotions; the battle ground of deception centers in our minds (though even here we can't get away from our emotions).

We're not enticed into sin by the prospect of committing evil; rather, we're enticed to believe evil is *not* evil; we're convinced there's some good in it. So we cheat on our taxes ("It's not stealing; the government is so wasteful, and besides, everyone does it"); we gossip ("only passing on truth from those of us who have mature discernment"); we hate and are unforgiving ("Someone must make them pay for what what they've done"); and we believe heresy and even generously support the heretic who teaches it, because they speak of joy, peace, triumph—who can be against such things?

Unless we understand this, we'll be pathetically gullible, sucked into sin, blown this way and that. Am I being too hard? "Let no one deceive you with empty words, for because of these things the wrath of God comes upon the sons of disobedience" (Ephesians 5:6).

SEEING THROUGH DISGUISES

See to it that no one takes you captive
through philosophy and empty deception.
—Colossians 2:8

It's not right, but it's a fact of life: The credibility of a message tends to stand or fall by the people who bring it. Our response is based not on whether the message is true, but rather on "Who said it?" and "Do we like the guy who said it?" That's the danger of the Mormons, the Jehovah's Witnesses, the new agers, the humanists—they're mostly nice people, some of the nicest people you'll ever meet.

The false teachers didn't want the Corinthians to like Paul, so they focused their attack on him as a person. They accused him of not being an apostle, since he wasn't part of the first twelve. They attacked his ministry because he wasn't a skilled speaker. They accused him of being a snob for not accepting money for his work. Because these attacks were affecting his ministry, Paul was forced in 2 Corinthians 11 to do something he hated to do: boast. This extreme to which he had to go is his defense is what he calls "foolishness" (11:1).

Paul wanted to expose these "likable" villains for who they really were and for why they were being so likable. He goes to the bottom line: "Such men are false apostles, deceitful workers, disguising themselves as apostles of Christ" (2 Corinthians 2:13). They had to disguise themselves because they still had the nature of their father Satan—"And no wonder, for even Satan disguises himself as an angel of light" (11:14).

Do you know how to see through the disguises?

MIND GAMES

*...that you may be able to resist in the evil day,
and having done everything, to stand firm.*
—*Ephesians 6:13*

Paul fleshes out his concern for the Corinthians with the picture of a father presenting his daughter to her new husband: "I betrothed you to one husband, that to Christ I might present you as a pure virgin" (11:2). At the coming of Christ, Paul wanted to present to Him this bride — the Corinthian believers—in purity and faithfulness. He had "a godly jealousy" (11:2) for them. Jealousy is a vice if it's only a rage over self-interest; but if it's a holy rage over the well-being of the one who is loved, it's a virtue. Paul was fearful for them: "I am afraid, lest as the serpent deceived Eve by his craftiness, your minds should be led astray from the simplicity and purity of devotion to Christ" (11:3).

How was Eve deceived? It had something to do with the mind—mind games, if you will. And it had something to do with Satan's "craftiness," a word meaning "deceit." Satan is a liar! (Jesus said so—John 8:44). Look in Genesis 3 at what Satan did: He *questioned* what God had said ("Indeed has God said..."); he *confused* what God had said ("or touch it..."); he *denied* what God had said ("you surely shall not die..."); he *substituted* what God had said ("you will be like God..."). Nothing has changed. It worked then, so Satan still uses it. The battle ground is in the mind, and begins with *what we think* about *what God has said*. That's how we get moved away from "the simplicity and purity of devotion to Christ." We must be a people of the Word! Tell yourself the truth—and the truth is His Word. But first, you must know the Word.

NO FOOL

The fool has said in his heart, "There is no God."
—Psalm 53:1

Satan attempts to make us fools, but he's no fool himself; he knows there is a God.

What would happen if Satan came to us in demonic appearances, as we're told he appears in other cultures? After the shock, we would be confirmed in our faith by sight! A culture which already believes in the spirit world can be controlled by fear; but our culture doesn't, so Satan's control is by deception. The "prince of darkness" appears "as an angel of light" (2 Corinthians 11:14). As he attacks, he makes people think they're dealing with the truth of God. He must convince us that his words are God's words. We can counter with "the sword of the Spirit, which is the word of God" (Ephesians 6:17), but our sword gets rusty when the Book is closed, and Satan's attacks confuse and deceive. *Beware of those who claim revelation from God that does not come from the Book!*

"His servants also disguise themselves as servants of righteousness" (11:15). Where would we expect to find these? In the cults and occult movements. If they were calling themselves Christians and even Christian leaders in Paul's day, they'll be doing the same today. *Beware when they call us to unity, and then accuse us of being divisive when we do not join with them!* These are the people, Paul says, "whose end shall be according to their deeds" (11:15).

His warning is like the words of Isaiah: "Woe to those who call evil good, and good evil; who substitute darkness for light and light for darkness" (5:20).

A WAY TO SAY WHAT IS DEEP

Whenever you fast...anoint your head, and wash your face,
so that you may not be seen fasting by men.
—Matthew 6:16-18

Because of that deep need we all have to be admired, the Pharisees used fasting to show just how spiritual they thought they were. But Jesus said, "When you fast, do not put on a gloomy face as the hypocrites do." His point: Look normal when you fast; bring no attention to yourself.

Throughout the Scriptures we find godly people fasting, among them Moses, Samuel, Hannah, David, Anna, John the Baptist, Paul, and most importantly, Jesus Himself. Their fasting was always linked with prayer. They fasted when there was grief, in times of danger, when they were penitent, when they were seeking God's will, or when a great task was before them. Fasting was not some sort of magic for them, but *demonstrated the sincerity of their prayer*. You can pray without fasting, but you cannot fast biblically without praying. Fasting is an affirmation of the intensity of your prayer, your desire to see God's desire. Have you ever second-guessed your sincerity at something? When you are consumed with concern, you fast.

Fasting isn't a shortcut to spirituality. It isn't a way to manipulate God to do your will, but rather, it's a way to help you seek *His* will—to genuinely express your desire for it. God has provided the fast as a way for you to say what is deep within your heart. Do you have something deep you want to say to God? Do you need to fast one day to say it? When you do...no one need know but your Father in heaven.

THE LAST WILL BE FIRST

The eye cannot say to the hand, "I have no need of you";
or again the head to the feet, "I have no need of you."
—1 Corinthians 12:21

An attitude of independence doesn't cut it in the body of Christ. The reality is that we're dependent on all of us—even the "weaker" members.

The Corinthian church had failed to recognize this, and placed a premium on the prominent, up-front spiritual gifts and those who had them. These were the gifts receiving all the honor and appreciation.

But Paul is saying to the Corinthians, "Our unity doesn't come in all conforming to one gift, as some would have you believe—but rather, just the opposite: Our diversity creates our unity." Paul says we are therefore to "bestow more abundant honor" on the "unseemly" members (1 Corinthians 12:23), the ministries in Christ's body that are not attractive or popular. The attractive, public-appreciated ministries receive their honor by virtue of the display of their gifts. But for these other parts, our responsibility as a body is to give them honor, as God does: "God has so composed the body, giving more abundant honor to that member which lacked" (12:24).

There will be some real surprises when we get to "the judgment seat of Christ, " where each of us will be "recompensed for his deeds in the body, according to what he has done, whether good or bad" (2 Corinthians 5:10). For some it will be the greatest shock of heaven. For Jesus said, "But many who are first will be last; and the last, first" (Matthew 19:30).

VITAL AND VULNERABLE

The members of the body which seem to be weaker
are necessary.
—1 Corinthians 12:22

As important as some of the prominent members of the human body are, it is still possible to live without them. The eye, the ear, the feet and arms are important, but not "necessary" for life. You cannot live, however, after losing the heart, the liver, the lungs, or the brain. These organs are more hidden and less attractive than the others, but also more vital. Consequently they are more guarded by the skeleton and the rest of the body. Even our bodily design acknowledges their position of importance. They are more vital and more vulnerable, and are therefore to be given more protection.

The vital parts, the vital ministries in the body of Christ, tend *not* to be the obvious ones: faithful, dedicated saints praying and serving. They're sometimes called the "hidden" ministries, and they are often the more reliable and productive channels of spiritual influence in the lives of others: loving children in the nursery and children's classes, preparing meals for the hurting, visiting the sick, rejoicing with the blessed, keeping in touch with the struggling—just being there with encouragement and counsel.

These vital parts are to be protected by fellow believers just as the body protects its vital organs. Let's do that by acknowledging our dependence upon them, and by expressing honor and deep appreciation. We have a mutual dependence on *each* other.

Remember: A master artist sometimes uses the smallest brush to achieve the greatest effect.

CARE, NOT COMPETITION

...that there should be no division in the body,
but that the members should have
the same care for one another.
—2 Corinthians 12:25

As we depend on each other's unique part in our lives, we draw upon each other's gifts with a mutual care. This "care" in 2 Corinthians 12:25 speaks of concern for another's welfare. There is no division when there is no competition, and how can you compete when you're caring for each other's welfare?

"And if one member suffers," Paul said, "all the members suffer with it" (12:26). Once, after a bad ski injury, my leg became swollen and very sore; the rest of my body was so concerned that it sat up all night to keep it company. In the functioning body of Christ, the one who hurts is comforted—and the one who is blessed is joined in rejoicing: "If one member is honored, all the members rejoice with it" (12:26). This is a command from Paul: "Rejoice with those who rejoice, and weep with those who weep" (Romans 12:15). Are you doing your part to enter into the sorrows and joys of others in the body?

Paul reminds us again: "Now you are Christ's body, and individually members of it" (1 Corinthians 12:27). We are one, and we are committed to the blessing and success of every part. That's why we "admonish the unruly, encourage the fainthearted," and "help the weak" (1 Thessalonians 5:14).

Only when we understand this mutual dependence, mutual honor, and mutual care in the body can we begin to understand spiritual gifts and our diverse ministries.

BY APPOINTMENT ONLY

God has appointed in the church, first apostles, second prophets,
third teachers, then miracles, then gifts of healings,
helps, administrations, various kinds of tongues.
—1 Corinthians 12:28

Our diverse ministries have nothing to do with our
seeking them. The design is God's. "God has placed
the members, each one of them, in the body, just as
He desired" (1 Corinthians 12:18). The gifts are God-
appointed (12:28). The first of those gifted men in the
church were the apostles, and second, the prophets.
Paul says the church is "built upon the foundation of
the apostles and prophets" (Ephesians 2:20). They
laid the foundation of faith in Christ; they received
and declared the revelation of God's Word and the
"mystery of Christ...as it has now been revealed to
His holy apostles and prophets in the Spirit" (3:4-5).

Third on the list in 1 Corinthians 12 are teachers—
those who instruct others in the revelation of God. A
similar order is in Ephesians 4: "He gave some as
apostles, and some as prophets, and some as evange-
lists, and some as pastors and teachers." First are
named the gifts that laid the church's foundation, then
those that bring growth to the church, both in mission-
ary outreach and spiritual inreach to the body.

The point is that whatever your gifts, it is *God* who
appoints (12:28), *God* who places (12:18), and *God* who
distributes (12:11) your gift and your part in the body.
And whatever your part, whatever gift comes down
to you, there must be a servant's heart with it—a heart
of love to serve the body. After teaching about gifts,
Paul says, "I show you a still more excellent way"—
and the next chapter is all about one thing: *love.*

FILLED WITH THE SPIRIT

And do not get drunk with wine…
but be filled with the Spirit.
—Ephesians 5:18

Do you know what Paul means here by "filled with the Spirit"? Just two verses earlier in this passage we read, "Do not be foolish, but understand what the will of the Lord is." To be filled with the Holy Spirit means to be empowered to supernaturally obey anything God has told you to do.

Anytime I disobey, anytime I do what Jesus would never do, it is *pride*—because I believe I have a better way to respond. God will resist this pride. He will say, "All right—you're on your own. Since you are not poor in spirit, since you think you can pull it off, I'll give you over to the consequences of your actions."

And then, after the lesson is learned, we come to Him in humility:

"God, I can't—apart from You I can't do anything. Therefore my confidence and my belief is that *You will do it through me.* You will give me the thoughts, and then I will speak. You will give me the desires, and then I will act. And You will give me the peace and the patience I need."

If you have committed your life to Christ, your spirit is alive, but only because the Holy Spirit makes your spirit alive. Don't quench the Spirit, but be filled—by constantly communicating with God: "Lord, what would You have me do?"

If this is your attitude, then when you get stretched and irritated, when you get bumped in life—and you *will* get bumped—what spills out will be the perfume of Jesus Christ.

LOVE THAT HURTS AND HEALS

Faithful are the wounds of a friend.
—Proverbs 27:6

What is the essence of a good relationship? That question doesn't have a simple answer, because good relationships are tough to find and examine. We tend to look for something safe, comfortable, and not painful. But relationships mean vulnerability, which means you can get hurt. Why pursue something that hurts? At least lonely is safe.

But safe isn't always living, nor is it fulfilling. Is painful always bad?

Significant love—honest love—may hurt at times because significant love will confront. But genuine love will never cause injury. Love may hurt at times —but it will never harm.

When Paul confronted the sin of the Corinthians, he knew there was much pain on both sides. He spoke of his own "affliction and anguish of heart" (2 Corinthians 2:4). Paul loved them, and to see them in pain caused *him* pain. There is nothing enjoyable in confrontation; it's painful, and should always be painful—to both sides! Paul hated it, but he did it "that you might know the love I have especially for you" (2:4). He wanted them to know the depth of his love; he was saying, "My love for you means I will risk the relationship *for your sake.*" To the one who had caused him offense, Paul then offered restoration and forgiveness (2:7-10).

There are many who will wound you—but not in love. For love to be love in confrontation—to ensure that it never harms—it must be sensitive to needs, reaffirming in care, and forgiving in spirit.

A BIGGER DEAL

The body is not for immorality, but for the Lord;
and the Lord is for the body.
—1 Corinthians 6:13

Greek philosophy argued that everything physical, including our bodies, was evil. There was no value in it. What was done with or to the body didn't matter. Biological needs are biological needs. No big deal. Paul quotes what was likely a popular proverb of the day: "Food is for the stomach, and the stomach for food." From there you could easily argue, "The body was made for sex"; sex was just another biological function, like eating, to satisfy a bodily appetite.

But Paul says the relationship between stomach and food is temporal: "God will do away with both of them. Yet the body is not for immorality, but for the Lord" (1 Corinthians 6:13). Biological processes have no eternal state, and will disappear from existence—but not so the body! It's not like the stomach. And it does not exist for sex, but for the Lord.

When God created the body He had more in mind than the satisfaction of a passion. (Your world gets pretty narrow and limited if you really believe sex is what makes it go round.) God created your body to use for something greater than a biological drive. The world God created for us to enjoy is a lot bigger than that!

Paul gives a better proverb for today: "The body for the Lord, the Lord for the body." Our bodies are to be an instrument for the Lord's use and the Lord's glory.

Can other people get an idea of what God is like by seeing Him through your body?

THE SPECIAL BOND

Do you not know that your bodies are members of Christ?
—1 Corinthians 6:15

Our bodies are designed to serve not only in this life, but also in the life to come. There will be changes —"We shall all be changed" (1 Corinthians 15:51); "Jesus Christ...will transform the body of our humble state into conformity with the body of His glory" (Philippians 3:21)—but it's *these bodies* that will be changed.

Your body is special because it's eternal. And it's special because it is a part of the Lord's own body. We in the church are His body, the incarnation of His Person. We are "His body, the fullness of Him who fills all in all" (Ephesians 1:23). His Spirit lives within us in some special way, and is changing us into people who reflect that Person. Your body is called "a temple of the Holy Spirit" (1 Corinthians 6:19) because the Lord's presence is there. It follows that if your body is part of Him and you commit immorality (6:13-18)—you join Him with your sin. Such a thought is repulsive to Paul: "May it never be!" (6:15).

You are bonded to the Lord in a special union— "the one who joins himself to the Lord is one spirit with Him"—and you join Him to whomever you join yourself. Knowing that your body is eternal, your body is part of Christ, and your body belongs to God ...therefore be responsible. "Flee immorality" (6:18). *Run!* Immorality begins with flirtation—a touch, a hug—and that's not "fleeing."

God made you something special; therefore act like something special.

YOUR SPECIAL GIFT

*As each one has received a special gift, employ it
in serving one another, as good stewards
of the manifold grace of God.*
—1 Peter 4:10

How do you discover your spiritual gift? Let me give you some guidelines:

(1) Don't worry about a title for your gift. None of the lists of gifts in the Scriptures (Romans 12, 1 Corinthians 12, Ephesians 4) is complete. Realize that there are a variety of gifts—all kinds of unique, Spirit-given abilities for being used in other people's lives. And realize that you *are* gifted! The Spirit gives gifts "to *each* one individually just as He wills" (1 Corinthians 12:4).

(2) Your gift is for ministry to others. Where are you burdened for others? What are you sensitive to in others? What are the needs you perceive in others?

(3) What confirmation do you receive from others of the effect your ministry has in their lives? Ministries come by responding to opportunities placed before us, not by grabbing for positions in other people's lives.

(4) Does the effect, the ministry, the gift serve others, rather than yourself? Our gifts were given by the Spirit to create unity in the Body.

The "still more excellent way" (12:31) is our love for each other—that's why there's a mutual dependence, a mutual honor, and a mutual caring within the body. The gifts are appointed by God, diverse in design, and motivated by our wanting to serve in love.

You *are* gifted for your part—and you *will know* your part if you have a heart to serve.

BECAUSE OF GOD

I hate and despise falsehood.
—Psalm 119:163

Someone has said that our society "is largely built upon a network of fabrication." Do you agree or disagree? Daniel Webster wrote, "There is nothing as powerful as truth, and often nothing as strange." We actually begin to get used to this "network of fabrication" we've built. Do these famous fibs sound familiar? *The check is in the mail... We service what we sell... One size fits all... Your table will be ready in a minute... I promise it won't hurt a bit... I'll start my diet tomorrow... I just need a few minutes of your time... This will hurt me more than it hurts you.*

In his book *Integrity*, Ted Engstrom wrote, "When we can no longer depend on one another to do what we said we would do, the future becomes an undefined nightmare."

How different it could be if, instead of reviewing our *plans* and *objectives*, we thought in terms of reviewing *the promises we have made*, and then talked about making and keeping new ones. "Promise-keeping," it has been said, "is one of the most fundamental acts of a society."

All of us want others to use the word *integrity* to describe us—and yet would it? Integrity is *meaning what you say and doing what you promised to do.* That may not sound profound, but what *is* profound is the *why* you do it. You love truth because *God* loves truth: "Behold, Thou dost desire truth in the innermost being" (Psalm 51:6). You hate lies because *God* hates lies: "Lying lips are an abomination to the Lord" (Proverbs 12:22).

PROFANITY

You shall not take the name of the Lord your God in vain.
—Exodus 20:6

Have you ever wondered what's meant by this third of the Ten Commandments?

The word translated "vain" is the Hebrew word *shav*, which was used interchangeably for that which was empty ("vain") or that which was a falsehood—a lie. The commandment refers to a false swearing in the name of God. The essence of profanity is to treat with contempt that which is sacred. A warning is given in Leviticus 5:4 to anyone who "swears thoughtlessly with his lips to do evil or to do good." And in Leviticus 19:12 is this command: "You shall not swear falsely by My name, so as to profane the name of your God; I am the Lord."

But what happened? Ezekiel records this judgment from God upon Israel: "I am about to act...for My holy name, which you have profaned among the nations where you went. And I will vindicate the holiness of My great name...which you have profaned in their midst" (36:22-23).

Who we are—our integrity—reflects upon who or what we worship. We are all defined by our worship. If you worship money, then in your life you will represent how good money is as a god. If you worship yourself, you'll show the rest of us how good a god you make. And if we worship the Holy God, we will show how holy a Holy God is.

"Like the Holy One who called you, be holy yourselves also in all your behavior; because it is written, "You shall be holy, for I am holy" (1 Peter 1:15-16). What is your life saying about who you worship?

A CASE OF THE NORMALS

Let your statement be, "Yes, yes," or "No, no";
anything beyond these is of evil.
—Matthew 5:37

Jesus says integrity for the Christian should be a case of the normals.

The Pharisees had twisted Old Testament teaching about oaths and vows to the Lord. The idea they developed was that if God's name was used in my oath, God became a partner in the transaction; if God's name was not used in my oath, then I'm free to "change my mind." Swearing became a pathetic attempt at lying. It was more of a confession of dishonesty than integrity. The Pharisees had reduced the law of oaths to a game of rules on how to break a promise and get out of what you said you were going to do.

Do you hear the response of Jesus? "But I say to you, make no oath at all, either by heaven, for it is the throne of God, or by the earth, for it is the footstool of His feet, or by Jerusalem, for it is the city of the great King..." (Matthew 5:34-35).

You can't separate life into little compartments, some having to do with God and others not. *Everything about you represents Him!* If you say you're a Christian, what people think about you will have everything to do with what they think about your God. When truth is profaned, the God of truth is profaned.

But what about "white lies"—lies that "do no harm"? Is it possible for lies not to harm? No—they eat away and eventually destroy your name...and thus profane His.

Is your integrity such that your "yes" is as good as an oath, and so is your "no"?

A CHOICE OF VALUES

Love one another, just as He commanded us.
—1 John 3:23

I've heard many times that "Love is the answer." The answer to what? Probably no concept is referred to more often and understood less than love.

The Greeks had four words for love (our language has just the word *love*, which can mean just about whatever you want to make it mean): *Eros* described the emotion of passion, sometimes thought in terms of lust, physical desire. *Phileo* described the emotion of friendship. *Astorgos* described the emotion of family ties. But the word used predominantly in the New Testament, especially in the command of Jesus taught by John, does not describe an emotion at all, because how can you command an emotion? That's why, at first shot, a command to love appears a bit ridiculous. The word John uses is *agape*. In that *agape* is commanded, it's not initially an emotion for it has to do with the will, a choice; the word speaks of a value system, what you believe to be important and why. *Agape* love is treating someone or something with worth.

The worth of something is either inherent, because of who made it and put the worth into it, or else it's determined by the price someone is willing to pay for it. Who made you and everyone else? "The rich and the poor have a common bond: The Lord is the maker of them all" (Proverbs 22:2). People are more important than things because God made people, and people make things. And what was God willing to pay for you and everyone else? "You were redeemed... with precious blood...the blood of Christ" (1 Peter 1:18-19).

FRESH AND NEW

I am not writing a new commandment to you, but an old
commandment which you have had from the beginning…
On the other hand, I am writing a new commandment to you…
—1 John 2:7-8

How can an "old" be a "new"? John says this new
commandment is actually old, and one his readers
have long known about—even "from the beginning."
The beginning of what? Some say the beginning of
Jesus' teaching, others the beginning of their faith in
Him. I believe John uses "the beginning" as he did in
his gospel, meaning "from the beginning of creation,
the beginning of God's revelation to us." Jesus made
reference to it when He was asked about the greatest
commandment in the Law. The first, Jesus answered,
was to love God; "And a second is like it, 'You shall
love your neighbor as yourself'" (Matthew 22:37-39).
This phrase was a precept from Mosaic law (Leviticus
19:18), so was not really "new"; yet John says it is.
Why?

Two words in Greek can be translated "new." *Neos*
speaks of something never before around. But John
uses the other word, *kainos,* "new in quality," which
could be translated "fresh." John is saying this is a
"fresh" commandment. What makes it fresh? Compare the Mosaic command Jesus quoted with His
words in John 15:12. One says to love your neighbor
"as yourself"; the other, "Love one another *just as I
have loved you."* Do you see the difference? From "as
yourself" to "as I have loved you."

The command is fresh and new because Jesus
gives us a whole new standard, a new model to follow: His own love for us.

THE STABILITY OF LOVE

Love never fails.
—1 Corinthians 13:8

It is the Spirit of God within believers who causes us to value what God values, to choose to place value on what God says has great worth. This is love: a commitment to a value system.

But, you say, *it sounds so cold and unemotional.* As an emotional Cajun Frenchman, let me answer with two points:

(1) Because love is initially not an emotion but an act of my will, I never have to worry about not being able to love someone. For it has nothing to do with how I feel about him or her. This is the stability of love.

(2) There is a principle within us that works this way: Whatever we treat as precious *becomes* precious to us. That's why the feelings of affection will follow the act of my will to love.

John writes, "The one who loves his brother abides in the light and there is no cause for stumbling in him" (1 John 2:10). The one who loves will not trip up by getting confused over whether or not he really knows Jesus Christ.

Earlier in this letter, John established the first birthmark of every genuine Christian: a deep desire to keep the commandments of Jesus Christ. The second birthmark—genuine love for others—helps you out with the first. If you're having trouble wondering which commandment to start practicing, start with this: "Love one another, as I have loved you."

NO SUCH THING AS NEUTRAL

The one who loves his brother abides in the light...
But the one who hates his brother is in the darkness.
—1 John 2:10-11

There is no such thing as a neutral relationship among believers. Either you love or you hate.

Isn't that a bit strong? you ask. But understand what it really means to *love* and to *hate*.

The love John speaks of is an issue of obedience, of choice, and initially has nothing to do with emotion. It is a commitment to a value system, the value system that places great worth upon people because they are created by God and redeemed by the blood of His Son, Jesus Christ.

Hate is simply the opposite of that. Initially, hate also has nothing to do with emotion. Hate is also about choices, about what I choose to value and not to value. *Whatever I am indifferent to, I hate*, regardless of whether I feel anything about it.

John's point in 1 John 2 is that genuine Christians cannot be indifferent to one another. It is love, in the light—or hatred, in the darkness. As someone has said, "There is no twilight in the spiritual world."

The one who hates "walks in the darkness," John says, "and does not know where he is going because the darkness has blinded his eyes" (2:11). Indifference to one another marks one who is still consumed with himself, walking in the darkness, blinded. His life is an illusion, and it will end with a nightmare. If all is done and the only one you value is you—you'll be left in the darkness alone with your precious self, feeling worthless.

CHOICE OR FEELING?

Love must be sincere.
—Romans 12:9

For each of these commands in Romans 12:9-21, ask yourself: Is this a choice…or a feeling?

Hate what is evil; cling to what is good.

Be devoted to one another in brotherly love.

Honor one another above yourselves.

Never be lacking in zeal, but keep your spiritual fervor, serving the Lord.

Be joyful in hope, patient in affliction, faithful in prayer.

Share with God's people who are in need.

Practice hospitality.

Bless those who persecute you; bless and do not curse.

Rejoice with those who rejoice.

Mourn with those who mourn.

Live in harmony with one another.

Do not be proud, but be willing to associate with people of low position. Do not be conceited.

Do not repay anyone evil for evil.

Be careful to do what is right in the eyes of everybody.

If it is possible, as far as it depends on you, live at peace with everyone.

Do not take revenge, my friends, but leave room for God's wrath.

Do not be overcome by evil, but overcome evil with good.

What choices are you making today?

THE TRUE NEW AGE

The darkness is passing away...the true light is already shining.
—1 John 2:8

When Jesus first came to earth it was to establish the true "new age" people. When He comes again it will be to establish the new age, the kingdom of God. If we are "new age people," people of the kingdom of God, people of the kingdom to come, we should act like kingdom people *in this age,* marked out from others by the way we practice the new command of Jesus: "Even as I have loved you, that you also love one another. By this all men will know that you are My disciples, if you have love for one another" (John 13:34-35).

As God's "spiritual offspring," we've been placed in a new relationship not only with God, but with each other as well. If you're a genuine Christian, you have no excuse not to love. Treat each other with the worth God has placed upon each of us.

Jerome tells us that when the apostle John was very old, he continued to say again and again, "Little children, love one another, love one another, love one another..." When asked why he said nothing more, his response was, "Because it is the commandment of the Lord, and because when this is done, all is done."

Tertullian in the second century reported the pagans of his day saying this about Christians: "See how they love one another! How ready they are to die for one another!" But as the church began to organize and controversies arose, the impression changed. Pagan historian Ammianus wrote in the fourth century, "The enmity of the Christians toward each other surpassed the fury of savage beast against man."

Today, do you have any excuses not to love?

TRUE CLEAVING

*A man...shall cleave to his wife; and the two
shall become one flesh. This mystery is great.*
—*Ephesians 5:31-32*

True cleaving in marriage means mutual sanctification and mutual nurture.

Mutual sanctification is marriage's spiritual life—
husbands are commanded to love their wives "just as
Christ also loved the church and gave Himself up for
her; that He might sanctify her" (Ephesians 5:25-26).
Sanctification is to set apart as one "cleansed...by the
washing of water in the word" (5:26). It is the kind of
spiritual interest Paul expressed in Colossians 1:9-12
("We have not ceased to pray for you and to ask that
you may be filled with the knowledge of His will...so
that you may walk in a manner worthy of the Lord");
it is the mutual desire to see our mate develop spiritually. How are you showing concern for your mate's
spiritual maturity? Be open to talk about spiritual
things. Allow one another opportunities for spiritual
growth.

Mutual nurture is marriage's physical life—"So husbands ought also to love their own wives as their own
bodies. He who loves his own wife loves himself; for
no one ever hated his own flesh, but nourishes and
cherishes it" (5:28-29). It is realizing my spouse is now
my flesh; we are bonded into one, we share in and are
committed to each other's success—in health,
strength, vocation, and more. We are concerned for
one another's physical and emotional maturity. My
wife is part of me. I am part of her. As she is successful, I am successful through her; and she is successful
in my success.

HUSBAND AND WIFE

He who created them from the beginning made them male and
female, and said, "For this cause a man...shall cleave to his wife;
and the two shall become one flesh."
—Matthew 19:4-5

If you are married, there are active spiritual forces opposing your union, for Satan would destroy anything good that God has designed, including the becoming of "one flesh" in marriage. "Let a man have his own wife," Paul writes, "and let a woman have her own husband" (1 Corinthians 7:2). This is God's design of marriage—so enter it! But, he cautions, you may not be getting a husband or a wife by just marrying. Before we can understand becoming "one flesh" with our mate, we must understand that "leaving and cleaving" comes first.

God designed marriage from the beginning: "A man shall leave his father and his mother, and shall cleave to his wife; and they shall become one flesh" (Genesis 12:24). The next verse says that Adam and Eve "were both naked and were not ashamed." Why were they not ashamed? Because they weren't consumed with themselves.

Marriage may not be a fairy tale, but if you commit yourself to the Creator's design for it, it can be a taste of heaven on earth.

To you, a husband, I ask: Does your wife know you have her best interests at heart in what you do? (Ask her!) Are you providing her the resources to succeed in her goals?

To you, a wife, I ask: Are you modeling "chaste and respectful behavior...a gentle and quiet spirit, which is precious in the sight of God" (1 Peter 3:1-6)?

ONE FLESH

They are no more two, but one flesh. What therefore
God has joined together, let no man separate.
—Matthew 19:6

Paul says, "Let the husband fulfill his duty to his wife, and likewise also the wife to her husband" (7:3). This word "duty" actually means bringing sexual satisfaction to the other. God created sex and designed it for marriage, and to abstain from it in marriage is not spiritual, but rather evil in the sight of God. Paul says it is a responsibility of marriage to serve the other sexually. But why is this a spiritual issue?

When there are problems in the sexual relationship, there are problems in the relationship.

In Genesis 2, "one flesh" flows naturally from cleaving. *Cleaving* means "glued, in common, welded together as one." Paul says, "The wife does not have authority over her own body, but the husband does; and likewise also the husband..." (7:4). The right of each other is to each other, for when two cleave they become a part of each other. We have authority over each other's body as we have that authority over our own body, and that authority means we are responsible for that united body. This is the foundational attitude we begin with in marriage.

"Stop depriving one another," Paul says, "except by agreement for a time that you may devote yourselves to prayer" (7:5). It is not God's design for you to be separated from each other; if you must from time to time, for the purpose of prayer, don't let it be long. And it should be "by agreement"—it comes down to sensitivity to each other.

"REMAIN EVEN AS I"

I say to the unmarried and to widows
that it is good for them if they remain even as I.
—1 Corinthians 7:8

It is well known that in Corinth there were many who had married and were divorced before they had become Christians; now they were asking Paul the question, What should we do?

Paul uses the word "unmarried" in 1 Corinthians 7:8, and it is believed he includes in this term both those who had been married before and those who had never married. (He also specifically mentions "widows," who were the most vulnerable in their needs.) Paul is speaking to all unmarried people in this verse, including those divorced before coming to Christ. (He'll focus later—in verses 25-26 — on those never married.)

Paul says it is good for them who are now free of marriage to remain so, even as he has done (Paul may well have been married before, his wife either having died or having left him after he became a believer.) "It is *good*" Paul says, "if they remain even as I." Marriage is not necessarily superior or inferior to singleness.

But Paul does add, "If they do not have self-control, let them marry, for it is better to marry than to burn" (7:9). A person cannot live a happy life, much less serve the Lord, if he or she is continually inflamed with strong sexual passion.

There appears, therefore, to be a biblical basis for remarriage for a Christian who had been divorced before coming to Christ (as well as for widows—Romans 7:2-3). This would fit with 2 Corinthians 5:17—"If any man is in Christ, he is a new creature."

A BOND NOT TO BE BROKEN

To the married I give instructions, not I, but the Lord,
that the wife should not leave her husband.
—1 Corinthians 7:10

Marriage is a bond not to be broken, a "becoming one flesh" that was never intended to be torn apart. To break that bond is the tearing of flesh, leaving broken pieces of everything everywhere.

In 1 Corinthians 7:10-11, Paul gives Christian couples the Lord's instruction against separation. God spoke clearly through the prophet Malachi when He said, "I hate divorce!" In Matthew 19:5-6, Jesus made it clear that the bond of marriage was not to be broken. (There is debate over what Jesus meant by "immorality" in Matthew 19:9—"Whoever divorces his wife, except for immorality, and marries another woman commits adultery." Some say He was referring to immorality found during the engagement period before the marriage. Others believe He refers to unlawful marriages never recognized by God in the first place. Many others believe He is protecting the innocent one, and saying that if the other partner continues in adultery, the marriage bond can be dissolved. The possibility in such a case of remarriage being permitted by God is thus left open.)

Paul is very straight here: *Christians are not to be separating and divorcing each other.* (In the cultural context of Corinth, usually the wife did the leaving and the husband did the sending.) If a Christian couple is separated, they have only two options: Either remain unmarried (single), or become reconciled to each other. They are not free to remarry, because in the eyes of God the union cannot be broken.

UNBELIEVING SPOUSES

God has called us to peace.
—1 Corinthians 7:15

In 1 Corinthians 7:12-14, Paul writes to those who, when they became Christians, were married to unbelievers. (*Take note:* He makes it clear Christians are not to marry unbelievers in 7:39 and 2 Corinthians 6:14.) They wanted to know if they should divorce. Some thought this union with a non-Christian might somehow defile them or their children, and dishonor God. Jesus had not directly taught about this problem—but Paul, directed by the Holy Spirit, does ("I say, not the Lord..."). Paul was saying, "Don't worry about your spouses' affect on you; think about your affect on them." If the unbelieving spouse "consents"—agrees, approves, even sympathizes with you—then don't break that bond. The union is still of God. Being unequally yoked can be frustrating, discouraging, even costly, but it need not be defiling, since it takes only one believer to sanctify a home (7:14)—to "set it apart" in God's eyes for His blessings, for no other reason than that you are a part of it. The other members of that home can enjoy the splash of your blessings and your care. If, however, an unbelieving spouse wanted a separation, "Don't fight it," Paul was saying (in 7:15). "Let them leave; submit yourself to the mighty hand of God and His care for you." (The text in this verse authorizes only separation, without containing clear instructions as to a new union.)

Paul concludes: "God has called us to peace" (7:15). We are not to war over this. Even in bad marriages there are good purposes of spiritual significance for preserving the bond of marriage.

CLEAR THINKING

Walk no longer as the Gentiles also walk,
in the futility of their mind.
—*Ephesians 4:17*

More than we want to admit, we are moved and molded by the desires of others in our opinions and convictions. It's important to stand for things...but not fall for things! Do you do your own thinking, or let others do it for you? (I'm not trying to insult your intelligence, but to encourage you to use it.)

We're all influenced by the thoughts of others, and none of us thinks totally in isolation. But we should at least be aware of how our thinking is being affected by them. Paul warned us about others controlling our thinking when he penned these words: "Do not be conformed *to this world,* but be transformed by the renewing of your mind, that you may prove what the will of God is, that which is good and acceptable and perfect" (Romans 12:2). This text says literally, "*Stop conforming* to this world..." It means to "stop being molded by this age," stop assuming the outward appearance of something or someone you are not.

The only way to break out of this tendency is to be "transformed"—changed—"by the renewing of your mind." I like the old English on this: "Renew your wits about you." So much of everything—what you do or don't do, what you commit to or don't commit to—has to do with *how you think.* "Renew" means to make fresh, to come alive and think clearly and correctly! To do that we must be released from conformity to the world and become freed-up thinkers.

By what process did you arrive at your convictions —or was there a process at all?

THE GREAT WORTH

Whoever believes that Jesus is the Christ is born of God;
and whoever loves the Father loves the child born of Him.
—1 John 5:1

See how this verse flows logically:

Person "A" believes Jesus is the Christ.

Person "A" is born of God (as in John 1:12).

Person "B" loves God.

Person "B" therefore also loves Person "A".

The point is that if someone loves God, he will love those who are "the children of God."

"Whoever *believes*"—I put my confidence in the fact that I am a sinner, separated from God; my sin will be judged; it was Jesus whom God judged for my sin (as Oswald Chambers says, Jesus "bore the sin of the world by identification, not by sympathy") so I could be *forgiven*. Forgiven people understand God's love for them *and for others*.

The way to beat the world's system, to dislodge from your mind this age's thinking, is *love*—recognizing and incorporating the great worth of people into your thinking. *The world doesn't think in these terms.*

John says it's an issue of obedience—"We love God and observe His commandments" (5:2). Our thinking is not always based on how we feel, but on what is right.

Love is defined as initiating acts of self-sacrifice which meet the felt needs of others. How do we love Someone who doesn't have felt needs? How do we love God? "By observing His commandments." Jesus said, "If you love Me, you will keep My commandments... If anyone loves Me, he will keep My word" (John 14:15,23).

RIGHT TO GOD, RIGHT TO ME

For this is the love of God,
that we keep His commandments;
and His commandments are not burdensome.
—1 John 5:3

What commandments is John talking about? The Ten Commandments—the Law? The Law was given not to make us good, but to show us we weren't (Romans 3:20). On the other hand, there's nothing evil about the Law of God. It's the standard of His righteousness, of what's right. Jesus said He came not to abolish the Law, but to fulfill it; Jesus was never in tension with the Law of God—only the laws of men.

Don't get me wrong. The Law is not a way to go to heaven, but it will give you a good idea of what God expects from us. When was the last time you took a close look at the Ten Commandments? As a Christian who loves God, do you find yourself struggling with any of these? (1) Worship no other god. (2) Don't make images and worship them as God. (3) God's name is sacred; don't shame it. (4) Keep the seventh day separate for God. Paul warned that this was not to be an issue of contention (Colossians 2:16), but of personal conviction (Romans 14:5-6). The point: Don't get caught up in "business as usual" in the world and forget your God! (5) Honor your parents. (6) Don't murder; life is sacred. (7) Don't commit adultery. (8) Don't steal. (9) Don't lie. (10) Don't covet the things of others, but be content with what you have.

This is what loving God is all about. What's right to God is right to us. And doing what's right is not some kind of punishment: "His commandments," John says, "are not burdensome."

BEAT THE SYSTEM

For whatever is born of God overcomes the world; and this
is the victory that has overcome the world—our faith.
—1 John 5:4

The verb here translated as "overcome" is *nikao*, for
which the noun is *nike*—it means "conqueror." We
find the name on some of our aerial missiles as well
as our running shoes. John spells out for us just how
we can be conquerors in this world, how we can overcome the pressures of this age and beat the world's
system: We overcome by *love* (1 John 5:1), knowing
people are the Great Worth. We overcome by *obedience* (5:2-3), knowing God's commands are the Great
Concern. We do what is right, no matter what others
say, or how we're feeling about something; our thinking is clear and we obey God rather than man. And
we overcome by *faith* (5:4)—which is the key to the
whole thing. The key to loving others and obeying
God is our faith! A child of God who loves his God
will continually overcome the moving and molding
pressures of this age. We aren't overcomers because
we're smarter or sharper; we're overcomers because
we have placed our confidence, not in the opinions of
a hundred different people, but in the truth of One—
Jesus the Christ. We have trusted Him for our salvation; we honor Him as our Lord.

Overcoming this age is a central issue for eternity:
"To him who overcomes," Jesus says in Revelation, "I
will grant to eat of the tree of life... I will give him
some of the hidden manna... I will give him the
morning star... I will grant to him to sit down with
Me on My throne, as I also overcame and sat down
with My Father on His throne" (Revelation 2-3).

JESUS IS FOR REAL

For there are three that bear witness, the Spirit and the water and the blood; and the three are in agreement.
—1 John 5:8

Scholars have called 1 John 5:6-12 the most perplexing passage in that epistle. Yet John didn't write it to be perplexing. A recurring word in the passage is "witness"—*marturia* in Greek, a testimony of evidence, a witness to fact. What fact? "That God has given us eternal life, and this life is in His Son" (5:10). John gives here three witnesses from God for this fact, for "on the evidence of two or three witnesses a matter shall be confirmed" (Deuteronomy 19:15).

First, John says Jesus "came by water" (5:6). This was Jesus' baptism, when God's voice from heaven said, "This is My beloved Son, in whom I am well-pleased" (Matthew 3:17). *Second*, John says Jesus also came by "blood" (1 John 5:6). Blood spoke of death, for "the life of the flesh is in the blood...it is the blood by reason of the life that makes atonement" (Leviticus 17:11). False teachers in John's day were saying Christ did not have a human body because bodies were evil, and good would never take on evil. But if Jesus Christ did not have a body that would bleed, He could never die as "the Lamb who takes away the sin of the world." His blood, His death on the cross, proved that He was the promised Messiah and the Son of God. The *third* witness from God, John says, "is the Spirit" (5:7), who bore witness to Jesus in His miracles, and continues to bear witness in the Bible.

The credibility of your faith rests in the credibility of the One you say you believe in. God's own witness confirms it: Jesus is for real.

GIVEN TO EACH ONE

There are varieties of gifts, but the same Spirit.
—1 Corinthians 12:4

As designed by God, the ministry of spiritual gifts is the greatest prevention to division. So you know we've got real problems when we start fighting over them! More often than not, arguments over gifts come from jealousy or competitiveness. That's why Paul says there are "varieties of gifts...varieties of ministries...varieties of effects" (1 Corinthians 12:4-6). This is no time to form Gift Clubs, for each gift is so unique to each individual.

Gifts are the Spirit-given enablements to effect the growth of another. The word *ministries* is from a word meaning "to serve"; there are all kinds of ways we can serve with each gift. *Effects* in Greek is *energema*— energized; literally, "what is worked out." The results! *Results are part of the gift He empowers*—which is why we must leave the results to Him. With all these possibilities for touching each other's life with the Spirit within us, we must be aware of God's design for these gifts. Two things can destroy the design: (1) *Non-use*—Paul says, "To *each one* is given the manifestation of the Spirit" (12:7). No one is excluded. No believer is without a Spirit-given ability to help another believer grow more like Christ. To ignore one's gift will only breed division. (2) *Misuse*—In each gift the Spirit is manifested "for the common good" (12:7). It's critical to understand that these gifts are not for self-edification. If you have the gift of teaching—don't teach yourself. If you have the gift of giving, don't give to yourself. Whatever gift you have, it's not to help you grow, but for others.

BEWARE SEDUCTION

*More bitter than death is the woman whose heart
is snares and nets, whose hands are chains.*
—Ecclesiastes 7:26

Solomon speaks of a woman whose personality is dominated by her hunter instincts—snares and nets to trap like prison fetters. This is the "adulteress" he warns us about in Proverbs 5. The problem began back in Genesis 3. Paul said Adam was not deceived like Eve (1 Timothy 2:14); Adam knew exactly what he was doing: He wanted the woman more than he wanted God. After their sin, the fallen woman would seek to control the man with her seduction (Genesis 3:16).

The seduction of a woman has everything to do with exposing a man's true character. Solomon said, "One who is pleasing to God will escape from her, but the sinner will be captured" (Ecclesiastes 7:26). The man who fears God wants to please God, and it will be seen in his sexual behavior; he will escape the seduction. The man who lives to please himself will not.

Solomon is speaking of the dark side of woman, and how it is used to control a man. Why is Solomon picking on the women? Because he's a man. But the converse is true as well. Look again at Genesis 3:16. The dark side of man is to rule over the woman, to have her serve his sensual needs. Sexual seduction brings out the sin problem in both.

O man, beware of the way the media degrades you into a lustful animal. (Or are they simply exposing the lustful animals we are?—it's one or the other.)

O woman, don't fall into our "cultured seductiveness" in your dress or manner. You don't know how difficult that makes it to get to know you as a person!

SEARCHING BUT NOT FINDING

While I was still searching but not finding—
I found one upright man among a thousand,
but not one upright woman among them all.
—Ecclesiastes 7:28

Solomon said that in his lifetime it was rare to find a man who wanted only to please God with his life—only one in a thousand. And in his relationships with women he never found even one. Let me hasten to say this is probably more of a comment on the way he *approached* women than a comment on women. His wives and concubines were trying to please him, not God. Despite the Lord's warning, Solomon "held fast" to his hundreds of women, and they "turned his heart away after other gods" (1 Kings 11:1-4).

As Ray Stedman notes, Solomon "was trapped by sexual seductions... Sex outside of marriage arrests the mutual process of discovery. You cannot discover who you are or who another person is when you are involved together in wrongful sex." When another person is viewed only as an object of personal pleasure, there can be no discovery of wisdom from one or the other. We do not relate or learn from objects of mere sensations.

God's design for relationships between the sexes is not centered on sex, but on mutual respect and honor before God. That's why Peter says what he does to men: "You husbands...live with your wives in an understanding way...and grant her honor as a fellow heir of the grace of life" (1 Peter 3:7). That's why Paul says what he does to men: "Treat older women as mothers, and younger women as sisters, with absolute purity" (1 Timothy 5:2).

OUR DARK SIDE

Do not take seriously all words which are spoken,
lest you hear your servant cursing you.
—Ecclesiastes 7:21

People bad-mouth each other—it's as certain as sin. Solomon's counsel is to choose to see it for what it is: a demonstration of the problem of sin. Some of us always want to know what people are saying about us, but that's not healthy. First, it sets up a false standard that will choke you to death. Second, it controls you like a puppet—and the strings are the cursings of others. David had some good advice for when others speak reproach: "I, like a deaf man, do not hear" (Psalm 38:13). But don't be too surprised to hear it, because you do it too: "You likewise," Solomon says, "have many times cursed others" (Ecclesiastes 7:22). We speak ill even of those we like. We prove the point: All of us have the same sin problem within.

Not only do we say dumb things; we also *do* dumb things—"folly and the foolishness of madness," Solomon calls it (7:25). *Folly* speaks of being "plump in the head," sluggish. I was taught never to use the word *stupid*, but that's the correct translation here—living in a stupor, dazed, dulled, not understanding. *Madness* speaks of being unable to use our mind because our emotions and drives have taken over.

"God made men upright," concludes Solomon, "but they have sought out many devices" (7:29). Man was created to be wise and good, but our decisions have brought out our dark side of sin. The solution is also a decision we make, by God's grace provided in Christ: "We beg you on behalf of Christ, be reconciled to God" (2 Corinthians 5:21).

FEAR

My friends, do not be afraid of those who kill the body,
and after that have no more that they can do.
But I will warn you whom to fear: fear the One who
after He has killed has authority to cast into hell;
yes, I tell you, fear Him!
—Luke 12:4-5

"Beloved, let us cleanse ourselves from all defilement of flesh and spirit, perfecting holiness *in the fear of God*" (2 Corinthians 7:1).

What is fear?

The Hebrew word is *yaré*, referring in the Old Testament to "that which is awesome, which creates a sense of awe." It's the mixed feelings of reverence and being fearful. The Greek word in the New Testament is *phobos*, "to put to flight, to run." God has created within us a capacity to fear, moving us away from the things that will harm us and toward the things that will protect us. The issue then becomes: What do we choose to fear? What to we choose to run *from?* What do we choose to run *to?*

It all began back in the Garden when man chose not to fear God. What happened? "They became fools, and exchanged the glory of the incorruptible God for an image in the form of corruptible man and of birds and four-footed animals and crawling creatures" (Romans 1:22-23). If man was not going to fear the Creator, he would begin to fear the creation. Both creation and the Creator can hurt you; but if you're forgiven, one of them won't. The balance fear brings to godliness is that I know I'm not perfect, *but I am forgiven —* and the One who can destroy me won't. It's this grace that moves me to please Him with my life.

THE EXCHANGE

"Bad company corrupts good morals."
—1 Corinthians 15:33

We like to believe we're having a great influence on others around us—and we are. But we tend to forget they're also having a great influence on us.

We also tend to seek companionship with those who will agree with us and justify what we want to do, even if we know it's wrong.

Pick your companions carefully. A simple rule to follow is to always ask yourself: *Do I want to be like them?* Remember the exchange that happened when you were a kid and skinned your knee on the sidewalk: From that close contact, your knee picked up some dirt from the sidewalk, and the sidewalk kept some skin from your knee. So it is with companions, close friends. There's always an exchange in relationships; and sometimes it's skin for dirt.

Paul quotes an ancient proverb: "Bad company corrupts good morals." Is he saying we shouldn't have any non-Christian relationships? No, he makes that issue clear in 1 Corinthians 5:9-10. We can't step out of the world. But he asks us to "become sober-minded as you ought" (15:34). Don't be dulled in your thinking, as one who is drunk, doing whatever you feel like doing, believing that how you feel determines right and wrong.

Paul adds, "Stop sinning; for some have no knowledge of God. I speak this to your shame." Don't act as if you don't know God or what God has to say about you. Recommit yourself to a life of purity—and that will make the picture much clearer about who your closest companions should be.

THE LAST HOUR

Children, it is the last hour...we know that it is the last hour.
    —1 John 2:18

It's the last hour, John wrote. Has it been the last hour for the past 1,900 years, or did John slip a little in his old age?

If John is confused, so are Paul, James, and Peter: "The end of all things is at hand," Peter said (1 Peter 4:7). Paul spoke about the godless ones in "the last times," then immediately told Timothy to avoid them now (2 Timothy 3:5). James said, "The coming of the Lord is at hand" (5:8). Have these men been running around for nearly two millennia with a placard over their shoulders saying, "We're doomed, the world is coming to an end"?

They are talking about the *character* of this age we live in. We need to understand it: We're in "the age of grace," the time when God is calling a people of His own for the kingdom of His Son. The complete fulfill-ment of the "abomination of desolation" spoken of in Daniel and by Jesus (Matthew 24:15) is yet future, but history is coming to a conclusion, the establishing of the kingdom of God on this earth. And the mysteri-ous character of this age is that *we do not know how long it is to last*. God has revealed no dates. Jesus said, "It is not for you to know times or epochs which the Father has fixed by His own authority" (Acts 1:7).

This age will snap shut with the rapture of the church *in a moment*. That's why Peter, James, John, and Paul are all correct in saying this is it — this is the last age. It could conclude at any moment, even be-fore you finish reading this page—or it could last a thousand years more.

THE NAME

"It is the last hour, and just as you heard that antichrist is coming, even now many antichrists have arisen" (1 John 2:18). John means that there are many even now who are under the same influence as the coming Antichrist who will ultimately oppose Christ.

If Satan knows that the kingdom of Jesus Christ is next on God's calendar...where will he focus his guns? What would he make the most sensitive of all subjects, implanting fear in us to even speak Christ's name before others? (Have you noticed in a conversation with nonbelievers that if you keep the subject on God, there seems to be little problem; but bring up Jesus Christ, and we get nervous? The problem usually is with us, not them.)

The "antichrists" deny two things about Jesus: The first is that He is the Christ, the promised Messiah, God's provision for our sin (Isaiah 53:4-12) who would die in our place for the consequences of our sin so we might enter into a personal relationship with our God.

Second, they deny that Jesus is the Son of God—not *a* son of God, but *the* Son of God. It's been said that many trails lead to God, that each religion of the world is just another way. *But that's not what Jesus said.* "He who believes *in the Son* has eternal life; but he who does not obey the Son shall not see life, but the wrath of God abides on him" (John 3:36). "The Father loves the Son," Jesus said, "and has given *all things* into His hand" (3:35).

SAINTS AND AINTS

I have not written to you because you do not
know the truth, but because you do know it.
—1 John 2:21

"I'm an American. I go to church from time to time. I try to do more good than bad, and I believe in God. Doesn't that make me a Christian?"

This planet is made up of two kinds of people: *saints* and *aints*. What a person *believes about Jesus*—Is He the Messiah sent to die for our sins? Is He the Son of God?—marks the difference.

When we think of *saints*, who we do think of? Usually the best shot is our mothers. Other than our mothers, is it possible for anyone else to be considered one? Can anyone ever be *that good?* (In fact, does being a saint have anything to do with "being that good"?) Apparently, according to the Bible, there are more of these folks running around than we realize. More than sixty times in the New Testament, all who believe in Jesus are referred to as saints.

In 1 John we read about the birthmarks of those who have experienced spiritual birth: The first is the *mark of obedience*, the deep desire to keep the commandments of Jesus Christ; the second is the *mark of love*, recognizing the worth God has placed upon people. The third is *the mark of belief.* We can obey all the commandments of Jesus, we can love everything with two legs, but this third mark proves the first two as genuine. This determines whether you are *in* or out of the family of God. *What you believe about Jesus* determines your eternal destiny. This is how you know.

John's purpose is not to raise doubts or to condemn, but to *raise confidence* in your faith.

THE QUESTION OF WORRY

...casting all your anxiety upon Him,
because He cares for you.
—1 Peter 5:7

"Anxiety" in 1 Peter 5:7 is *merimnao* in Greek, "a dividing, a pulling apart," tearing you in the middle. Jesus uses the verb form in Matthew 6:25—"For this reason I say to you, *do not be anxious* for your life." ("For this reason" refers back to the previous verse: "No one can serve two masters... You cannot serve God and mammon." If God is your master, then don't be anxious; if money is your master, then be anxious, for you have reasons to be.)

Our English word *worry* comes from an old German word meaning "to strangle, to choke." Dr. Charles Mayo of the Mayo Clinic wrote, "Worry affects the circulation, the heart, the glands, and the whole nervous system. I have never known a man to die of overwork, but I have known a lot who died of worry."

Jesus said not to be anxious—apprehensive, fearful, distressed—"for your life." *Life* here is not the word for your heart pumping, but *te psuche,* the *experience* of living, our emotional response to life. There's a lot of things to be concerned over, and we all have our own way of dealing with them—humor, crying, talking, nervous mannerisms, eating, drinking, anger, depression, hobbies, vacations, sports, withdrawal, drugs, television... or, we can cast all our anxiety upon Him, knowing that *He cares.*

If and when you worry, meditate on Psalm 94:19— "When my anxious thoughts multiply within me, Thy consolations delight my soul."

HE KNOWS, AND HE CARES

Be anxious for nothing, but in everything
by prayer and supplication with thanksgiving
let your requests be made known to God.
—Philippians 4:6

"Look at the birds of the air," Jesus says (Matthew 6:26). Birds put a lot of energy into gathering food, but they don't appear to worry much about it. Jesus says God feeds the birds; He also says they sometimes fall from the sky and die (Matthew 10:29). *But not without Him knowing about it!* "Not one of them will fall to the ground apart from your Father." Christians also die and some do starve, but not without God knowing about it. David says, "In Thy book they were all written, the days that were ordained for me, when as yet there was not one of them" (Psalm 139:16).

Observe too, Jesus says, "how the lilies of the field grow" (Matthew 6:28). Wild flowers graced the hillsides of Galilee. Even Solomon in all his glory was not decked out like them, and yet we worry about clothing.

Jesus says, "O men of little faith"—literally "little-faith ones" (6:30). *Faith in God* has something to do with how not to worry. Worry is a characteristic of unbelief. The people of the world worry because they have no other choice, no one other than themselves to rely on. That's why "all these things the Gentiles eagerly seek" (6:32). It's every man for himself. They're fearful of missing out on their share of life.

"Your heavenly Father knows," Jesus says (6:32). It comes down to this: Do you trust the fact that He knows? And do you trust the fact that He cares?

THE UNCEASING QUEST

Seek first His kingdom and His righteousness;
and all these things shall be added to you.
—Matthew 6:33

Here's the resolution to worry. "Seek" means an unceasing search. This is *always* the issue for us, an unceasing quest after *His kingdom and His righteousness*—His will, His pleasure, the things that bring Him glory, the things that are right in His sight. *That* is the resolution to worry. "Thy kingdom come, Thy will be done." With this set purpose as a personal conviction, I don't have to worry about what I'm going to do. I know what I'm going to do: that which is right in His sight. This is no "optional Christianity"; there is no opting out. I will do what brings the greatest glory to God.

That takes care of most of the anxiety right there. And I add to that this conviction concerning my needs: *I know God knows* and *I know God cares*. It's okay, *even if I lose everything.*

When the decision to glorify God with my life has been made, other decisions are easier: Should I divorce my wife? Should I be faithful and pure? Should I take drugs? Should I get drunk? Should I steal, cheat, lie?

And what about tomorrow? "Therefore do not be anxious for tomorrow; for tomorrow will care for itself" (6:34). Worrying about tomorrow paralyzes you. It distracts you from what you need to be accomplishing today to bring God glory. "Each day," Jesus said, "has enough trouble of its own"—and enough grace from God to meet them: "His compassions never fail. They are new every morning" (Lamentations 3:22-23).

JESUS AND THE LAW

"Do not think that I came to abolish the Law or the Prophets;
I did not come to abolish, but to fulfill.
—Matthew 5:17

Jesus knew many of His followers misunderstood His confrontations with authorities. Because He didn't follow the rabbinic traditions, they assumed He wanted to do away with the Law as well. He was called an outlaw, a law-breaker.

In the time of Jesus "the law" most commonly meant the Jewish scribal laws, the thousands of rules and regulations deduced for just about every situation in life. It was this that Jesus condemned.

When He said He didn't come to abolish the Law, he meant God's Law, not the laws of men. Men are always adding to God's Law their own laws, calling it religion, and trying to make others follow it as if it was all originally God's. Think about it: Isn't it easier to carry out rules than it is to worry about your heart? A man could lust out of his mind, but to the Jews it was okay as long as he didn't commit the actual act of adultery. You could hate someone with an acid bitterness and still feel righteous if you didn't kill him.

Jesus said He came not to destroy, but to fulfill the true Law of God. He did that in His own life: He *modeled* it, showing us the true intent of God's Law and living it out; and He *consummated* it by being the answer to the Law's true intent. "The Scriptures," He said, "bear witness of Me" (John 5:39). "The Law," said Paul, "has become our tutor to lead us to Christ, that we may be justified by faith" (Galatians 3:24).

What are you more concerned with: rules, or your heart?

HERE TO STAY

Truly I say to you, until heaven and earth pass away,
not the smallest letter or stroke shall pass away
from the Law, until all is accomplished.
—Matthew 5:18

The word *Truly* here is literally "Amen"—intense affirmation. Jesus was saying, "I affirm with absolute authority that until the end of time as you know it, not the smallest letter in the alphabet or the smallest stroke of a pen—not even the tiniest, seemingly most insignificant part of God's Word—will be removed or modified until all is accomplished."

The Word of God is here to stay. "The Scripture cannot be broken" (John 10:35).

Jesus went on, "Whoever then annuls one of the least of these commandments, and so teaches others, shall be called least in the kingdom of heaven; but whoever keeps and teaches them, he shall be called great in the kingdom of heaven" (Matthew 5:19). This word *annuls* means to loose yourself from its requirements. If you mess with this Word by changing it—or merely ignoring it—you'll be called "the least in the kingdom of heaven."

John Stott writes, "Because He has come not to abolish but to fulfill, and because not an iota or dot will pass from the Law until all has been fulfilled, therefore greatness in the kingdom of God will be measured by conformity to it."

Getting *into* heaven has to do with your relationship with Jesus Christ (your belief in the gospel); but *what you'll be doing there* has to do with how you value this Word in your life.

How do you value that Word today?

DEEPER AND DEEPER

Are you so foolish? Having begun by the Spirit,
are you now being perfected by the flesh?
—Galatians 3:3

The Jews had a saying: "If only two people go to heaven, one will be a scribe, the other a Pharisee." But Jesus said, "Unless your righteousness surpasses that of the scribes and Pharisees, you shall not enter the kingdom of heaven" (5:20). How is it possible to be more righteous than "the professionals"? By being assured that your righteousness is *genuine.* "This people honors Me with their lips," God says, "but their heart is far away from Me" (Matthew 15:8).

Remember the promise of Jeremiah 31:33—"I will put My law *within them,* and *on their heart* I will write it." Remember Ezekiel 36:27—"I will put My Spirit *within you,* and cause you to walk in My statutes, and you will be careful to observe My ordinances." It's not "Obey more and more," but rather, "Obey *deeper and deeper* from the heart."

Beware the Great Temptation: to go outside, not inside. Be aware, and be warned that rules are the easiest way to develop false righteousness. A "works" system will always be tempting to fall into, and many, many have done it. "You have been severed from Christ," Paul says to them, "you who are seeking to be justified by law; you have fallen from grace" (Galatians 5:4). He reminds us: "It was for freedom that Christ set us free" (5:1).

Remember the picture Jesus used of the cup? On the outside of our cups there may be Bible-reading, prayer, church attendance, service. What's on the inside? Any hatred? Lust? Lying? Selfishness?

MURDER

Cain...was of the evil one, and slew his brother.
—1 John 3:12

Why do people murder? Why would someone have the desire to destroy another person? Where did the thought come from? Jesus tells us the thought is from Satan—"You want to do the desires of your father. He was a murderer from the beginning" (John 8:44). Satan hates the image of God and will do whatever he can to destroy it in whomever it's found. That's why God says in Proverbs 6:17 that He "hates" murder—"hands that shed innocent blood."

Numbers 35:32 says that a murderer "shall surely be put to death." Go back even further to Genesis 9:6 —"Whoever sheds man's blood, by man his blood shall be shed, for in the image of God He made man." The issue was "the image of God"; man and woman were created "in the image of God" (1:27); murder is an assault to the sacredness of God's image upon them. Therefore, by the command of God, when you murdered someone, your life was forfeited.

Murder goes deeper than an act of taking a life. Murder begins in the heart, not with the hands. John said, "Everyone who hates his brother is a murderer" (1 John 3:15).

Satan hates the image of God and will attempt to destroy it any way he can. If he can't change it or pervert it, he'll abuse it.

If pure hatred is the assassination of one's intellect and character—then what is pure loving? It is recognizing God's image in one another by listening to what they say, and valuing who they are.

HATRED

You have heard that the ancients were told,
"You shall not murder."
—Matthew 5:21

Jesus quoted one of the Ten Commandments, then continues: *"But I say to you…"* He is not setting Himself up against the Law of God; rather, He will tell how the Law of God reads when it is written on the heart; here is the intent of the Law, here's why God commanded, "You shall not murder."

He says, "Everyone who *is angry* with his brother shall be guilty before the court; and whoever *shall say to his brother,* '*Raca,*' shall be guilty before the supreme court; and whoever *shall say,* '*You fool,*' shall be guilty enough to go into the fiery hell" (5:22). From anger to "Raca" to "You fool"—the progression of hate. Murder is an assault *with the hands* on the image of God within another; hatred is an assault *with the lips* on the image of God. With our tongue, James says, "we curse men, who have been made in the likeness of God" (3:9).

Raca means "empty-head." We might say "brainless idiot." It's an attack on a person's intelligence. It is saying, "Your thinking amounts to nothing; your thoughts and opinions are of no worth to anyone." On the contrary, you value what others think by *listening to what they say.*

"Fool" is the word *moré,* from which we get *moron.* It means "outcast"; it's an attack on one's character and worth. "You are worthless, without any meaning or purpose." The purest form of hate is indifference to the worth of another. The purest form of love is recognizing that another is created in the image of God.

ANGER

Be angry, and yet do not sin.
—Ephesians 4:26

Is it sometimes right to get angry at someone?

There were times when Jesus got angry. In Mark 3, when the Pharisees were watching to see if Jesus would heal on the Sabbath a man with a withered hand, Jesus healed the man "after looking around at them with anger, grieved at their hardness of heart" (3:5). When He cried out in the temple court, "It is written, 'My house shall be called a house of prayer,' but you are making it a robber's den," I don't think He was smiling. David prayed, "Arise, O Lord, in Thine anger," and then said, "God is a righteous judge, and a God who has indignation every day" (Psalm 7:6,11). There is a righteous anger that drives you to confront evil for what it is, and to do something about it.

But that's not the anger Jesus speaks of in Matthew 5:22—"Everyone who is angry with his brother shall be guilty." This is the fruit of bitterness, the anger Paul speaks of in Ephesians 4:31—"Let all bitterness and wrath and anger and clamor and slander be put away." Notice the progression: from bitterness to slander. "Slander" in Greek is *blasphemia*. You're blaspheming if you verbally attack someone. This is assaulting the image of God stamped on that man or woman. With my mouth I either recognize or repudiate the image of God within others. I either humanize or dehumanize them.

We have the great privilege to recognize the image of God in others because we know the image!

Does your mouth spur on the spirit of life...or the spirit of murder?

HYPOCRISY

Even so, you too outwardly appear righteous to men,
but inwardly you are full of hypocrisy and lawlessness.
—Matthew 23:28

You've heard the famous excuse for not coming to church: "Because it's filled with hypocrites!" Why don't we in the church take a look around us, and see if the charge is accurate? The Greek word means *one who separates the truth from the truth.* It was used of an actor who played a part and pretended the part was true of him. Are you a hypocrite? Hardly a man or woman dares to be just what he or she is without doctoring up the impression somehow. Pretense becomes a rope around our necks. How many of us are free to be just the way we are? To dress the way we want to dress? To say what we want to say? To do what we want to do?

Jesus called the Pharisees "hypocrites." Their substituted "righteousness" condemned people to hell. It was a religiousness feeding itself by observing man-made rules and regulations. It was an external thing having nothing to do with what was going on inside.

To the pure in heart, hypocrisy and deceit are abhorrent. God is concerned about what is *genuine*, what is genuinely *in you*—your heart. Listen to the Psalms of David, a "man after God's own heart": "Who may stand in His holy place? He who has clean hands and a pure heart" (24:4); "My heart trusts in Him, and I am helped; therefore my heart exults" (28:7); "The righteous will inherit the land... The law of his God is in his heart; his steps do not slip" (37:31); "I delight to do Thy will, O my God; Thy Law is within my heart" (40:8).

SET YOUR SACRIFICE DOWN!

Leave your offering there before the altar,
and go your way; first be reconciled to your brother,
and then come and present your offering.
—*Matthew 5:24*

Jesus gives the picture of a Jew bringing a sacrifice to God as an offering. He brings the animal to the priests, then places his hands on it and presses down as an act of transferring his sins to the animal, confessing that he knows he has sinned against God. Then he says, "I entreat Thee, O Lord; I have sinned, I have done perversely, I have rebelled." He tells the sin he had committed, then adds, "But I return in penitence, and let this be for my covering."

While he stands there at the railing, a problem comes to mind: He's not at peace with his brother. The Lord tells him, *"Set your sacrifice down right there."*

"But...but I'm already here!"

"Set it down right there."

"But...I'm about to give the man my sacrifice."

"Set your sacrifice down right there."

"Oh, but...you don't understand! Can't you see I'm already worshiping?"

"YOU don't understand. You aren't worshiping anyone —other than yourself. Set your sacrifice down! Go and be reconciled to your brother!"

When Jesus says "brother" here, he is speaking of all those who are made in the image of God. You can't worship God when you hate His image.

Enhancing worship doesn't mean better music or prayer or messages. When all is said and done, it means better relationships with each other.

Reconciliation always comes before worship.

YOUR BEST

If I regard iniquity in my heart,
the Lord will not hear.
—Psalm 66:18

If "your brother has something against you," Jesus says, "Go ... be reconciled to your brother, and then come and present your offering" (Matthew 5:24).

But what if it's not my problem? *She's the one who's angry, not me.* Do I run around trying to make everything right with everyone who has a problem with me?

Jesus didn't. When did He get reconciled with the scribes and Pharisees?

Then when is it an issue? When you know your brother has a *reason* for blaming you.

What does "reconcile" mean? The word is *diallassomai*. The first part of it, *dia*, means "between two." The rest means "to alter, to change." Reconciliation is changing two people from mutual hostility to mutual concession. It's a yielding of anger and hurt, in agreement.

But what can I do if I'm not the one angry?

Remember first that if you are the more mature of the two, it's your responsibility to initiate the peace. You know that peace is God's desire—and His desire means something to you!

Second, remember that your responsibility is only to do everything you can to bring the peace. Peace can only be offered, as God offered it; the response to your offer will always remain the other person's responsibility.

When you have done *your best*...you have done enough.

RECONCILIATION PRINCIPLES

When a man's ways are pleasing to the Lord,
He makes even his enemies to be at peace with him.
—Proverbs 16:7

Here are three principles for the way you seek reconciliation with your brother:

(1) Keep it *a private matter.* "Do not reveal the secret of another, lest he who hears it reproach you, and the evil report about you not pass away" (Proverbs 25:9-10).

(2) Use *a quiet voice.* "A gentle answer turns away wrath, but a harsh word stirs up anger. The tongue of the wise makes knowledge acceptable, but the mouth of fools spouts folly... A soothing tongue is a tree of life, but perversion in it crushes the spirit" (Proverbs 15:1-4).

(3) Become *a humbled self.* "Go, humble yourself, and importune your neighbor" (Proverbs 6:3). Have the attitude, "What can I do to make it right?"

This is the God-like attitude. "Blessed are the peacemakers," Jesus said, "for they shall be called *sons of God*" (Matthew 5:9).

If there's a strained relationship—pursue reconciliation *now*. Remember: It won't get better with time! That's the point of the progression in Ephesians 4:31 —bitterness becomes wrath, then anger, then clamor, then slander.

Jesus said, "Make friends quickly with your opponent..." (Matthew 5:25). Don't delay in making every attempt to make a relationship right before God—before you come before God for anything else. When relationships go wrong, in nine out of ten cases, immediate action will mend them.

FIND US FAITHFUL

The church…is His body,
the fullness of Him who fills all in all.
—Ephesians 1:22-23

God took a great risk when He decided to use primarily Christians in making Himself known to this world. It's amazing that He uses *us* to show the world who *He* is—but He does! He doesn't do it, however, through our religion.

Most people are turned off by religion, and for the most part they should be. Jesus was. He attacked the rules and regulations, the religious exercises designed to make us feel righteous.

God wants to know what is going on in our hearts. What is it that we deeply believe? Everything we think and do begins with—and is rooted in—*what we really believe.* It's not always what we *say* we believe. If you want to see what I believe, watch what I do and why I do it. Our belief system is the sum of the assumptions and judgments we hold to be true. It contains what we think about ourselves, what we think about God, what we think about people, and what we think about relationships. From that belief system we make our plans and our decisions. We interpret other people's actions. We make meaning out of life experiences, solve problems, pattern our relationships, develop our careers, establish our priorities. This is the heart of the matter. This is your faith.

Ask God to find you faithful. Ask Him to mold you into a man or woman who wants always to follow Jesus, growing in your faith, becoming more and more selfless and less and less selfish.

LOOKING FOR THE LUSTING

Everyone who looks on a woman to lust for her
has committed adultery with her already in his heart.
—*Matthew 5:28*

The Pharisees had a conveniently narrow definition for sexual sin and a conveniently broad definition of sexual purity. They imagined that as long as you did not actually commit the act itself, you were sexually pure. But Jesus says adultery is more than an act—it has something to do with the heart. "Everyone who looks on a woman to lust for her has committed adultery with her already in his heart" (Matthew 5:28).

Jesus is not saying the sexual desire is evil; Paul warned about those who would teach such a thing (1 Timothy 4:3-4). God neither created nor commands evil. Nor is Jesus saying men are not to be looking at women. There was a group of Pharisees called "the Bruised and Bleeding" because they would not look upon women and kept running into walls. Some had gone into isolation, a monastic type of of living, to remove the temptation to lust from their sight; but it didn't work, because temptation has to do with the heart.

The whole phrase is "to *look* on a woman *to lust* for her." In Greek it refers to a continual looking, as in a habit, and indicates that the whole reason for the looking is for the lusting. The intention of looking is for sexual satisfaction. Lust is uncontrolled sexual passion that changes the other person into an object. Lust denies relationship. Lust turns the other person into a thing, a nonperson. It denies the image of God in that person.

STRONG LANGUAGE

If your right eye makes you stumble, tear it out,
and throw it from you… And if your right hand
makes you stumble, cut it off, and throw it from you.
—*Matthew 5:29-30*

Jesus continues: "For it is better for you that one of the parts of your body perish, than for your whole body to go into hell." The word for "stumble" in the passage is *skandalizo*, which was used of the bait stick springing the trap which lured an animal to its destruction. The word came to mean anything which causes a man's own destruction.

There are few things for which Jesus uses such strong language; we had better take an honest look at this. Guilt over the past is not the issue; but you are responsible for what you know *now*.

What is this stuff about plucking out the eye and cutting off the hand? This was evidently a favorite saying of Jesus, for He quoted it more than once. It recurs later in this same gospel (18:8-9), and there He adds the foot.

But if the problem of lust is in the heart (5:28), what good is plucking out an eye or cutting off a hand or foot? If the right eye were lost, the left would continue to lust, and if the right hand were cut off, it would be amazing how quickly one could learn to be left-handed.

To the Jew, the "right eye" represented your best vision, and the "right hand" your best skill. Jesus' point is this: We should be ready to give up whatever is necessary, *even the most cherished things we possess*, if doing so will help protect us from this evil.

Are you prepared to do that?

A GOOD REASON

Now flee from youthful lusts.
—2 Timothy 2:22

Do something about lust now, or it will consume you. Lust has been described as the athlete's foot of the mind. It never goes away. It's always asking to be scratched, promising relief. But to scratch it is to cause greater pain, to intensify the itch.

There are times when you just have to remove yourself, when you must "flee from youthful lusts." But you can't always do that. Maybe we need a *good reason* not to lust, so that when we're tempted, we'll know what to do and *why*.

Remember that Satan hates the image of God in you and in me. Through both anger and lust he can cause you to assault it in others. Anger and sexual lust are two of the most powerful influences on mankind. One goes after the sanctity of *life*, the other after the sanctity of *marriage*. The person who gives reign to either will soon find himself more *controlled* than in control. Both anger and lust become obsessive and all-consuming if we don't understand them.

Satan hates purity. Why? God loves with a pure love, and at great risk He has chosen to use us Christians to make His love known. Most human love is selfish. But the day I believe there is no purity in love is the day I stop believing God loves me!

That's why Satan hates virginity if you're single, and purity if you're married. He wants to destroy the beautiful picture of God's pure love for all of us.

Paul writes, "For *the love of Christ* controls us... Therefore from now on we recognize no man according to the flesh..." (2 Corinthians 5:14-16).

LORD, MAKE ME CLEAN

I have made a covenant with my eyes;
how then could I gaze at a virgin?
—Job 31:1

Lust destroys relationships because all relationships become "sexualized." People become nonpersons, objects that are dehumanized, a collection of body parts. How then do you restore that life, that image of God which others bear as a creation of God?

You change an *object* back into a *person* by mentally placing others back into the context of their relationships—as the wife or husband of someone else, the child of someone, the parent of someone — and most importantly, as the creation of God. Paul gave Timothy these guidelines for how to treat others: "the younger men as brothers, the older women as mothers, and the younger women as sisters, in all purity" (1 Timothy 5:1-2).

A word to sisters: It would be silly to legislate fashions, but wise to ask you to make the distinction in the way you dress between what makes you look attractive and what makes you look seductive.

And a word to brothers: When you see an attractive woman and face the mental temptation to lust, begin praying: "Lord, You created a beauty there. If she knows You, she is my sister; if not, she is still a creature created by You, and bearing Your image..." It's hard to lust while you're talking to God.

Many have prayed as Walter Chalmers Smith did:

One thing I of the Lord desire—
For all my way has darksome been—
Be it by earthquake, wind, or fire,
Lord, make me clean; Lord, make me clean!

A DARK SIDE TO OUR RIGHTS

Do not resist him who is evil.
—Matthew 5:39

Probably no other nation under heaven is more concerned with personal rights than ours. This is one of the fibers of the freedoms we have enjoyed in this country. Many have suffered and many have died defending these rights.

But freedom is not synonymous with "personal rights." There is a dark side to personal rights which produces more bondage than freedom.

When self-interest becomes the dominating force behind rights, those rights have become a bittersweet experience. The consuming passion to protect your personal rights breeds a sense of personal vengeance when those rights are violated. Vengeance is that feeling of outrage you have when one of your rights has been trampled upon. Vengeance at the time may taste sweet, but it leaves behind a bitterness that sours your whole life.

What Jesus had to say about vengeance in Matthew 5:38-42 is one of the most distinguishing characteristics of the Christian ethic. From this the love of God can be seen more clearly than with any other response we have to life.

This is one of the "hard sayings" of our Lord— hard, because initially everything within us fights against what He says.

But let us now "be quick to hear, slow to speak, and slow to anger" (James 1:19).

Take a look at Matthew 5:38-42 today—after praying for readiness to hear what may well seem hard to take.

RETALIATION

You have heard that it was said,
"An eye for an eye, and a tooth for a tooth."
—Matthew 5:38

This law is mentioned in the Old Testament in Exodus 21, Leviticus 24, and Deuteronomy 19. It's been accused of being among the most bloodthirsty, savage, and merciless laws of the Bible, but that's because the intention behind it has been overlooked or twisted. Instead of being bloodthirsty and savage, it was given for *mercy*. The law was to limit vengeance, to curb the vendettas and blood feuds characteristic of tribal societies. It was given for helping a court to assess a just punishment. God has always been deeply concerned with the evil of vengeance: "You shall not take vengeance, nor bear any grudge against the sons of your people, but you shall love your neighbor as yourself" (Leviticus 19:18); "Do not say, 'I'll do to him as he has done to me; I'll pay that man back for what he did'" (Proverbs 24:29).

The Pharisees, however, tried to use the law to justify personal revenge. Once again they took a law of God and twisted it from its original intention. The question became, How far can I go with my retaliation without breaking the law? What was meant for courts of law to determine was being dragged into the personal arena; vengeance, not justice was the issue.

Jesus responds, "But I say to you, do not resist him who is evil…" (Matthew 5:39). Jesus rescues this law of God and writes it on our hearts. How does it look? It is the renouncing of all *personal vengeance*, the releasing of personal rights.

NO PERSONAL VENGEANCE

*Do not resist him who is evil; but whoever slaps you
on your right cheek, turn to him the other also.*
—Matthew 5:39

Some take this to mean that Jesus is calling us to total nonresistance to evil; when evil hits, we're to do absolutely nothing. Luther was among those who reacted to this; he spoke of "the crazy saint who lets the lice nibble at him…maintaining he had to suffer and could not resist evil." The Scriptures make it clear that evil is to be resisted; God established government for that purpose (Romans 13:4, 1 Peter 2:13-14).

In Jesus' statement, the word *resist* means "to set yourself against," not against evil in general, but against "one who does evil." (This can't mean *the* Evil One—Satan—because we're told to resist him in James 4:7.) Jesus says, "Don't set yourself—as an enemy—against the one who does evil to you." The issue for us: How do we respond, not to the evil itself, but to the person doing the evil against us?

The right response is no personal vengeance. Why? Because taking revenge creates evil *within you*. We're to see to it "that no root of bitterness springing up causes trouble" (Hebrews 12:15). Expectations of always preserving your rights will eat you up. It sets you up for continual anger and resentment, as well as a creeping paranoia that won't let you go. As Emerson wrote, "For every minute you remain angry, you give up sixty seconds of peace of mind." It also reduces you to reproducing that evil in others. Evil does not overcome evil; evil can't destroy evil. All it can do is reproduce itself in you … then again in the one whose revenge will be excited by your own.

RELEASE FROM REVENGE

Let him give his cheek to the smiter.
—*Lamentations 3:30*

If the evil of revenge comes about from my holding on to my rights—then freedom from it must come from releasing those rights. It begins first with releasing your right to *honor and respect*. "Whoever slaps you on your right cheek, turn to him the other also" (Matthew 5:39).

Look at Christ on the day of the cross: "While being reviled, He did not revile in return; while suffering, He uttered no threats" (1 Peter 2:23). We absorb the insults and dishonor with dignity.

How? If I've already given up my right to honor, I no longer expect to be treated with honor.

It also means releasing your right to *comfort:* "If anyone wants to sue you and take your shirt, let him have your coat also" (Matthew 5:40).

Jesus is not talking about someone robbing you, but one who has a legitimate claim—he's *suing* you. The point: We should be willing to offer even more in order to show our regret for any wrong we did, and to show that we are not resentful against the one who has sued us. By responding this way we are saying, "You are more important to me than my comfort."

It means releasing your right to *choice:* "Whoever shall force you to go one mile, go with him two" (5:41). Palestine was occupied by Roman soldiers, and civilians often were ordered to carry their equipment and weapons. There was no choice on the people's part; you just did it. Jesus says, "So do it, and then do more."

MAKING A LIFE

Give to him who asks of you, and do not turn away
from him who wants to borrow from you.
—*Matthew 5:42*

This means releasing your right to *possessing*.

Jesus is speaking of a genuine generosity that wants to meet the other person's need—not a tokenism that does a good deed to buy off one's own conscience.

The world is full of two kinds of people, the givers and the takers. The takers eat well, but the givers sleep well.

We protest: *But it's mine!*

The issue here is a right understanding of what a steward is. We possess nothing, yet enjoy what we have been given. And what we have been given is for us to *steward*.

You can sow in confidence, because "He who supplies seed to the sower…will supply and multiply your seed for sowing and increase the harvest of your righteousness" (2 Corinthians 9:10). "He who is gracious to the poor man lends to the Lord, and He will repay him for his good deed" (Proverbs 19:17).

Is it the Christian's responsibility to give to the professional beggar, to pay for the drugs or the booze that ruin another man's life? Remember that it's God's money—and it is to be stewarded in a way that brings thanksgiving to God (2 Corinthians 9:12-13).

We make a living by what we *get;* we make a life by what we *give*.

TO BE AN ANVIL

You have been called for this purpose,
since Christ also suffered for you, leaving you
an example for you to follow in His steps.
—1 Peter 2:21

How is it possible to give up our rights?

By changing platitudes into convictions. Look at Galatians 2:20—"I have been crucified with Christ; and it is no longer I who live, but Christ lives in me." Dietrich Bonhoeffer described this as the "visible participation in His cross."

George Mueller wrote, "There was a day when I died, utterly died to George Mueller and his opinions, his preferences, and his tastes and his will. I died to the world, to its approval and its censure. I died to the approval or the blame of even my brethren and friends. And since then I have studied only to show myself approved unto God."

Are your opinions, preferences, and tastes alive and kicking? Or have you learned to give them up at the cross?

To be a doormat is one thing; to be an anvil is something else.

Look carefully at Romans 12:21—"Do not be overcome by evil, but overcome evil with good."

How do I release vengeance? By releasing your right—your expectation—of being treated to honor, comfort, choice, and possession.

Jesus "did not regard equality with God a thing to be grasped." Jesus "emptied Himself." Jesus "humbled Himself." Paul says, "Have this attitude in yourselves which was also in Christ Jesus" (Philippians 2:5-9).

DIVORCE

Because of your hardness of heart, Moses permitted you
to divorce your wives; but from the beginning
it has not been this way.
—Matthew 19:8

Men were already divorcing their wives when
Moses set down his words on divorce in Deuteronomy 24. There is nothing in his words commanding
divorce. It was because of their "hardness of heart"
that the instructions were given. They were designed
to protect women from slander, and to give them
freedom to marry another. It was also to dissuade impulsive divorces: "Think about it," Moses was saying.
"Once you send her away and she marries another,
there's no way you can have her back again!"

Did you realize that, of the Ten Commandments,
two have to do with protecting the sacredness of marriage? "You shall not commit adultery" and "You
shall not covet your neighbor's wife" (Exodus
20:14,17).

For the Pharisees, however, the ease of divorce
made it possible to avoid open adultery. Only a little
paperwork was required to legalize their lust.

In the Sermon on the Mount, Jesus brings up the
issue of divorce while talking about *adultery*
(Matthew 5:27-32). That's the point! Jesus warns that
there are three ways adultery is committed: (1) the act
of sexual union with another person; (2) the lusting
after another who is not your mate; and (3) divorcing
your mate.

Committing adultery is mocking God's creation
and design, for it destroys what God created in "two
becoming one."

NO BAILING OUT

And we know that God causes all things
to work together for good to those who love God,
to those who are called according to His purpose.
—Romans 8:28

Called according to His purpose... And what is His
purpose? "For whom He foreknew," Paul continues,
"He also predestined *to become conformed to the image*
of His Son" (8:29).

But how are we shaped into that image of Christ,
that image of the glory of God? How do we become
more and more like what God first created us to become?

Proverbs 27:6 says, "Faithful are the wounds of a
friend"—"friend" is *ahav*, "one who loves."

Look at James 1:3-4—"When you encounter various trials...let endurance have its perfect result, that
you may be perfect and complete, lacking in nothing."

Perfect and complete... Look what that image of God
looks like in man: "Love, joy, peace, patience, kindness, goodness, faithfulness, gentleness, self-control"
(Galatians 5:22-23).

Where do you learn these things?

How about in marriage?

But the pain is too great... I want out!

Out of what? Out of what God is doing in your
life?

Bail out on your mate, and in essence you are bailing out on God's plan for your life. The consequences
can be devastating—for you, and for those you say
you love!

WHEN THINGS GET TOUGH

The testing of your faith produces endurance.
—James 1:3

Two becoming "one flesh" in the presence of God by covenant is more than something sexual. Jesus makes that clear in Matthew 19:6—"What therefore God has joined together, let no man separate." The mystery is not the "one flesh," but the two becoming one. This oneness is never to be broken because it is *spiritual*.

Why is God so serious about this thing called "marriage," "one flesh," "two becoming one"?

Because things get real tough between two people living together. The pain at times is too great. *Why not divorce?* We would do it continually.

Philip Yancey writes, "Pain narrows vision. The most private of sensations, it forces us to think of ourselves and little else." We can make a lot of serious mistakes when trying to make decisions while we're in pain. But what might that pain be? It was George MacDonald who wrote, "Everything difficult indicates something more than our theory of life yet embraces." In the pain that comes in a married relationship, we need to ask ourselves the question, Why am I married?

The answer: Because it is good, and I am completed in marriage. I am to grow into all that God has for me; I am to learn all I can from this sacred union.

Let the law of God be written on your heart: *I will not commit adultery by divorcing my mate.*

Why am I married?

To glorify God! *I made a covenant with God...*

HIS MIND ON MARRIAGE

But I say to you that everyone who divorces his wife,
except for the cause of unchastity, makes her
commit adultery; and whoever marries
a divorced woman commits adultery.
—*Matthew 5:32*

Jesus isn't talking about loopholes here for getting out of marriage, and He's not addressing those who are already divorced. God is a God of forgiveness to the repentant heart, and *your* situation has to do with the grace of God and you.

Jesus in this passage is speaking to all who are married or thinking about getting married. This is "the mind of Christ" on the issue of the sacredness of marriage.

In Genesis 1 we read, "And God created man in His own image, in the image of God He created him; male and female He created them." Why male and female? He tells us why in Genesis 2: "It is not good for the man to be alone; I will make him a helper suitable for him." This "not good" was in contrast to the good of all the rest of creation, the completeness of it. Why was it "not good" for man to be alone? How would the creation of woman, and the "two becoming one," correct that which was "not good"? The woman would be similar in nature, and yet different—his converse, so as to complete the good by completing him. (That's why men and women are so different— opposite—in our ways.)

Thus, after creating the woman God said, *"For this cause* a man shall leave his father and his mother, and shall cleave to his wife; and they shall become one flesh" (Genesis 2:24).

OUT OF THE ASHES

Blessed be the God and Father of our Lord Jesus Christ,
the Father of mercies and God of all comfort;
who comforts us in all our affliction
so that we may be able to comfort...
—2 Corinthians 1:3-4

Why do we have to hurt sometimes? Can anything good come out of the ashes of suffering?

We suffer, we hurt, because we live in a world we've built ourselves; because we thought we didn't need God. And so, as Paul puts it, "Even though they knew God, they did not honor Him as God, or give thanks; but they became futile in their speculations, and their foolish heart was darkened... Therefore God gave them over..."

But even in this fallen world, God comforts His own. When we hurt, there is no wasted suffering, for He will not permit you to suffer needless pain.

He knows!

He cares!

He's there!

He is there to bring out of the ashes the *compassion* in us to comfort others.

He is there to bring out of the ashes the *trust* in Him instead of ourselves.

He is there to bring out of the ashes the *thanksgiving* offered to Him for His deliverance.

God is the author of mercies, and that's why He is the "God of all comfort." He values what He has made, and does not desire to destroy us. He comes alongside us, giving strength.

He is our hope in our pain.

BOUND IN SUFFERING

The sufferings of Christ are ours in abundance.
—2 Corinthians 1:5

Would you have ever known comfort if you had never known pain? Comfort has to do with the *removal of pain.*

That doesn't always mean your removal from painful circumstances. But it does mean *the presence of God there with you in the pain.*

He is there to cause purpose and design to come out of it. He will not let you suffer needlessly or alone. He will bring out of it all the residue of beauty.

Paul tells about some of these purposes. One of them is that we might be able to comfort others. He's alongside *us*...so we can come alongside someone else. *God does not comfort us to make us comfortable, but to make us comforters.* Where else do we learn compassion? Where else do we learn sensitivity? Where else do we gain the depth of feeling to be able to touch another with a tear?

It would be nice to believe that only bad people suffer. Then we could respond to all suffering by simply saying, "You had it coming." (What did Christ have coming?) But the truth is that sorrow and pain are no respecters of persons. Good people get hurt, and hurt badly.

"The sufferings of Christ are ours in abundance," Paul says. His intense sufferings came as a result of bringing people the gospel. Then he says, "You are sharers of our sufferings" (1:7). Not only are we bound as a people to Christ, but we are bound to each other.

Whose suffering are you sharing today?

HITTING BOTTOM

For My thoughts are not your thoughts,
neither are your ways My ways…
For as the heavens are higher than the earth,
so are My ways higher than your ways,
and My thoughts than your thoughts.
—Isaiah 55:8-9

We try too often to figure it all out, and keep it all under control—in other words, to deliver ourselves from our affliction. We try to handle the fear, run from the pain.

God says, "Humble yourselves under the mighty hand of God" (1 Peter 5:7).

What's going on — on the inside?

The issue is total dependence on God. Paul spoke of great affliction: "We were burdened excessively, beyond our strength, so that we despaired even of life; indeed we had the sentence of death within ourselves…" Why? "…in order that we should not trust in ourselves, but in God who raises the dead" (2 Corinthians 1:8-9). When Paul's own strength was gone, there was nothing else he could do. He had to trust God…or else curse Him, and die (Job 2:9-10).

When we finally hit the bottom, we realize the bottom is the palm of God's hand.

It's been said that pain plants the flag of reality in the fortress of a rebel heart. Pain reduces us to a primary level, the level of dependence on our God.

That's why some of us have to hit bottom before we're willing to look up.

GOD'S INTERVENTION

*Thanks be to God, who always
leads us in His triumph in Christ.*
—2 Corinthians 2:14

What is our fear in sharing our faith in Jesus Christ
with others? Isn't it ultimately the fear of being rejected, or thought to be foolish? (Believe it or not, the
apostle Paul felt the same way; that's why in Ephesians 6:19 he asked prayer for boldness in sharing
the gospel.)

On the other hand, as a Christian, what is it that
most keeps you from spiritual apathy? *Sharing our
faith!* Evangelism puts sparkle into the Christian life.
When we're sharing the gospel, we pray specifically,
laying hold on God for victory in the spiritual struggles within the soul of an individual we care about.

We live in a real world. So prepare yourself to understand the real world instead of being fearful of it
or surprised by it. Not everyone responds to anyone,
and if they do respond, realize that they will respond
in many different ways. And for the most part, it has
nothing to do with you.

There are some things that will not happen unless
God intervenes. A person's salvation is one of them.
"No one can come to Me," Jesus said, "unless the Father who sent Me draws him" (John 6:44). *We* don't
convert another to Christ.

In thanksgiving for God's intervention, Paul in 2
Corinthians 2 gives the picture of a Roman victory
processional. He acknowledges that the battle is His,
the triumph is His. Paul says, "Who is adequate for
these things?" None of us. It's God who leads the triumph.

THE SCENT GOES GODWARD

We are a fragrance of Christ to God.
—2 Corinthians 2:15

Paul speaks of how "the sweet aroma of the knowledge of Him" is manifested through our lives (2 Corinthians 2:14); we are vessels or instruments through which the fragrance is released. "We are the fragrance of Christ *to God* among *those who are being saved* and among *those who are perishing*" (2:15). The scent goes Godward, and is to pleasing to Him, regardless of the response. Just having His Son shared is joy to the Father, though the response of people will vary. God is pleased whenever His Son is declared.

Paul then lays down the ultimate exclusives: "...to the one an aroma from death to death, to the other an aroma from life to life." When all the dust settles and the philosophical chattering ceases, it comes down to this: Either you are moving in life to life, or in death to death—literally "out of life into life," or "out of death into death." Whether those living in death will respond to the message of Christ is not your responsibility, but His. It is He who draws, and the Holy Spirit who convicts of sin (John 16:8-9).

Paul says, "For we are not like many, peddling the word of God, but as from sincerity, but as from God, we speak in Christ in the sight of God" (2 Corinthians 2:17). Ours is not to market this thing, to "peddle" the Word of God. Personal gain, fame, or even acceptance is not our aim.

We share *in sincerity*. The fragrance is to please Him by sharing and declaring His Son!

MAN OF PERSPECTIVE

Who is like the wise man
and who knows the interpretation of a matter?
A man's wisdom illumines him
and causes his stern face to beam.
—Ecclesiastes 8:1

No one has an edge on the man who has wisdom. He knows the art of life, and has the skill to live it. He has the "interpretation," the right understanding of how things around him fit into the scheme of his life, how they all—the good and the bad—have their needful place in his living. He has the right *perspective*.

You can see the uniqueness of this guy by his face. Because he understands what's happening to him, there's illumination there, a peace, a joy. There's a nonfearing presence about him. He's actually cheerful, which will cause him to stand out from the crowd like a flagpole.

That "perspective" has changed his hard, "stern" look to one of restfulness and contentment...because he knows the worth of wisdom.

"Wisdom," Solomon says, "is good, and an advantage to those who see the sun. For wisdom is protection just as money is protection" (Ecclesiastes 7:11-12). Literally the phrase is "In the shade, is wisdom, in the shade is money" ("shade" in eastern thought represented *protection*). In other words, with wisdom and money, you've got it made in the shade!

"Wisdom preserves the lives of its possessors" (7:13). Wisdom protects not only the wise, but those around them: "He who walks with wise men will be wise" (Proverbs 13:20).

THE ONLY CREDENTIAL

...written not with ink, but with the Spirit
of the living God; not on tablets of stone,
but on tablets of human hearts.
—2 Corinthians 3:3

Legalism leads to death, because either you live your whole life condemned, or when you realize there's no happiness in legalism, you move to license. If keeping all the rules doesn't work, maybe breaking all the rules will!

What demonstrates the truth of the gospel of grace? Paul says it in 2 Corinthians 3: *changed lives!* This is the only credential. The change in my life is the same as the change in your life, and the same gospel of grace changed us both. It's a change that "all men" (3:2) can read and see in us! This is the undeniable reality of the truth of the gospel of Jesus Christ.

Paul reminds us that when God gave the Law (the Ten Commandments), it was written "on tablets of stone," and recopied later "with ink" onto papyrus. The Law was given to communicate something about us ... but it never changed us.

But this *new thing*—Paul calls it "a new covenant" (3:6)—is written by the Holy Spirit on our hearts. The ministry of grace changes the heart—where lie the deep desires and attitudes from which we perceive the world.

Paul was a brilliant and well-educated man, yet he did not depend on himself to bring about this change in anyone. "Not that we are adequate in ourselves to consider anything as coming from ourselves, but our adequacy is from God" (3:5). God must do that deep work within the heart of another.

ASK, AND BE OPEN

The Spirit gives life.
—2 Corinthians 3:6

Whenever you find something truly genuine, you can usually find someone coming along promoting a counterfeit. There is the authentic, and there is that subtle perversion.

The counterfeit has a lot to do with what we do. We Christians tend to do a lot: We pray; we read the Bible; we get baptized; we take communion; we go to church; we give of our resources; we pursue purity; we clean up our language; we smile more and try to act like we generally have it all together.

We may discover what millions of others have: that it's possible to avoid the pain and humiliation of genuine repentance and renewal by maintaining an outward facade of spiritual commitment to orthodox behavior.

An authentic Christian life, however, *changes* your life; the change is *from within*, and the change is *real*, not passing. That's the heart of the matter.

Have you slipped into believing a counterfeit—a legalism which leads only to guilt and fear? Or because keeping all the rules didn't bring you happiness, have you given up and moved into license— and yet still feeling miserable inside?

As I grow in my own Christian walk, I am finding it less and less complicated: To begin each step you first *ask for the desire*, and then *be open to the change*.

Are you ready for a new step — a new step of authentic Christian living?

Are you ready to wake up to the will of God?

RIGHTEOUS SERVANTS

The fruit of the righteous is a tree of life,
and he who is wise wins souls.
—Proverbs 11:30

A righteous man or woman will have influence on those around them because it becomes apparent that they possess something others want. In their righteousness they experience life to its fullest. It is that credibility that affects others.

Righteousness is being in a right relationship with God, yourself, and with others. What follows is a desire to carry out your righteousness in obedience to the Word of righteousness.

A right relationship with God is as a child. A right relationship with yourself is to be at peace. And a right relationship with others is as a servant. It is as we are recognized as a servant that we have the greatest influence on others.

We are called to be servants, not hired hands (there's a difference).

In 2 Corinthians 5:20-21, Paul tells us what kind of servants we are to be: ambassadors for Christ, committed to the ministry of reconciliation, helping people to have a personal relationship with God, personal intimacy with God.

An ambassador is a representative of a *person,* not a religion, and is commissioned to speak and to do in behalf of that person. We are ambassadors for Jesus, and that's what it means to be called a servant. Jesus is the focus of what we say and what we do as servants.

NECK PAIN

Do not be bound together with unbelievers.
—2 Corinthians 6:14

What is it to be "bound together"? The King James Version translates this "unequally yoked." The picture is from Deuteronomy 22:10—"You shall not plow with an ox and a donkey together." The natures of these two beasts were different, and they want to go different ways. One wasn't better than the other, just different.

The point of being "bound" or "yoked" is that of mutual dependence. If the full impact of your influence depends on someone else, you had better take a good look at that someone else!

Picture yourself with your neck yoked with that person's. Is he headed where you are headed? If not, it could cause you some real neck pain!

Paul is simply saying that there are times when "saints" and "aints" don't mix well. The believer and unbeliever have totally different reasons for living. And if I yoke myself up with an unbeliever, in truth I have begun to separate myself from the One who is the center of my life.

Therefore, Paul says in 6:17, "come out from their midst and be separate." How? "Do not touch what is unclean." How? By not being bound or yoked to what is unclean.

James says, "Whoever wishes to be a friend of the world makes himself an enemy of God" (4:4). He is a Father to us, and we are His sons and daughters (2 Corinthians 6:18). He's the last Person you would ever want to separate yourself from...the last Person you would ever want for an enemy.

JESUS WAS NOT A MONK

I have made myself a slave to all, that I might win the more.
—1 Corinthians 9:19

Many in history have wanted desperately to be pure before God (which is a wonderful thing). But it became an issue of paranoia. Those seeking purity feared they would be diseased by the world, forgetting that we are supposed to be the ones with the infectious cure. And so the concept of *separation* came into being. Christians began to cut themselves off from other Christians whom they believed had diseased themselves by being part of the world. People began to draw up lists of things they considered worldly. Naturally the lists all differ from one another. Whenever someone struggled with some temptation or some kind of recreation or activity, it was marked down on their list as "worldly." Personal prejudices and biblical convictions got confused. In centuries past, many decided the only way to avoid the temptations of the world was to completely seclude themselves from it. They built high-walled monasteries and lived their lives inside. Still today we have many who live like twentieth-century monks, behind walls of their own making.

Jesus was not a monk! And He said His followers were to live *in* the world (John 17:14-15), and to let "all men know" by their love that they were His disciples (13:35). That's why the apostle Paul wasn't a monk either, but instead became "all things to *all men, that I may by all means* save some" (1 Corinthians 9:22).

If we are to win the world, we have to be *in the* world.

DIFFERENT REASONS

For we are the temple of the living God, just as God said.
—2 Corinthians 6:16

Paul says there are times when "saints" and "aints" don't mix well. He gives five reasons why (in 2 Corinthians 6:14-16):

(1) "What partnership have righteousness and lawlessness?" One wants to obey God's Law, the other is indifferent to it. They follow totally different desires.

(2) "What fellowship has light with darkness?" Fellowship here is *koinonia*, "fellow share-holders," sharing in common. The Christian is in the light as God is in the light. Darkness is ignorance; there is no capacity to discern goodness, righteousness or truth. In other words, we have totally different value systems.

(3) "What harmony has Christ with Belial?" The voices are different; and for the believer, what is *most important* is different. For the Christian, Jesus is Lord. Everything he does ultimately has the purpose of glorifying God. Jesus is not Lord for the non-Christian. Who is? The word *Belial* means "worthlessness," and was used as a name for Satan.

(4) "What has a believer in common with an unbeliever?" The believer has a sense of love and acceptance from God, a sense of purpose in bringing others into God's kingdom, and a sense of future — eternal life in that kingdom. The unbeliever has none of that.

(5) "What agreement has the temple of God with idols?" The believer has "cast his vote" for God; the unbeliever has committed his life to idolatry.

How does this apply to: Business partnerships? Marriage? Friendships? Work relationships?

VINDICATION

Just as he is Christ's, so also are we.
—2 Corinthians 10:7

In answering criticism of himself, Paul gives us in 2 Corinthians 10 some guidelines for how to answer it ourselves.

(1) Keep the focus on the accusers, not on others who are influenced by them and thus confused, and having questions.

(2) Defensive self-justification looks weak and is an embarrassment to you and to others. We answer criticism when it comes down to questioning our credibility and testimony in serving Jesus Christ.

(3) The weapons of defense are not of the flesh—power plays, emotional temper tantrums, or manipulative intimidation.

(4) The divinely empowered weapons bring out the truth of the matter: our specific obedience to Christ, which is the very thing that causes the criticism. The rest of the defense belongs to God.

Have you been criticized lately?

Was any of it true? ("Reprove a wise man," Solomon says, "and he will love you. Give instruction to a wise man, and he will be still wiser"—Proverbs 9:8-9). If it wasn't true—is it really affecting your credibility and freedom to serve our Lord?

Go and explain your obedience to Jesus Christ, and leave the rest of the defense to the One who judges righteously.

"No weapon formed against you shall prosper, and every tongue that accuses you in judgment you will condemn. This is the heritage of the servants of the Lord, and their vindication is from Me" (Isaiah 54:17).

LITTLE TO WORK WITH

If I boast, I will boast of what pertains to my weakness.
—2 Corinthians 11:30

Paul was determined to boast of the things that would show his weakness: "I'm weak, shamed, beaten up, hated, and humiliated. But with all this you can see one thing clearly: Jesus is my Lord, and I am His servant. The glory goes to God for everything!" Paul's weaknesses were on display so that others could see what God had done with the little He had to work with. Is the issue of Christ's lordship something you feel good about, or something you shy away from? Do you understand what it is?

The gospel of Jesus Christ is salvation through faith alone, not of works. "For by grace you have been saved through faith, and that not of yourselves; it is the gift of God" (Ephesians 2:8-9). And yet look at what Paul says in the next verse: "We are His workmanship, created in Christ Jesus for good works, which God prepared beforehand, that we should walk in them." There must be some evidence of genuine faith—or have I only tried to appease God with a prayer?

Lordship is the evidence of genuine faith, and lordship is simply carrying out the things Jesus has told us to do. Sometimes the things He has told us to do will cost us something. Are we willing to pay the price? What is our commitment to Jesus as our Lord?

"God highly exalted Him, and bestowed on Him the name which is above every name, that at the name of Jesus every knee should bow...and every tongue should confess that Jesus Christ is Lord, to the glory of God the Father" (Philippians 2:9-11).

A THORN AND A PROMISE

There was given me a thorn in the flesh, a messenger of Satan to buffet me — to keep me from exalting myself!
—2 Corinthians 12:7

Whatever Paul's infirmity was, it evidently was quite painful. The word *thorn* means "a sharpened stake." It came to him after he experienced "revelations" of "surpassing greatness"; Paul said they were given "for this reason, to keep me from exalting myself!" (12:7). There's something worse than sickness. It's sin and pride.

Paul saw the thorn as both the work of God and the work of Satan. It was sent by Satan to wound, limit, and defeat Paul; at the same time, he says it was permitted by God. Paul prayed three times for its removal; God did not give Paul explanations; instead He gave him a promise: "My grace is sufficient for you, for power is perfected in weakness." We do not live on explanations. We do live on promises.

Do you have a thorn? If so, what do you really want from it? To have it removed, and have it count for nothing? Or to let the power of Christ be seen in you as the grace of God gives what you need to realize God's intentions in your life.

How does this thought hit you? *I am most useful to others when I am hurting in some way.*

The greatest honor is to be used in the lives of others. And yet God "resists the proud and gives grace to the humble" (James 4:6). How has God honored you by using you in the lives of others? And how has God humbled you? What thorn was needed for Him to be able to use you?

DAILY THORNS, DAILY GRACE

My grace is sufficient for you.
—2 Corinthians 12:9

What is this "sufficient grace"? It is God's provision for our every need, when we need it!

For example, it's God's faithfulness in providing a "way of escape" when we face temptation (1 Corinthians 10:13). James speaks of "a greater grace" (4:6) when we submit to God, knowing that He gives grace to the humble. When we are doing what God says—exactly what He says—the power is greater, because of the greater control God has of the situation to accomplish His will.

It's not a great, final triumph, but rather this is *daily grace* dealing with daily thorns, our daily weaknesses. For "Power," God told Paul, "is perfected in weakness" (2 Corinthians 12:9).

When faced with a thorn, we usually pray for substitution and not transformation. Paul was asking for substitution—removal of the thorn, health instead of sickness, deliverance instead of pain. Sometimes God does substitute. Yet at other times God *transforms* by not removing the affliction, but giving the grace needed to use it for His good.

After praying three times for the thorn's removal, Paul came to the point of being "well content" with it. He was determined and resolved that this was a good thing from the hand of God, even though delivered by Satan. By it he was made a dwelling place of the power of Christ. And what is the power of Christ? The ability to accomplish God's intentions in any situation.

TAKEN FOR GRANTED

I have not taken advantage of you.
—2 Corinthians 12:17

We should never have to defend ourselves; there ought to be enough people around who know us well enough to make a defense for us. But nobody was standing with Paul as he was forced unjustly to defend himself in 2 Corinthians 12, and that must have hurt. Paul tells the Corinthians, "There's nothing special about me, but there's nothing wrong with me either." He was getting no commendation, no loyalty from the Corinthians. That's being taken for granted! "If I love you the more," he said, "am I to be loved the less?" (12:15). Love is designed to kindle love. A healthy response to being loved is to respond. A sick response to being loved is to take it for granted.

Paul loved the Corinthians ("I wrote to you with many tears…that you might know the love which I have especially for you"— 2:4). Loving like that leaves you vulnerable; you just might get hurt and taken for granted. And yet the only other option is to protect yourself by manipulating power over everyone else. (No thank you! Why play sick games with sick people?)

Ever feel like you're taken for granted?

If so, what are you going to do about it? What will you do with the feeling of it? What will you do with the fact of it?

Remember Matthew 7:12—"Whatever you want others to do for you, do so for them."

And remember that all relationships begin with one higher relationship—with One who has never and will never take you for granted.

LOVE IS NOT A FEELING

The greatest of these is love.
—1 Corinthians 13:13

It's been said that love isn't what makes the world go round; it's what makes the ride worthwhile.

Jesus gave the new command to all His disciples: "Love one another, even as I have loved you. By this all men will know that you are My disciples" (John 13:34-35).

The word is *agape!* Love is the very mark of the Christian. They will know us by our love.

The Greeks elevated a man for what he knew—his intellect. The Romans worshiped a man for what he could do—his power. But in 1 Corinthians 13, Paul's great hymn of love, it's what you *become*— your character. The issue is *significant being.*

Understanding what it means to love is such a focal point in God's plan for your change, that Paul says, "Love therefore is the fulfillment of the law" (Romans 13:10).

Notice where we find Paul's great hymn of love— it's nestled in controversy. These Corinthian Christians have been fighting over spiritual gifts and how spiritual the gifts made them feel. In all this divisive arrogance, Paul reminds them in the closing words of 1 Corinthians 12, "I show you a still more excellent way…"

If you're really desirous of being Spirit-filled and Spirit-controlled, then look at the first and foremost manifestation of it: "The fruit of the Spirit is love…" (Galatians 5:22).

LOVE IS NOT A FEELING

If I...do not have love, I am nothing.
—1 Corinthians 13:2

Significant *doing* flows out of significant being, and significant *being* flows out from our new nature of love. As we submit our responses to that nature, the Spirit of God can begin to bring about spiritual growth in us. Love is something you *become*. It's a description of a new nature reflected in the way we relate to others, ourselves, sin, and circumstances.

Love in my response to others:

Love is patient...
Am I retaliating?

Love is kind...
Am I being useful?

Love is not jealous...
Am I being envious?

Love in my response to self:

Love does not brag...
Am I trying to make others envious of me?

Love is not arrogant...
Am I rude in not recognizing the equal worth of another?

Love does not act unbecomingly...
Am I caring how others feel?

Love does not seek its own...
Am I centering the attention around me?

(1 Corinthians 13:4-5)

LOVE IS NOT A FEELING

If I…do not have love, it profits me nothing.
—1 Corinthians 13:3

Love is the seeking of another's good at your own expense. We seek the good of others at our own cost so that they may come to know the worth of a soul, and the change that's wrought by the touch of the Master's hand.

Love in my response to sin:

Love is not provoked…
Am I losing my temper?

Love does not take into account a wrong…
Am I returning hurt to others?

Love does not rejoice in unrighteousness…
Am I enjoying the hurts of others?

Love rejoices with the truth…
Am I committed to the success of others?

Love in my response to circumstance:

Love bears all things…
Am I protecting the reputation of others?

Love believes all things…
Am I believing first the best of others?

Love hopes all things…
Am I expecting God to do good things for others?

Love endures all things…
Am I faithful in my commitments to others?

(1 Corinthians 13:5-7)

CREDIBLE LOVE

*This is the message which you have heard
from the beginning, that we should love one another.*
—1 John 3:11

It's been said that everyone shares two fears: that we will never be loved, and that we will never know how to love. The two fears go hand in hand; if I don't know how to love someone else, how will I ever know if I am being loved?

We can know how to show affection and how to speak the "sweet nothings" in each other's ears—but few know how to love. And when we don't know how ... we leave damaged people.

John says, "Little children, let us not love with word or with tongue, but in deed and truth" (1 John 3:18). Most of what we think is loving has to do with things we say. But the absence of love in deed and truth can be fatal. Deed and truth give credibility to love. Personal self-sacrifice is the very blood of those words. It's the deed of self-sacrifice that shows love to be true.

In the next verse John says, "We shall know by this that we are of the truth, and shall assure our heart before Him" (3:19). By this self-sacrificial behavior I will be able to "assure" or persuade my heart that I am truly a genuine Christian. When I find myself doing what I know I would not be doing if it was only me— giving up something for someone else—I know there has been a change in my life.

If I'm loving in *deed*, there's some self-sacrifice in evidence — and I'm loving in truth.

There should be people close around me feeling good about themselves. If not, why not?

A LOVE CALLED HATE

Cain…was of the evil one.
—1 John 3:12

To help us understand love, John contrasts it with another kind of love that the Bible calls "hate." Hate is actually a love.

"Everyone who hates his brother is a murderer, and you know that no murderer has eternal life abiding in him" (3:15). Hate begins with an attitude of self-consumed ego, and ends up inflicting damage to the worth of others. John mentions Cain as the classic example of hating one's brother.

Abel's obedience of God's will rebuked Cain's disobedience. Cain could have made it right, but instead wanted to get rid of what was making his life miserable: Abel. "Cain…slew his brother" (3:12). The word for "slew" is *sphadzo*, "to cut the throat in a sacrifice." This is the attitude behind the murder: "Okay, God; You want a blood sacrifice? Here, I'll give You one— my brother." Why did he do that? "Because his deeds were evil, and his brother's were righteous" (3:12).

Hate is a love for yourself, a love that is exclusively committed to your own success. Therefore anything or anyone who threatens that success is a threat and must be removed, or at least punished. When Cain saw his brother's success, he was only reminded of his own failure. That which threatens me must be removed. Hate is threatened by the success of anyone else, so we continually do what we can to remove those threats. Murder is simply the natural result of hate.

What do you learn about love by seeing its opposite? (Look today at Philippians 2:1-4.)

THE HERO

We know that we have passed out of death into life,
because we love the brethren.
—1 John 3:14

Here's how you can know you're spiritually alive:
You are not indifferent to what God says has great
worth. You "love the brethren." As I see myself loving others I know that it is not my old nature; something has happened to me, and that something is my
salvation.

"We know love by this, that He laid down His life
for us; and we ought to lay down our lives for the
brethren" (3:16). Here is the element that cuts the line
clearly between love and hate: *self-sacrifice*. Self-sacrifice is a somewhat foreign concept to man. That's
why we're so shocked when we see it in another. We
call him a hero. To deny yourself something for the
good of another is what self-sacrifice is all about. It's
what love is all about. There is no other way to communicate worth to another individual.

When everything has been said, including the
"sweet nothings," it's what has been done in self-sacrifice that truly has significance.

Your worth to me is what I'm willing to give up
for your good.

"Whoever has the world's goods, and beholds his
brother in need and closes his heart against him, how
does the love of God abide in him?" (3:17). When we
refuse to sacrifice anything for others, the door is
slammed shut in their faces. This is what hate looks
like, whether you intended to express it or not. We do
damage to the worth of others without even trying.

FOR THOSE CLOSE AROUND

Love one another, just as He commanded us.
—1 John 3:23

What you know about loving says a lot about you. It shows to whom you belong—whether or not you're a child of God. John said, "Everyone who hates his brother is a murderer" (3:15). How can John say that? Because Jesus said it in Matthew 5:21-22. But how can Jesus say that? Because God looks at the heart of a man, and the full spectrum from social ostracism to murder represents simply different degrees of the exact same attitude of hate.

John speaks of the "confidence before God" (3:21) that results from loving others out of a genuine Christian commitment, thereby proving I'm a follower of Jesus. This confidence means freedom—I'm freed up, knowing I'm part of the family of God. I don't have to be plagued with doubts any longer.

"We have confidence before God," John continues, "and whatever we ask we receive from Him" (3:22). With this freedom, knowing God is my heavenly Father, I can ask for those things I deeply desire, and He will respond—"because we keep His commandments and do the things that are pleasing in His sight. And this is His commandment, that we believe in the name of His Son Jesus Christ, and love one another, just as He commanded us" (3:22-23).

Some questions to ask yourself: (1) Do those closest to me feel valuable, important, of great worth...because of how I treat them? (2) Do they feel intimidated or fearful of me? (3) What can I do in the way of self-sacrifice to further the success of those close around me?

LOVE IS NOT A FEELING

*If I speak in the tongues of men and of angels…If I have
the gift of prophecy…If I give all my possessions
to feed the poor…but do not have love, it profits me nothing.*
—1 Corinthians 13:1-3

Paul gives a formula for greatness (in the sight of men, not God)—to be able to speak eloquently, to know all things, and to be generous in giving. Sounds like a wonderful person to me. But Paul puts it all in right perspective: There is a necessity for love.

Let's suppose I could speak with great fluency in many languages, Paul says, and speak even with the eloquence of one of the angels who spoke to men in the Old Testament. I would be only as a "noisy gong or a clanging cymbal." If it is not spoken from a heart of love, it resembles only the resonant sound of a dead and hollow instrument. It may be loud and impressive, but it all means nothing!

Let's say I had the gift of prophecy, the ability to know "all mysteries and all knowledge"; nothing was hidden from me, whether God's knowledge or man's; and with this knowledge my confidence in God was so great, I could move mountains. Yet still no love?… Then I'm nothing. There is no significance to any of it. A full head with an empty heart is worthless!

Lastly, suppose I did the ultimate act of benevolence and compassion by giving all my possessions away to feed the poor, and even gave my life to be martyred. If it was done without love it would profit me nothing in the eyes of God.

These things may win you the admiration of men; but the person void of love produces nothing, is nothing, and gains nothing in the sight of God.

LOVE IS NOT A FEELING

Love is patient…
—1 Corinthians 13:4

Patient here means "patient with people"; literally, "long-tempered." Chrysostom, an early church father, said the word is used "of the man who is wronged and who has it easily in his power to avenge himself, but will never do it."

Patience never retaliates.

This doesn't go with our natural flow. We would much rather flow with what was taught by Aristotle, who saw virtue in refusing to tolerate insult or injury, and in striking back in retaliation for the slightest offense. Vengeance is sweet.

That sounds more like our style.

That's the point: It is! But Jesus said, "You have heard that it was said, 'An eye for an eye, and a tooth for a tooth.' But I say to you, Do not resist him who is evil; but whoever slaps you on your right cheek, turn to him the other also" (Matthew 5:38-39).

What if God was more like our style? How long would we still be here?

Robert Ingersoll, well-known atheist of the last century, often would stop in the middle of his lectures against God and say, "I'll give God five minutes to strike me dead for the things I've said." He then used the fact that he was not struck down as proof that God did not exist. Theodore Parker said of Ingersoll's claim, "And did the gentleman think he could exhaust the patience of the eternal God in five minutes?"

Love does not retaliate.

LOVE IS NOT A FEELING

Love is kind, and is not jealous; love does not brag...
—1 Corinthians 13:4

Love is kind. This means actually doing good to the very ones who can irritate you. The word means "to be useful to others and gracious." It is active good will.

Kindness is the counterpart to patience. What Jesus says about turning the other cheek in patience, He says in the next few verses of Matthew 5 about kindness. It is as Paul said in Romans 12—not taking your own revenge is patience, and what follows is kindness.

Love is not jealous. Love isn't bothered when others receive a blessing from the hand of God. Love and jealousy are mutually exclusive. William Shakespeare in *Othello* warned about jealousy: "O! Beware, my lord, of jealousy: It is the green-eyed monster which doth mock the meat it feeds on."

There are two forms of jealousy: The first is wanting to have what others have. Sometimes we call it "envy." The second kind is more degenerate— when we wish others didn't have what they have, because we don't have it.

Love does not brag. It's a shame that we feel the pressure to convince each other that we're lovable. What is bragging? It's the other side of jealousy. Jealousy is wanting what someone else has; bragging is trying to make others jealous of what we have.

A test: How often, when you have the opportunity to introduce the topic of conversation, does the topic end up being about you?

LOVE IS NOT A FEELING

Love is not arrogant, does not act unbecomingly;
it does not seek its own, is not provoked...
—*1 Corinthians 13:4-5*

Love is not arrogant. This is a lack of respect for others, an ignoring of the equal worth of another; in other words, *rude!* God hates it when we devalue what He considers to be of great worth.

Love does not act unbecomingly. This is poor manners! The loveless person cares nothing for the feelings of others, so he is careless in the way he acts. Love is sensitive to the feelings of those around you. This is the *act* of the *attitude* of arrogance.

Love does not seek its own. There's an inscription on a tombstone in a small English village which reads, "Here lies a miser who lived for himself, and cared for nothing but gathering wealth. Now where he is or how he fares, nobody knows and nobody cares." Here's another inscription, this one from a tombstone in the courtyard at St. Paul's Cathedral in London: "Sacred to the memory of General Charles George Gordin, who at all times and in every way gave his strength to the weak, his substance to the poor, his sympathy to the suffering, his heart to God."

It was Dr. Lenski who said, "Cure selfishness and you have just replanted the Garden of Eden."

Love is not provoked. Love is not driven to an outburst of anger when we are not pleased from not getting our own way. What are we offended at? *Our rules* have been broken. In love we are not the intimidating type, forcing people around us to walk on eggshells for fear of giving rise to our wrath.

LOVE IS NOT A FEELING

Love does not take into account a wrong suffered,
does not rejoice in unrighteousness,
but rejoices with the truth.
—1 Corinthians 13:5-6

Love does not take into account a wrong suffered. This is a bookkeeping term, speaking of entries in a ledger for the purpose of a permanent record that can be consulted whenever needed.

Keeping track of things done against us—"I don't get angry, I get even"—is a sure road to misery. Peter says, "Love covers a multitude of sins" (1 Peter 5:3). Chrysostom observed that a wrong done against love is like a spark that falls into the sea and is quenched. Love covers over wrongs; it doesn't record them.

Love does not rejoice in unrighteousness. This is similar to what Jesus said in Matthew 5:4—"Blessed are those who mourn, for they shall be comforted"—in other words, Happy are the sad.

Isaiah warned about a form of rejoicing in unrighteousness: "Woe to those who call evil good…who substitute light for darkness and darkness for light" (5:20). These are like the people Paul described in Romans 1:18-32, who were "filled with all unrighteousness, wickedness, greed, evil, full of envy, murder, strife, deceit, malice," and who "not only do the same, but also give hearty approval to those who practice them." What entertains you?

Love rejoices with the truth. Love deeply desires hearing what is right in the sight of God—success and blessing—rather than showing a morbid interest in the failures and sufferings of others.

LOVE IS NOT A FEELING

Love bears all things, believes all things,
hopes all things, endures all things.
—1 Corinthians 13:7

Love bears all things. The word means to support and protect others from exposure, ridicule, or harm.

Our human nature takes pleasure in exposing someone's faults and failure. That's why gossip is so appealing. In love, we confront sin in each other in private; in public we protect each other's reputation. The reason? Because...

Love believes all things. Love is not suspicious or cynical. Love is not blind, but will believe the best first. This is a rarity, when one will first believe the best of you when they hear the worst!

Love hopes all things. In love, our expectation of the future is good (as it was for the godly woman in Proverbs 31: "She smiles at the future"—31:25). Love is not fearful of the future, but expectant of what God will do in His sovereignty over it.

Love endures all things. Love understands the word *commitment*—literally, "to hold under." Love doesn't bail out on others or on God. Another way of saying it: Those who love are *responsible to* and *honest about* their commitments.

What is the nature of love? Love is the kind of person we become as we mature in our faith. If you read 1 Corinthians 13:4-7 and substitute your name for the word *love* — does it ring true?

How is it possible to become that kind of person?

Make sure you're letting God define your value system.

LIVING PRINCIPLE

I am the vine, you are the branches…
apart from Me you can do nothing.
—John 15:5

Jesus says you can do…*nothing*. Spiritually you are like a poverty-stricken beggar who can make or earn nothing. Anything he has he must beg for…and wait for. In that same way, Jesus says, when it comes to your spirit—when it comes to being alive, when it comes to pleasing God, when it comes to doing what is right, when it comes to doing something significant in the life of someone else—you, we, I…*can do absolutely nothing.*

You cannot find fulfillment away from Christ. You can, of course, manipulate behavior. You can move emotions. You can numb feelings, or you can stimulate them. You can laugh, you can enjoy sensations of ecstasy. But as far as fulfillment, genuine happiness, being what God wants you to be, enjoying what you were created to enjoy—you cannot do one thing about it, no matter how religious you are, how many verses you know, how often you pray, what background or spiritual heritage you have. We can do absolutely nothing.

It's hard to say, "I can't do it," because we're doers. We're fix-it men and women. But we go nowhere until we come to the point of saying, "God, I can do absolutely nothing. I am absolutely dependent on Your intervention in my life for *everything*. This is my mindset, my ethic, my principle for life."

Today…is this the living principle in *your* life? The more it is—the more it becomes a consistent dynamic in your life—the happier you'll be.

SONG OF DELIVERANCE

The Spirit of the Lord God is upon me,
because the Lord has anointed me...
He has sent me to bind up the brokenhearted.
—Isaiah 61:1

Jesus said He came to fulfill these words of Isaiah the prophet. He was anointed to help those who are broken, to bring them comfort.

David knew the comfort. In Psalm 32 he tells of the agony he felt at first, the anguish: "When I kept silent about my sin, my body wasted away through my groaning...my vitality was drained away..." But then: "I acknowledged my sin to Thee...I said, 'I will confess my transgressions to the Lord'; and Thou didst forgive the guilt of my sin." Now he could sing of the comfort: "How blessed is he whose transgression is forgiven, whose sin is covered!... Thou dost surround me with songs of deliverance."

When we get serious about sin, God gets very serious about comforting us. And He brings His comfort by taking away the anguish. The mystery is that He takes the sting out of the pain. He takes the hopelessness out of the despair, the bitterness out of the hurt.

There will come a day when He will take it all away: the pain, the despair, the hurt. "He shall wipe away every tear...and there shall no longer be any death; there shall no longer be any mourning, or crying, or pain" (Revelation 21:4).

For now, however, the pain is here. And yet, God can take away the sting. He can take the agony out. Let Him do that for you today. If you are brokenhearted over the things that break *His* heart too—let His loving hands bind it up.

STRENGTH SURRENDERED

Blessed are the gentle [the meek, the humble],
for they shall inherit the earth.
—Matthew 5:5

"Oh, the happiness," Jesus is saying, "of those who are gentle, who are humble, who are meek."

The word *meek* conjures up the image of weakness, and yet the concept Jesus is talking about is as far from weakness as it could possibly be.

But if it isn't weakness—what is it?

The Greek word used here was used in ancient times in reference to the breaking of a wild animal. It meant *strength put under control.* It's the same strength spoken of in Proverbs 16:32—"He who rules his spirit is better than he who captures a city." If you want to be truly successful, then understand how to rule your spirit.

Gentleness does not mean weakness, but rather the use of strength fully surrendered to God's control and pleasure. Gentleness flows from mourning, which flows from being poor in spirit. I must come to realize, "God, I can do nothing without You; I understand my sinfulness and grieve over it; and I know that all I have left is to please *You.*" Martin Lloyd-Jones put it like this: "We are to leave everything—ourselves, our rights, our cause, our whole future—in the hands of God, *and especially so if we feel we are suffering unjustly.*"

Gentleness is using my inner strength only to serve Him who is God, and no other gods—including myself. It is accepting the position of being "poor in spirit," and desiring only for God's will to be done.

WAGER EVERYTHING

How can a man be in the right before God?
—Job 9:2

Job asked a basic question: How can we be right with God? How can we know *righteousness?*

The answer is that righteousness is both a *gift* and a *command*. It is a gift because we can't achieve it without the intervention of God. "All our righteous deeds are like a filthy garment" (Isaiah 64:6). The gift of righteousness is salvation through Jesus Christ. "He made Him who knew no sin to be sin on our behalf, that we might become *the righteousness of God* in Him" (2 Corinthians 5:21). The gift comes by our faith: Abraham "believed in the Lord; and He reckoned it to him as *righteousness*" (Genesis 15:6).

But righteousness is not just something you believe; it must be something you live out. Paul says, "The righteous man *shall live* by faith," (Romans 1:17). The evidence that we have received the gift of righteousness is in living out life in keeping with that righteousness. So there's a gift of righteousness, and there's a practice of righteousness, a passion to carry out the will of God. "The command," wrote Martin Luther, "is not to crawl into a corner or into the desert, but to run out...and to offer your hands and your feet and your whole body, and to wager everything you have and can do."

Today—are you looking to do God's will...to run out and do what is *right?*

What is more important to you: to do right, or to get others to treat you right?

THE RIGHT ROAD

I delight to do Thy will, O my God.
—Psalm 40:8

"Feel better about yourself," the world says, "so you can be happy." Wrong road. Don't spend your time contemplating how you feel about *you*. Rather, contemplate how you feel about righteousness, about doing what is right in the sight of God. Think: *What is right in Thy sight, O Lord?* That is righteousness.

Concerning the circumstances of our lives today, what's on our minds?

Someone has betrayed me, wounding me deeply… What should I be thinking? This: *What is right in Thy sight, O Lord?*

My child is rebelling against my authority… What should I be thinking? *What is right in Thy sight, O Lord?*

I lost my husband a month ago, and I'm so alone… My wife left me for another man; in fact, she's with him right now… The temptations at work are all over the place, so strong… I have a relationship with this guy I love, and it's getting heavy… I'm losing my business, my home, my savings; even my retirement is down the tubes… I've been out of work for months, and I'm hopeless; I have no idea how to put food on the table… I'm pregnant, and not married, and my folks are upset, and the guy won't marry me; I don't know what to do… I'm frustrated, depressed. Life is so painful, I feel so alone, so worthless. I want to take my life…

What's to be my thinking?
What is right in Thy sight, O Lord?

FALSE MERCY

Blessed are the merciful, for they shall receive mercy.
—Matthew 5:7

Mercy does not ignore sin. If it did, it would be a false mercy—as unmerciful as it is unjust. Mercy is not apathy.

It was this sort of false mercy that David showed when he failed to deal with the sin of his rebellious son Absalom. His attitude toward his son was unrighteous sentimentality—neither justice nor mercy. It served only to confirm Absalom in his wickedness.

This sort of false mercy is common today. We think it's unloving and unkind to hold people responsible for their sins. But because it merely overlooks sin, it *leaves* sin.

In every true act of mercy, someone pays the price. God did!

Jesus said, "Be on your guard! If your brother sins, rebuke him; and if he repents, forgive him" (Luke 17:3). But when you reprove your sinful brother, remember that your attitude is key. The aim is to *reclaim,* not to destroy. Sir John Seeley said, "When the power of reclaiming the lost dies out of the church, it ceases to be the church."

There is no need for this power to die out, however. God is "rich in mercy" (Ephesians 2:4). *His* continued mercy is the key to our own.

Learn what David learned: "Thou, O Lord, art a God merciful and gracious, slow to anger and abundant in lovingkindness and truth" (Psalm 86:15).

Do you practice God's mercy—or false mercy?

THIS GREAT PRIVILEGE

Purify your hearts, you doubleminded.
—James 4:8

Are you doubleminded? The word means "two-souled." The doubleminded man is one who is wavering in his loyalties, divided in his interest, undecided in his intentions. He's a mess. *Confused* is a good word for him. And he's blinded to God.

When it comes to following God, is your will undecided? Are your intentions mixed, your motives divided?

Jesus says those who are "pure in heart"—and only those who are pure in heart—will have the opportunity to actually *see* God (Matthew 5:8). There are two aspects of this great privilege: one present, one future.

When our hearts are purified as believers, we begin right now to live in the presence of God. We comprehend Him as never before. Just as Moses saw first the "back" of God, so we also begin with His "back," before we see Him face to face. Paul said that while we behold "as in a mirror" the glory of God, we are "being transformed into the same image from glory to glory" (2 Corinthians 3:18). With purity of heart—which means a singleminded commitment to obeying God's word—I am being conformed into the image of Jesus. And the more I am conformed, the more I will see clearly the glory of the Lord around me.

And this is our future: "We shall be like Him, because we shall see Him just as He is" (1 John 3:2). In the future new Jerusalem, at "the throne of God and of the Lamb...His bond-servants shall serve Him; and they shall *see His face*" (Revelation 22:3-4).

THE STEPS OF THE STRONG

In this is love, not that we loved God,
but that He loved us and sent the Son to be
the Savior of the world.
—1 John 4:10

Love initiates peace. God set the pattern. He, the Strong One, offered peace to us, the weak ones.

In peacemaking, in resolving conflict, the burden is on the stronger person to initiate reconciliation. For peace is an act of self-sacrifice, and only the mature sacrifice willingly. In a broken relationship, the stronger one takes the responsibility and does what needs to be done to offer peace.

But be careful about offering the wrong kind of peace. It must be just, righteous. "Righteousness and peace have kissed each other," the psalmist wrote. There is a cheap peace that is brought about by a cheap forgiveness.

God forgives only the repentant, and Jesus tells us to do the same: "If your brother sins, rebuke him; *and if he repents*, forgive him" (Luke 17:3).

Genuine peace can only be offered. It cannot be simply declared. There will be times when the offer of peace will not be accepted, and there is no repentance. We can only be at peace as much as lies within us. "If possible," writes Paul, "so far as it depends on you, be at peace with all men." I can (and must) be at peace with *them;* it is their decision to be at peace with me.

Right now in your life, be an initiator of peace. Be strong, and sacrifice willingly. Take responsibility for offering peace where peace is missing now.

CLOSER TO GOD

I do not speak to condemn you.
—2 Corinthians 7:3

When you want to be everything God wants you to be, how do you get started? Is it by going out and doing some "holy" things?

No—it begins with how you respond to what's already around you. It begins, for example, with what you do when reproof and correction come your way (not an easy issue to tangle with!).

How do you respond or react to the wounds of a friend? It has so much to do with who you are. Have you learned to *respond* to reproof instead of always *reacting* to it—not reacting as a fool, but responding as someone wise?

A wise man or woman considers well the source of reproof, and asks, *Are the motives here for my good? Is this a friend who loves me and is willing to risk the friendship for my spiritual good?*

Yes, the process of reproof is painful. Even when godly reproof is met by godly repentance, there is grief on both sides. But Paul says, "The sorrow that is according to the will of God produces a repentance without regret, leading to salvation" (2 Corinthians 7:10). Sorrow which produces repentance is like a slap —"Thanks, I needed that."

Repentance is changing your mind and turning from what you did to what God wants you to do. It moves you literally "toward" salvation—closer to God, not further away. It means staying soft and moldable in the Master's hands.

Remember: The same sun that softens the wax, hardens the clay.

GODLY SORROW

I rejoice, not that you were made sorrowful, but that you were made sorrowful to the point of repentance; for you were made sorrowful according to the will of God.
—*2 Corinthians 7:9*

Paul's motives were pure in his reproof—and the Corinthians' responses were godly. Paul said he heard about it all from Titus: "your longing, your mourning, your zeal for me" (2 Corinthians 7:7). They hadn't rejected Paul; nor had they rejected his words, but rather were grieved over their sin. They responded with repentance—the deep desire to do what is right in the sight of God.

"Behold," exclaimed Paul, "what earnestness this very thing, this godly sorrow, has produced in you" (7:11). Paul retraces the effect:

"what *vindication of yourselves*..."—Their motives were pure; they wanted to be God's man or God's woman, and proved it by not being reactionary and defensive to the reproof.

"what *indignation*..."—In righteous anger they were motivated by their sin to correct what was wrong.

"what *fear*..."—They desired to remove the shame they had brought upon the Lord.

"what *longing*..."—They wanted to be reunited with Paul and with others whom they had alienated because of their sin.

"what *zeal*..."—They had a passion to do what was right in the sight of God.

"what *avenging of wrong*..."—This was not vengeance, which belongs to God (Romans 12:19), but rather bringing justice to the offenders, and dealing with them in discipline.

FREE EXPRESSION

Beyond their ability they gave of their own accord,
begging us with much entreaty.
—2 Corinthians 8:3-4

Sacrifice is one thing; willing sacrifice is something else. The Macedonians of whom Paul is speaking here were begging Paul for the opportunity to have a part in giving to the saints. They understood that the church is a community of people caring for each other and caring for what God is doing in this world—and that made them *enthusiastic* about it. They went beyond merely giving their money: "They first gave themselves to the Lord and to us by the will of God" (8:5). Paul says this was "not as we had expected," but the will of God was put into their hearts, and this was what they felt God wanted them to do. They understood "stewardship" and "lordship"; they knew to give all that they *had,* and all that they *were,* making it all available to God.

Paul wanted the Corinthians to understand: This is what giving is all about. He reminded them of their riches (are they yours as well?). "You abound in everything," he said (8:7): "in *faith*"—the capacity to believe and trust God; "in *utterance*"—the *logos,* the truth of what God has said; "in *knowledge*"—the discernment of good and evil; "in all *earnestness*"—pure motives, genuinely wanting to be what God wants us to be; "and in *love*"—recognizing the true and great worth of others. These are the riches from which true giving comes. This kind of giving is not a matter of law, not a command, but something expressed freely.

You don't satisfy your conscience with this kind of giving; you satisfy your loving gratitude.

ACCEPTABLE GIVING

There is one who scatters, yet increases all the more, and there is one who withholds what is justly due, but it results only in want. The generous man will be prosperous, and he who waters will himself be watered.
—*Proverbs 11:24-25*

From this passage it doesn't sound like a generous man will be struggling a lot over his finances. Maybe generosity—giving—is a good place to start in financial management!

Giving is simply managing what isn't yours. *Being a steward* is a Bible term for it. In Bible times a steward originally was a servant who superintended the household and property of his master. Later the same term came to refer to an estate manager or an accountant. The money and property never belonged to the steward; he simply administered it as the master directed. He was "entrusted" (Matthew 25:14) with the wealth, and expected to be "faithful" (25:21) in his management of it.

The first step in faithful stewardship concerns our attitude toward this whole thing of money. It has nothing to do with your bank account, but everything to do with your spirit. Giving isn't God's way of raising money; it's God's way of raising His children.

If you don't have much, don't grieve because you can't give much. "If the readiness is present," Paul said, "it is acceptable according to what a man has, not according to what he does not have" (2 Corinthians 8:12). Your "readiness" to give more than you have is accepted by God—though He may test that "readiness" sometimes by giving you extra, just to see what you would do with it.

STRAINED RIGHTEOUSNESS

Do not be excessively righteous, and do not be
overly wise. Why should you ruin yourself?
—Ecclesiastes 7:16

Is that a raw proverb, or is that a raw proverb?
What in the world is Solomon talking about?

We're creatures of extremes: *If I'm going to be good,*
I'm going to be good *at being good*—we fall so easily
into a trap. This is what Jesus was talking about: "I
have not come to call righteous men but sinners to repentance" (Luke 5:32). The scribes and Pharisees had
convinced themselves they were pretty good. This
"strained righteousness" bred arrogance and conceit,
even to the point that they would question God's
righteousness when it didn't match up to their own.

"Why ruin yourself?" Solomon says. Why get a
spiritual hernia? Your pursuit of righteousness just
may destroy the very character of true righteousness.
Your pursuit of being good is the very thing that will
create trouble with your arrogance.

Where does an honest godliness come in? Here's
the balance: I know I'm a sinner who has been forgiven by God because of what Jesus Christ did on the
cross for me. Because I am forgiven, that love and
grace motivate me to pursue pleasing God. My goal is
not to be good or righteous, but *to be pleasing to Him.*

"You were formerly darkness, but now you are
light in the Lord; walk as children of light (for the
fruit of the light consists in all goodness and righteousness and truth), trying to learn *what is pleasing to*
the Lord" (Ephesians 5:8-10).

We try so hard to be good. Why not just please
Him, and let Him take care of the good?

RELAXED WICKEDNESS

Do not be excessively wicked, and do not be a fool.
Why should you die before your time?
—Ecclesiastes 7:17

What is Solomon talking about? Is it okay to be a *little* wicked? (God says, "You shall be holy, for I am holy"—1 Peter 1:16.)

The real problem with the "excessively wicked" is that they don't admit they aren't righteous through and through. "If we say we have no sin, we are deceiving ourselves" (1 John 1:8). Believers have a new nature, and yet we still have the flesh, that bent toward evil. Some have tried to tell us we no longer have that bent. They quote Romans 6:6—"Our old self was crucified with Him." But what does Paul mean by that? He says in 6:11-13—"Do not let sin reign in your mortal body that you should obey its lusts, and do not go on presenting the members of your body to sin." He speaks to those who would not practice self-control or self-denial. "Don't be a fool," Solomon said. The life of a fool is to destroy himself by the consequences of his own sin. "For the one who sows to his own flesh shall from the flesh reap corruption" (Galatians 6:7-8).

Strained righteousness says, "I'm good and I know it; I'm righteous like I'm supposed to be." Relaxed wickedness says, "I'm bad and I know it; I may blow it, but at least I'm not a hypocrite like *you*." Both issue from pride and arrogance, and both will hurt you.

Understand them both. "It is good that you grasp one thing, and also not let go of the other," says Solomon, "for the one who fears God comes forth with both of them" (Ecclesiastes 7:18).

FIXING EACH OTHER

Sanctify them in the truth.
—John 17:17

Look closely at those words from Jesus' prayer in John 17. Who's the subject in that statement?

The subject is God—*not you*. It's God who sanctifies. It's *His* righteousness, as in 2 Corinthians 5:21—"He made Him who knew no sin to be sin on our behalf, that we might become *the righteousness of God* in Him."

We Christians try to fix each other. Here's how it works: The Spirit of God convicts me of some area in my life that displeases Him. *I then feel my call is to convict everyone else of it!*

Are we making Christians who want to please God —or Christians who only want to please us?

"Sanctify them in the truth; Thy word is truth" (John 17:17). Learn the truth of Scripture, and let the Holy Spirit within do the convicting in a heart that fears God. That's why we Christians do and don't do what we do and don't do.

How about you? Are you a Christian because you don't do certain things like get drunk, steal, mess with drugs, and be unfaithful to your spouse—or do you not do them because you're a Christian? How much of what we do or don't do as believers has to do with the Spirit of God within us, and how much has to do with what other believers will think of us?

Do we make up our own sense of good to satisfy our guilt—or else rationalize our guilt to satisfy our sense of being good?

Genuineness is honesty with yourself about what's true about you. So—what's true about you?

VIOLENCE TO THE COVENANT

Flee immorality.
—1 Corinthians 6:18

Today's philosophy of sexual hedonism is nothing new. Don't believe for a moment that man, even with all his technological advances, has changed much. In New Testament times, Paul addressed the same thing in Corinth. A common Greek notion was that sex was just another biological function with no other significance, no different morally from eating, drinking, or sleeping. Why would God make it a moral issue, one about which Jesus spoke in Matthew 5 as seriously as murder? Because adultery assaults a covenant with God. Adultery reduces your mate to being part of a herd for your pleasure. Adultery does violence to the "one flesh" that was formed by covenant *before* God and *to* God. "What therefore God has joined together, let no man separate." That's why, in 1 Timothy 3:2, one of the main distinctions of a godly man is that he is "a one-woman man."

Jesus makes a deeper point in Matthew 5:28—"Everyone who looks on a woman to lust for her has committed adultery with her already in his heart." His point is not that lust might lead you to commit the sinful act; if you lust, He says, you have already committed the act before God. Lust is the issue here.

From this perspective we begin to understand about pornography as evil. If the intent is to have a sexual fantasy in your mind, you have already committed the act of adultery. Opportunity is all you lack.

Deeds of shame are preceded by fantasies of shame, inflamed by the imagination of lust.

WHAT AM I HERE FOR?

I came that they might have life...
—John 10:10

Is this faith stuff something tangible, or are we all just playing some game and fooling ourselves? How would we know?

Apologetics is basically the defense of the Christian faith by the use of different kinds of evidence. This may be historical, like the evidence for the resurrection of Jesus. Or it may be prophetical, concerned with all the biblical references to fulfilled prophecy. Or it may be philosophical in nature, along the lines of the demonstration of the existence of God.

But when everything is argued, debated, and thought through, something else is still the greatest proof of the faith: a changed life. Who can justifiably argue about what has happened deep within a person's life?

Jesus said, "I have come that you might have life, and have it more abundantly." There must be something radically different about that life; if I see it *in me,* I have seen the proof of my faith.

Is there something radically different about us?

God calls us a holy people, not because we are better than anyone else (we aren't), but because we are set apart for a special purpose to be used by Him. We tend to get caught in identity crises—*Who am I really? Am I really successful? What happened to my dreams, my goals? Do I have any real direction for my life?*

Actually, "Who am I?" is not the issue; "What am I here for?" is.

Put the answer in your own words today: *What am I here for?*

THE RUBBER MEETS THE ROAD

You have heard that it was said,
"You shall love your neighbor, and hate your enemy."
But I say to you, love your enemies...
—Matthew 5:43-44

Here's where the rubber meets the road. If my faith is real and there is actually something different about me because of Jesus, this is where it's going to be seen.

The scribes and Pharisees went after this Old Testament law by leaving out a little and then adding a little. First they omitted the last two words of the command in Leviticus 19:18, which reads, "You shall love your neighbor *as yourself.*" To value and care for someone else as much as I value and care for myself —that alone is enough to make me stand out from the crowd real fast. Then the scribes and Pharisees added something that wasn't there: "...and hate your enemies." They had narrowed the idea of "neighbor" to mean "your own kin," or at the most, "those who shared your same race or religion," and it followed logically that if I'm going to love my neighbor, I must hate my enemy. All this was used to justify their own racial prejudice. No wonder the Romans accused the Jews of hating the human race. (Look further in Leviticus 19 for more that they ignored: "When a stranger resides with you in your land, you shall not do him wrong. The stranger who resides with you shall be to you as the native among you, and you shall love him as yourself"—19:33-34.)

When it comes to enemies, Jesus says this one thing: *Love them.* He doesn't use a word for affection or warm and fuzzy feelings, but the strongest Greek word for love: Consider that person's worth to God!

THE SUPREME DEMAND

Love your enemies,
and pray for those who persecute you.
—Matthew 5:44

It's been said that the way to defeat your enemy is by making him a friend. Have you ever asked yourself, "Why bother?"

Who is my enemy?

Jesus tells us: "Pray for those who persecute you." That's your enemy by definition. And who are they? Go back to verse 11—"Blessed are you when men cast insults at you, and persecute you, and say all kinds of evil against you falsely, on account of Me." It's those who abuse you with their speech, or abuse you physically in some way, or who lie about you behind your back. Sometimes it may be your family. Sometimes it may be those who claim to be your friends. Have you ever said under your breath, "With friends like this who needs enemies?"

But how do you ever love someone who treats you that way? That's the point. You can't, so don't try!

You think you know what I'm going to say next, don't you? "Let the Lord love them through you." Right?

That's exactly what I'm going to say, but Jesus tells us *how that's done:* "Pray for those who persecute you." Dietrich Bonhoeffer, a pastor murdered by Germany's Nazis, responded to this passage in this way: "This is the supreme demand. Through the medium of prayer we go to our enemy, stand by his side, and plead for him to God." Chrysostom saw it as "the very highest summit of self-control."

Who can you be praying for today?

SOMETHING HAPPENS

Pray for those who persecute you.
—Matthew 5:44

Why would I ever do such a thing? Why would I pray for my enemy? Because it's the only way I could ever be able to obey the Lord's command to "love your enemies"…and I don't want Jesus ever asking me, "Why do you call me 'Lord, Lord,' and do not do what I ask?" When it comes to loving family and friends, our love comes from our heart. When it comes to loving our enemies, it begins with our wills. Because of my love for Jesus, I will *to will* to pray for them. And in my praying for them, God does something supernatural in my heart: With the Spirit of God in me, it is impossible for me to continue to hate someone when I am consistently praying for them. When I take myself and the man I hate to God, something happens: I cannot go on hating him in the presence of God! And there is no way I can continue being bitter toward someone whom I'm serving, and whose best I'm pursuing. Those we choose to *treat* precious *become* precious to us!

We love our enemies by praying for them—so they will know *who we are:* "…that you may be sons of your Father who is in heaven" (5:45). Here's the purpose clause. It doesn't *make* you a child of God, but it does show you and others that *you are.*

In loving our enemies, we are *going beyond* (5:46-47). If I love those who treat me well, big deal. What makes me any different from anyone else? And why should there be a difference? Because you say Jesus is real and you're a Christian. The question is: What more are you doing than others?

YOUR PURPOSE AND DESIGN

Therefore you are to be perfect,
as your heavenly Father is perfect.
—Matthew 5:48

Do you have that one figured out yet? It's one of the most perplexing commands in the Bible. Few verses are more misunderstood than this one. It seems absolutely impossible. Why would Jesus, after telling us what *was* possible, blow us all away now with a final impossible command?

The Greek word here for "perfect" is *téleios*. When a man reached his full-grown stature, he was called *téleios*. When a student had matured in knowledge and mastered his subject, he was called *téleios*. When a sacrifice was fit to be offered, it was called *téleios*.

Téleios is a form of the noun *télos*, which means "an end, a purpose, an aim, a goal." A thing was "perfect" when it fully realized the purpose for which it was designed and made. When a man or woman realize the purpose for which they were created and sent into the world—they are "perfect"!

Jesus tells us to be perfect "as your heavenly Father is perfect." Look three verses earlier: God "causes His sun to rise on the evil and the good, and sends rain on the righteous and the unrighteous." God seeks nothing but man's highest good. To do the same as your Father in heaven—this is being "perfect."

Are you asking, "Who am I?" Get off it!

The question is, "What am I here for?"

What are you here for? *To be perfect.* To realize your purpose and design…to show the perfect love of God for those whom He has created.

THE ROYAL LAW

Bear one another's burdens,
and thus fulfill the law of Christ.
—Galatians 6:2

The religious leaders in the time of Jesus had developed traditions and convictions so important to them that the Scriptures themselves became secondary. They used their prejudices as standards for the righteousness of others.

We do the same thing today, don't we? It can be anything from the way of dressing to political views and theological positions. We get into trouble when we begin using these traditions and prejudices to evaluate the spiritual walk of another. Is that our role? Are we called to play Holy Spirit, to spy out each other's faults? If not—then are we to pretend there's never a problem?

"Faithful are the wounds of a friend," Solomon says in Proverbs 27, and "Iron sharpens iron, so one man sharpens another." When are wounds faithful, and when does iron sharpen?

If we are to love each other by going to each other when we are blowing it—how do we do that without a judgmental, unmerciful attitude?

The answer is in the royal law of Jesus, the fulfillment of His law: "Brethren, even if a man is caught in any trespass, you who are spiritual, restore such a one in a spirit of gentleness; each one looking to yourself, lest you too be tempted. Bear one another's burdens, *and thus fulfill the law of Christ*" (Galatians 6:1-2).

Do we love our brothers and sisters enough to be a friend who wounds only with faithful wounds, and who sharpens only with iron?

JUDGING

Do not judge, lest you be judged. For in the way you judge,
you will be judged; and by your standard of measure,
it will be measured to you.
—Matthew 7:1-2

Have you ever been warned, "Don't judge, lest you be judged"?

But is all judging condemning?

The word *standard* in Matthew 7:2 speaks of an instrument of measure. This is how you measure something…such as a spiritual walk.

In Matthew 7, Jesus is speaking against an attitude, one that is judgmental and unmerciful, one that uses personal standards as if they were law. James nails this: "Do not speak against one another… Who are you to judge your neighbor?" (4:1-12). And Paul: "Who are you to judge the servant of another? To his own master he stands or falls… Why do you judge your brother?" (Romans 14:4,10).

Jesus is not saying we are never to confront each other. Later in Matthew 7, He warns of those who are in rebellion (7:15-20). He also tells us (in 18:15-17) to go to our brother who sins. (As we carry out that command, it will often mean taking much heat from those who would condemn us as judgmental.)

In Matthew 7, this word for "judge," *krino,* simply means "to separate" or "to determine" something. Whatever attitude or standard you use in determining someone else's spiritual walk, Jesus is saying, that same attitude or standard will be used on you by God.

This is a reminder that we are not the final court. We do not know the whole story. We do not know enough to be able to render a final verdict on anyone.

LOG EYE

Why do you look at the speck in your brother's eye,
but do not notice the log in your own eye?
—*Matthew 7:3*

What is this "speck in your brother's eye"? The word doesn't mean dust or sawdust, but refers to a chip or splinter, something that can cause some real damage if not removed. The issue here: *There's a problem, and something needs to be done about it.* The question is, How do we do it?

The picture Jesus paints here is funny! (Relax—it's okay for Jesus to be funny.) The person coming to remove the splinter has a tree hanging from his own eye. If the chip can do damage, what will this rafter do? Jesus goes after that attitude of self-righteousness, whose nature is to justify self and condemn others. We're hard on others so we can be lighter on ourselves. We push others lower to lift ourselves higher.

Jesus says, "First take the log out of your own eye, and then you will see clearly to take the speck out of your brother's eye" (7:5). Before ever going to another who is blowing it, we must first make a judgment about our own self-righteousness.

And why am I going? The answer must be this: I am going for the purpose of loving my brother or sister, desiring nothing more than their well-being. David prayed, "Create in me a clean heart, O God, and renew a steadfast spirit within me... Then I will teach transgressors Thy ways, and sinners will be converted to Thee" (Psalm 51:10-13).

Do we permit others to take out the splinters in our eyes, so we might continue to grow and be all God wants us to be?

NOT FOR DOGS AND SWINE

Do not give what is holy to dogs,
and do not throw your pearls before swine,
lest they trample them under their feet,
and turn and tear you to pieces.
—Matthew 7:6

Here Jesus shatters the sentimental interpretation of never confronting anyone, lest you be judging. This is the other side of being undiscriminating.

In biblical times, dogs weren't the cuddly, caring pets we have today. While some were used in the fields of the shepherds, most were half-wild mongrels that acted as scavengers. They were often dirty, greedy, vicious, and diseased. The picture Jesus draws is this: As offerings were taken to the temple, a portion of the meat was placed on the altar which was consecrated exclusively for the Lord. It was holy. The thought of taking that and throwing it to the dogs would be the height of desecration.

The "swine" in the passage refers to the wild boars that would feed on the garbage dumps on the edge of town. They could become vicious if you came between them and their food. Throw them "pearls" for their food, and they would spit them out and come at you with their tusks. This is as Solomon said in Proverbs 9:8—"Do not reprove a scoffer, lest he hate you." Certain truths of faith are not to be shared with people who are totally antagonistic to the things of God. They have no desire nor appreciation for that which is holy and as precious as a pearl.

Unresponsiveness means unresponsiveness. There comes a time when you stop, and walk away.

PIETY PARADE

When you pray, you are not to be as the hypocrites.
—Matthew 6:5

No religious faith had a higher devotion to prayer than Judaism, but some things had crept into the Jewish prayer life that have also crept into our own.

For example: Prayer became ritualized with special wording and forms of prayer to be read or recited from memory. They could be spoken without attention to what was actually being said. Jesus condemns this "meaningless repetition" (6:7). Can you imagine someone talking to you and all he does is repeat the same phrases? What kind of communion with God is that?

Another problem was that prayer was limited to specific times and occasions. There was nothing spontaneous about it. There were set times to pray; that's when you prayed—and that was it.

Long prayers were esteemed highly. But the worst problem was praying and wanting to be seen praying. These were hypocrites who prayed for reasons other than for prayer. They used prayer to parade their piety. Can you imagine having someone talking to you while looking to see if others were noticing? If I were God, I'd walk away.

The point, Jesus said, is this: If you pray to display, you have your reward. If that's what you want out of prayer, that's what you get—and no more! Don't expect anything else from God. You've already received the answer to your prayer. Those whom you wanted to notice you—it was *they* to whom you prayed!

But when *you* pray—you are not to pray as the hypocrites.

YOUR INNER ROOM

When you pray, go into your inner room.
—Matthew 6:6

Isn't prayer simply talking to your heavenly Father? Why is something appearing to be so simple so difficult?

The theology of prayer continues to be a mystery. How does praying effect the sovereign hand of God? Isn't He going to do what He's going to do anyway?

Jesus doesn't talk about the mystery of the theology of prayer here. He takes a pragmatic approach.

Do it!

There are powers that want us *not* to pray, and when we don't, it is to those powers we yield.

When you pray, Jesus said, "go into your inner room." Jesus is not forbidding public prayer (Paul commands it in 1 Timothy 2). There are times when we all want to talk to God about the same thing. Jesus is talking about the *attitude* behind the praying. When you pray, *in your mind* go and shut the door and pray *to your Father.* Get your attention off yourself, and on to Him.

Prayer is in secret when, as far as we're concerned, God is the sole audience.

As for *how* we pray…let's purge ourselves from reciting those quip phrases and vain repetitions of many words.

And *what* to pray…talk to your Father about what *He* wants to talk about (6:9-13): People treating Him as God. Jesus coming again with the kingdom. Submitting to and carrying out His will. Our physical needs. Our sinfulness and rebellion. Our tough times and trials.

THE DISCIPLE'S PRAYER

Our Father, who art in heaven, hallowed be Thy name.
Thy kingdom come. Thy will be done, on earth as it is in heaven.
Give us this day our daily bread. And forgive us our debts,
as we also have forgiven our debtors. And do not lead us
into temptation, but deliver us from evil.
—*Matthew 6:9-13*

This is many times called the "Lord's Prayer." It is better referred to as the "Disciple's Prayer."

Jesus gives us a succinct but comprehensive outline of what we should be praying about. This is not given to be a recited formula. (He has just warned us about that in 6:7). "Pray along these lines," He says. In fewer than seventy words, here is the essence of what we should be talking to God about. The spirit of the prayer covers it all, when it comes to our relationship with God: devotion, reverence, loyalty, submission, dependence, penitence, humility, exultation, and hope. There are six petitions in the "Disciple's Prayer":

God's name, God's reign, and *God's will;*
our bread, our debts, and *our adversary.*

"*Our Father who art in heaven...*" There's a basic question every created being ought to ask once in his life: Is this a friendly universe? Is the Creator for us or against us?

There are more than a hundred names for God in the Koran, yet never is He referred to as Father.

Every time Jesus prayed in the gospels, He began with "Father," except for on the cross when He cried out Psalm 22, "My God, My God, why hast Thou forsaken Me?"

We come to God in prayer *as His children.*

THIS IS THE WAY

Pray, then, in this way...
—Matthew 6:9

"Hallowed be Thy name" — The archaic English "hallowed" is the Greek word *hagiadzo*, "made holy, set apart." We attribute to God the holiness that is already due to His name.

"Thy kingdom come" — This is the prayer that God's sovereign rule would come to this renegade planet—that *Jesus the King* will return. We talk to God about Jesus coming again—*Maranatha*, come Lord Jesus!

"Thy will be done on earth as it is in heaven" — that we might all return to the first will—that is, God's. Satan added a second will; Adam and Eve added theirs, then Cain, until "all of us like sheep have gone astray, each of us has turned to his own way" (Isaiah 53:6). We talk to God about submitting to and carrying out His will.

"Give us this day our daily bread" — We want a year's supply, don't we? We talk to God about our physical needs.

"And forgive us our debts, as we also have forgiven our debtors" — God applies daily His forgiveness for our daily sins, as we daily confess them. Forgiveness of others is central to this praying. Remember the point Jesus made in the parable of Matthew 18. The birthmark of a child who can address Him as Father is a forgiving heart. Don't soften what He says. *Forgive!*

"And do not lead us into temptation, but deliver us from evil" — The prayer is, "Lord, I'll be tested; my desire is not to do evil, thus help me not to fall into evil when the trials come." We ask God to help us not to blow it when times are tough.

RICH AND READY

Instruct those who are rich…to do good, to be rich in good works, to be generous and ready to share, storing up for themselves the treasure of a good foundation for the future.
—1 Timothy 6:17-19

But, you say, Paul is talking to the rich here. You don't know my financial statement.

Do you have *any* discretionary funds? Do you have some funds for fun? If so, then by the standards of those days (and these days too, in most of the world), you're rich.

And with those discretionary funds, Paul says, "do good." This is not some outburst of charity. This is a lifestyle of doing good with what you have to invest. "Good" is the idea of *shalom*, a state of peace and well-being. You bring peace and well-being into the life of someone else. You use your investments to create a sense of rest in the life of another. And what brings peace and well-being? The gospel brings peace with God. Ministries that help people grow physically, emotionally and spiritually bring them peace, a deep sense of rest in their lives.

"Be rich in good works"—the word "good" here is *kalos*, "winsome, beautiful, attractive." Let your light so shine…

"Be generous and ready to share"—Our English word *generous* comes from a Latin word meaning "of noble birth." The nobility provided well-being to those under their care. "Ready to share" is the Greek *koinonia*—we create a communion by sharing what we enjoy as a sense of well-being.

This is how treasures are sent ahead and stored as "a good foundation for the future."

THE DEEPEST HURT

Rejoice in the wife of your youth.
—*Proverbs 5:18*

No sin is more destructive to more people than sexual immorality—sexual intimacy outside God's design for marriage. It has broken more marriages, shattered more homes, caused more heartache and disease, and destroyed more lives by far than alcohol and drugs combined. It has authored lying, stealing, cheating, and killing, as well as bitterness, hatred, slander, gossip, unforgiveness, and suicide.

Yet nothing is more alluring, more promising of pleasure and satisfaction. "The lips of an adulteress drip honey," said Solomon, "and smoother than oil is her speech; *but in the end* she is bitter as wormwood, sharp as a two-edged sword. Her feet go down to death" (Proverbs 5:3-5).

Sexual union is more than a physical union. A man and a woman "become one flesh" (Genesis 2:24). As C. S. Lewis wrote, "Every time a man and a woman enter into a sexual relationship, a spiritual bond is established between them which must be eternally enjoyed or eternally endured." Because of this spiritual nature of sexual intimacy—the deepest uniting of two persons—the misuse of sex corrupts on the deepest human level, leaving deep scars which will remain for one's entire life on earth. It robs a believer of his freedom of feeling clean before God, which is what our salvation is all about.

If you are married and still struggle with sexual purity, then *get romantic* with your spouse—both of you! If you are single and struggle with your purity… then get married (1 Corinthians 7:2,9).

WHO'S WHO IN THE FAMILY

*I have written to you, little children, because your sins
are forgiven... fathers, because you know Him
who has been from the beginning... young men,
because you have overcome the evil one.*
—1 John 2:12-13.

We're commanded to love one another, but at
times we don't like each other. Expectations have a lot
to do with it. Sometimes we need to cut each other a
little slack, and back off from our expectations a bit.

We need to know "who's who in the family." How
do we all fit in and make up this thing called the family of God?

In 1 John 2:12-14, John says there are different
members of the family, and he divides us into three
groups, three maturity levels: "babies," "young men,"
and "fathers." *Wait a second,* you say, *where are the
ladies?* He's not leaving out the women; He's simply
describing spiritual levels of maturity.

(Let me point out a distinction between spirituality
and maturity. *Spiritual* means to be controlled by the
Holy Spirit instead of the flesh. Either you are spiritual or carnal. It has to do with your will: You want to
please God, or satisfy your flesh. Can a child in Christ
be spiritual? Can a father in the faith be carnal? Of
course! Spirituality is a moment-by-moment thing;
maturity is a process of growing in the faith.)

We need everyone in the family, and we can draw
from one another—

The *babies* in the faith give us the praise...

The *young men* give us the knowledge and stability...

The *fathers* give us the wisdom and rest.

FORGIVEN FOR HIM

I am about to act...for My holy name.
—Ezekiel 36:23

"Little children," the apostle John writes in 1 John 2:12, using a term meaning "little born ones." He continues: "I am writing to you because your sins are forgiven you for His name's sake." He makes this point because many of us still run around with our guilt, and it's that guilt that affects the way we treat each other in the family of God. *You are forgiven!*—It's still the most difficult truth in the Bible to believe. We struggle with it more than any other truth. (We're commanded to partake of the Lord's Supper so we'll remember that forgiveness.) If I don't release my guilt, in my pain and frustration I will punish everyone around me for it. If I don't understand my forgiveness, I won't recognize yours.

"And remember," John is saying, "that the reason you've been forgiven is not primarily for you, but *for His name's sake.* Get your eyes off yourself and your self-condemnation. The issue is God's name: who He is, and His reputation among the people. It is *our* forgiveness that shows *His* grace and mercy (it actually doesn't say a whole lot about *you*). "For Thy name's sake," David prayed, "pardon my iniquity, for it is great" (Psalm 25:11). "Help us, O God of our salvation, *for the glory of Thy name;* and deliver us, and forgive our sins, *for Thy name's sake*" (Psalm 79:8).

This is what makes us a family: We are all forgiven, and none of us deserved it. That's what we have in common that will bring the attention of others to Him—*for His name's sake.*

CHILDREN OF THE FAITH

I have written to you, children,
because you know the Father.
—1 John 2:13

These "children" are the immature ones in the family of faith, the inexperienced; literally, the "ignorant ones." These are the "babes in Christ." One of the first things babies learn is to recognize their parents. John says he writes to them because they have come to know God as their Father.

Babies are very in tune with their emotions; they are controlled by their affections more than their understanding. They tend to be honest about their desires (which is why Peter could say, "Like newborn babes, long for the pure milk of the Word, that by it you may grow"—1 Peter 2:2).

They can get quite excited, and even become intimidating to others as they become critical of any who do not share the same enthusiasm. They can then turn around and have great doubts about their faith.

The greatest threat to them is false teachers, cults that rip them away because they haven't learned to trust God's Word instead of their feelings.

They are of great worth to have around because they remind others of the joy of the Lord and "first love" affection. (That's why every church needs to experience "conversion growth," not just "transfer growth.")

We all began as babes in the faith; the problem is that too many remain as babies.

The word to them is this: *God wants you to grow!* "We are no longer to be children" (Ephesians 4:14).

YOUNG MEN OF THE FAITH

I write to you, young men, because you are strong,
and the word of God abides in you,
and you have overcome the evil one.
—1 John 2:14

The young men of the faith have "overcome the evil one," Satan. How? "Because you are strong, and the word of God abides in you." The young man of the faith is not feelings-oriented. His focus is elsewhere: He wants to know, What does God's Word say about this?

Does this mean the freshness and excitement of new faith is gone from him? Not necessarily, but they do need the babes in the faith around to remind them of that joy. At times they may even need to hear this word from the Lord, "I have this against you, that you have left your first love" (Revelation 2:4).

On the other hand, joy of the young man of the faith begins to come from seeing God's faithfulness to His Word, no matter what his feelings are. He knows that the danger in some teaching is that it solely gives thrills to the sensations, and only nurtures infancy.

You know you are a young man of the faith when false doctrine has no appeal. As a matter of fact, it begins to irritate you. You have outgrown any affection for it. You are no longer fascinated by it. In more immature days, the believer still wants to mix his opinions with what he believes, and so he tends to be looking for something that will let him do that.

The young man of the faith is strong; Satan can't overcome him by deceiving him any longer. "The glory of young men," wrote Solomon, "is their strength" (Proverbs 20:29).

A TEST FOR YOUNG MEN

Put on the whole armor of God,
that you may be able to stand firm
against the schemes of the devil.
—*Ephesians 6:11*

The young men of the faith (1 John 2:14) are strong because the Word of God "abides" in them, dwells within them, and remains there. God's Word has a home in their heart, for they "let the Word of God richly dwell" within them (Colossians 3:16). *They know what God says!*

John says these young men are strong. They have learned to be "strong in the Lord, and in the strength of His might" (Ephesians 6:10).

They have learned that "our struggle is not against flesh and blood, but against...the spiritual forces of wickedness" (6:12). They have learned that temptations are of the flesh, the emotions, and the spirit. They have learned that the way to meet them is the way Jesus met them (Matthew 4:1-4): with God's Word.

Here's a test: What is your greatest struggle right now? What is your greatest source of fear, anger, frustration? Now answer these questions: *What* does God say about it? *Why* is God permitting this in your life? *What* does God say you need to do about it?

When you can identify the attacks of Satan and not be duped by him, you have entered into spiritual manhood. You really don't struggle anymore with doubts about who God is and what He has said. You may not always like what God says, but you have no doubts that He said it.

FATHERS OF THE FAITH

I am writing to you, fathers, because you know Him
who has been from the beginning.
—1 John 2:13

These are the folks who have grown out of baby-hood, have been young men for years, and now have had time to prove God's Word in their own lives. They have had time to come to know the One who has been "from the beginning" (1:1)—Jesus.

This is not merely a knowledge about Him, but *of* Him. Knowledge itself has the tendency to puff up; wisdom humbles knowledge. Wisdom increases with the years of applying the knowledge of the Word, and seeing "the wisdom of the wisdom of God." Wisdom is God helping you apply what He has said, so you can begin to understand *why He said it!*

It's a shame so many of us are fearful of growing old, for only over time does one became a father of faith. The baby and the young man may have as much desire, but the father in the faith has had the time—the years and the pain—to actually see the faithfulness of Jesus in joys and in crisis.

There's a certain rest that fathers of the faith exhibit in the spiritual walk. Some really make it look so easy!

Solomon spoke of "the honor of old men" (Proverbs 20:29), and Job said, "Wisdom is with aged men; with long life is understanding" (12:12). The psalmist says of them, "They will still yield fruit in old age" (92:14).

Do you know any fathers of the faith?

Do you *value* those whom you know?

TRANSFORMATION

A time to tear down, and a time to build up…
—*Ecclesiastes 3:3*

There are times when we need to move over and give room for the new things that need to come into being.

Remember the seven last words of the church? "We've never done it that way before."

The very thought of change to some people strikes terror. But one thing that does need to keep changing is *us*. "Be transformed…" (Romans 12:2). The Holy Spirit authors this change by continually transforming our heart. How do we put ourselves in a place to permit the Spirit in us to bring about the change?

It begins with *an unveiled face*. If you can truly see the beauty of the glory of His image (2 Corinthians 3:18, 4:6), you'll want to be like Him, and to be "transformed into the same image" (3:18). "The one who says he abides in Him ought to walk in the same manner as He walked" (1 John 2:6).

There is also a *true self-perception:* A value judgment is made. It starts with a passion, a desire—I *want* to be changed from what I am. I don't like the way I am responding or behaving.

There is *a true world-perception*. Instead of defending the world, we see through it. We come to see the wisdom of confessing what is wrong with what the world is pressuring us to do.

There is also *a true Christ-perception:* We follow Him; in every situation we constantly ask, *How would Jesus respond to this?* We remember what Jesus said in John 16:14—the Holy Spirit will cause us to know what Jesus' response would be.

FROM GLORY TO GLORY

Having therefore such a hope,
we use great boldness in our speech.
—2 Corinthians 3:12

When Jesus Christ came to this earth, died, and was raised again, He brought into effect the new covenant, the new agreement between God and man: God would give us the life we need to be able to *do* what He desires for us to do. The very presence of God, the glory of God, would be *in us* to change us into what He wants us to be. Knowing that God, through this new covenant, is bringing life out of death—actually changing our lives by changing our hearts—Paul has "hope," and speaks with "great boldness." He has freedom to speak, and is uninhibited by anyone. He knows that God and only God can change a person's heart, so the pressure isn't on Paul to do it.

He continues, "We all, with unveiled face beholding as in a mirror the glory of the Lord, are being transformed into the same image from glory to glory, just from the Lord, the Spirit" (3:18). We are being changed into the holy image of God by the Spirit who is holy. We won't see the Lord face to face until we see Him in heaven, but even now we are being affected by the glory of that very image. The Holy Spirit reveals Him—"He shall glorify Me," Jesus said, "for He shall take of Mine and shall disclose it to you" (John 16:14).

This happens *from glory to glory.* We are in process. We are being changed, and when the vision is perfect, the transformation will be perfect.

The change is from within the heart. The desires change, the attitude changes, the responses change, the behaviors change.

DON'T LOSE HEART

As we have received mercy, we do not lose heart.
—2 Corinthians 4:1

Over a two-week period I asked several business-men, "Do you see spiritual significance in your work that will affect the kingdom of God?" The responses were either, "I've never been asked that question," or a flat-out "No." One man added, "If I could, it would be a lot easier to get up in the morning."

One historian recently described Christianity in America as "privately engaging but socially irrelevant." Is your faith and ministry irrelevant in the face of day-to-day, marketplace issues at the place where you work? Do you get discouraged at your job because you can't see anything spiritually significant about it?

Are professional ministers the only ones with a ministry?

It takes a lot of energy to be positive about living—and nothing will rob you of it faster than losing heart. None of us has escaped that common plague which gnaws at our enthusiasm for life—*discouragement.*

The fitting counsel from Paul in 2 Corinthians 4 can be summarized this way:

Don't lose heart. Just be there, work hard, be your best, and let God take care of your influence.

Don't deceive: Don't get cute with craftiness, adulterating your walk. Be honest about who you are.

Don't get distracted: The issue is Jesus and the fact that He is your Lord. Work that way and talk that way. Be distinctive in your work!

GOD'S PLAN FOR MY WORK

Do you see a man skilled in his work?
—Proverbs 22:29

There's no longer in life a dichotomy between the sacred and the secular. Every activity is an opportunity for the Christian to honor God, and that includes work—the place where you may spend sixty to eighty percent of your waking hours.

Work was ordained by God. Having created man in His image, God gave him work to do as a service to his Creator and to his fellow man. God created man to work; therefore work in itself has great dignity and value before God. "In all labor there is profit" (Proverbs 14:23). Paul wrote, "Make it your ambition …to work with your hands, just as we commanded you" (1 Thessalonians 4:11).

The new covenant Paul speaks about in 2 Corinthians is to be lived and shared in this marketplace. Paul said, "Since we have this ministry, as we received mercy, we do not lose heart" (4:1). *Losing heart* is when I fear failure and so become weary, despairing. But I need to remember that *we* aren't the ones who make it happen, anyway. I just need to know *what* I am supposed to do, and do that faithfully.

Out of discouragement and fear we often change from God's Plan A to our own Plan B in an attempt to make this thing fly. But Paul wouldn't do it. The battle cry in the marketplace is "Be distinctive"; Paul's commitment was to keep living out the new covenant and to let God's glory be seen. That's *your* ministry too, and the spiritual significance of your work. There's good reason for getting up tomorrow morning and hitting the asphalt!

TO EVERY MAN'S CONSCIENCE

Light shall shine out of darkness.
—2 Corinthians 4:6

Paul said, "We have renounced the things hidden because of shame" (2 Corinthians 4:2). These are the things we do that we feel are okay when we do them —until they're exposed. They are the things we're told are wrong only if you get caught. Things like kickbacks in business, or payoffs and drugs in collegiate sports. "It's all a part of it," we hear. "Don't be naive; these are things you have to do." But if everyone knows that, why is everyone embarrassed when it's brought out into the open?

Whether in or out of the marketplace, Paul says there are two things he would never do: (1) walk in craftiness, or (2) adulterate the Word of God (4:2). He would not compromise his *walk* or the *word* of what he believed. Rather, he says, he wants to manifest the truth, commending himself "to every man's conscience in the sight of God." In other words, "I am not going to change the way I live nor what I say I believe just because I'm in the marketplace. The fact that the new covenant exists and is real will be seen in how it has changed me."

Paul continues: "God, who said, 'Light shall shine out of darkness,' is the One who has shone in our hearts to give the light of the knowledge of the glory of God in the face of Christ" (4:6). God is the One who first created light out of physical darkness, and here Paul says He is the One who has brought light into spiritual darkness by sending us His Son. God's presence will be seen in our lives by the changes that reflect His lordship.

I'M UNDER AUTHORITY

Even if our gospel is veiled,
it is veiled to those who are perishing.
—2 *Corinthians 4:3*

How is the gospel, the good news of the covenant, "veiled"?

"Those who are perishing" cannot see the glory of the gospel, the presence of God in it. Why? "The god of this world has blinded the minds of the unbelieving, that they might not see the light of the gospel" (4:4). Jesus calls him the "ruler of this world" (John 12:31). How does he blind? There is a spiritual bias, a mental bent against the truth of the New Covenant. Satan has effectively designed a cloud of confusion around Jesus, so that Christianity has replaced Jesus, and so we spend our time talking and defending it rather than declaring Christianity's Lord. It is very easy to justify unbelief in Christianity when you take a good look at what Christianity has supposedly produced: the crusades of the Middle Ages, an authoritarian church, political arguments, hypocritical lifestyles, judgmental and condemning zealots—all distractions from the real issue. But Paul says, "We do not preach ourselves, but Christ Jesus as Lord." He wouldn't let himself be distracted.

Who is it that we want people to accept? Jesus, or us? If it's us, that's when it gets personal, and we get intense.

The issue is "Christ Jesus as Lord." There is only one point: He is Lord. People need to see one thing from me: that I am under greater authority, and that I deeply desire to please Him only.

CHRIST CRUCIFIED

Where is the wise man? Where is the scribe?
Where is the debater of this age?
Has not God made foolish the wisdom of the world?
—*1 Corinthians 1:20*

Where are your advisers, those in whose wisdom and cunning you trust, those who will tell you how to cope. Look and see how well *they* are coping. Are they producing good counsel for your life, or are they merely stimulating your thinking and curiosity?

Where are your learned ones, those who have accumulated much knowledge and information? They are knowledgeable…but are they wise?

Where are the debaters? What of real value have they truly accomplished with all their clever arguments, their impressive rhetoric?

Where have all our great thinkers brought us— our philosophers, sociologists, psychologists, economists, scientists, statesmen? What real progress have they made in solving mankind's problems of hatred, conflict, misunderstandings, crime, depression, fears, and selfishness?

Man's own sinful nature is the cause of his problems, and he cannot change his nature. Even if he could or would recognize the problem, he still does not have the power to correct it. *But God does!*

God chose to use truth that the world calls foolish to save those who will simply believe— those who will exchange their own wisdom, their futile efforts to change their problems, for *His* wisdom and answers.

Therefore, Paul says, "We preach Christ crucified" (1 Corinthians 1:23).

THE POWER OF GOD

For the word of the cross is foolishness
to those who are perishing, but to us
who are being saved it is the power of God.
—1 Corinthians 1:18

Why is the word of the cross considered foolish? That God would take human form, be crucified and raised in order to provide for man's forgiveness of sin and entrance into heaven is an idea far too simple. That one man (even the Son of God) could die on a piece of wood on a nondescript hill in a nondescript part of the world and thereby determine the destiny of every person who has ever lived—it seems ridiculous! It allows no place for man's merit, man's attainment, man's understanding, or man's pride. To those who are in the process of perishing, the whole message is absolute nonsense.

But to us who are being saved, who are in the process of living, growing in our understanding relationships with God, with ourselves, and with others—the message of the gospel is perceived as the power of God. Why? Because it had the power to change *me*.

Knowledge is not evil, as a scalpel is not something evil but good in the hands of a surgeon using it for what it was designed. So it is with knowledge. When we need the technical knowledge and skill that science has to offer and was designed to offer, it is a blessing of God. Wisdom speaks of the skill in knowing the right thing to do in producing a quality life. Knowledge is accumulating information, but wisdom is the understanding which produces living.

Are you willing to believe God's wisdom for every area of your life?

REVERSE, NEUTRAL, FIRST GEAR

Remember therefore…and repent and do …
—Revelation 2:5

Wisdom is the discernment to do what is right—to do what produces the greatest quality of life for you and for those around you. Wisdom produces goodness for you.

So why isn't there more goodness around? Because the wisdom of God is consistently passed over. Why? Because at first appearance it seems weak. That's the paradox of God's wisdom.

Do you have a habit of passing over the wisdom of God because you don't trust it yet?

Do you know something God has said about something you are into…and you think He really doesn't know what He's talking about?

For instance, what He says about: *revenge* (Romans 12:17-21); *forgiveness* (Luke 17:3-4); *lawsuits* (1 Corinthians 16:8); *divorce* (Matthew 19:6); *purity* (1 Thessalonians 4:3).

(1) *Why* do you think what He says is so ridiculous? Who or what supports that thought? *(Family? Friends?)*

(2) *What* are you getting out of believing it's so ridiculous? Do you see this as your last chance at independence from God? Is it a matter of maintaining your individuality?

(3) Some have said that the basis of all neurosis and sin is the avoidance of legitimate pain. Legitimate pain produces good in us (Romans 8:28-29). Are you running from legitimate pain? (Whenever we do, we only run into illegitimate pain.)

Look at Revelation 2:5, and think *Reverse; Neutral; First Gear* — (1) remember, (2) repent, and (3) do.

THE MIND OF CHRIST

We have the mind of Christ.
—1 Corinthians 2:16

What does Paul mean here by saying, "We have the mind of Christ"?

Perhaps it's best understood by the way the same word *mind* is used in Luke 24:45—"Then He opened their minds to understand the Scriptures." We can understand the Scriptures as Christ understands the Scriptures.

Does this mean we can know and understand everything? Deuteronomy 29:29—"The secret things belong to the Lord our God, but the things revealed belong to us and to our sons forever, that we may observe all the words of this law."

Does it mean we don't need teachers? Ephesians 4:11-12—"And He gave...some as pastors and teachers, for the equipping of the saints for the work of service."

Does it mean our study of the Bible will not be hard work? 2 Timothy 2:15—"Be diligent to present yourself approved to God as a workman who does not need to be ashamed, handling accurately the word of truth."

Do you realize what we have in the Bible? *The revelation of the very thoughts and purposes of God!*

Do you want to know them?

Do you want to grow in them?

Theodore Roosevelt, the man who said "Speak softly and carry a big stick," also said, "If a man is not familiar with the Bible, he has suffered a loss which he had better make all possible haste to correct."

IN THEIR MIDST

I do not ask Thee to take them out of the world...
They are not of the world, even as I am not of the world.
—John 17:14-15

How do you feel when you're around unbelievers?
Comfortable, you say? How comfortable?
Uncomfortable, you say? How uncomfortable?

Some Christians have treated the unbeliever as
someone diseased, and have separated themselves
from him. But Paul says, "Prove yourselves to be
blameless and innocent, children of God above reproach *in the midst* of a crooked and perverse generation, *among whom* you appear as lights in the world."
Are you "in the midst" of unbelievers? Are you
"among" them, so your light can shine and bring
glory to God?

How do people outside the faith perceive you?
What are you communicating to them? How do they
interpret you? Do you devalue them without your
even knowing it?

Try understanding them—In your actions and words
and manner, communicate this: "What you believe
and feel is important to me."

Try accepting them—Are your relationships with
unbelievers conditional? Communicate this: "You are
important to me for no other reason than that you are
you, a creation of God."

Try involvement with them—Communicate this: "I
am interested in what you are interested in."

We live with the tension of being called to identify
with others without being identical to them. We can
still affirm the good and care for the hurt, without con-
doning the bad.

LAWSUITS

It is already a defeat...that you have lawsuits with one another.
—1 Corinthians 6:7

Christians in Corinth were going to court against each other. Paul asks, Why look to the unrighteous—those without a relationship with God—to tell you what is right in God's sight? And is this what we want unbelievers to see about Christ's body—that we can't even resolve our own problems? Jesus laid out a better way for resolving our conflicts (Matthew 18:15-17). Yet there is still "a more excellent way." Paul says, "Why not rather be wronged?" (1 Corinthians 6:7). Jesus chose this way Himself, enduring injustice.

Does this mean a Christian should never be found in a courtroom? Even Paul, when he had been falsely accused before a Roman governor, declared, "I appeal to Caesar"; he stood upon his natural rights as a Roman citizen and insisted his case be heard in the imperial court. Paul tells us, "If possible, so far as it depends on you, be at peace with all men" (Romans 12:17-19). After giving such guidelines for our personal relationships with each other, he goes on: "Let every person be in subjection to the governing authorities" (13:1). God has established government to protect and serve us. That is why we are to pray for those in positions of great responsibility. There will be times when must go to court, for God has provided divine protection through the government. But even then, our purpose in court is to glorify God, not to gain selfish advantage. Remember Matthew 6:33? A Christian's primary concern is not to protect his possessions or rights, but to protect his relationship with his Lord and with his fellow believers.

ALCOHOLISM

…nor drunkards…shall inherit the kingdom of God.
—1 Corinthians 6:10

Do you carry a prejudice against the alcoholic? Do you hate him? He already hates himself, and tends to project that hatred onto others. His guilt perpetuates his drinking. What can you do to help him?

Paul says, "Restore such a one in a spirit of gentleness; each one looking to yourself, lest you too be tempted" (Galatians 6:1).

If you're an alcoholic, here's how you can turn away from your sin.

YOU MUST:
(1) Admit it.
(2) Stop drinking all alcohol. There is only one answer to alcoholism: total abstinence, forever.
(3) Admit you are unable to change by yourself.
(4) Turn it over to God and be willing to do whatever He asks of you.
(5) Look at your own defenses.
(6) Forgive those around you and stop blaming them for your problem.
(7) Seek forgiveness from those around you.
(8) Forgive yourself.
(9) Have a support group to talk about what is hurting you, and remove the delusions you carry.
(10) Begin to let God fill you with His truth of your worth, acceptance, and forgiveness.

"You were washed…you were sanctified…you were justified in the name of the Lord Jesus Christ and in the Spirit of our God" (1 Corinthians 6:11).

WITH ALL YOUR MIGHT

Whatever your hand finds to do,
verily, do it with all your might.
—Ecclesiastes 9:10

Be devoted to life. Learn that God is good by enjoying the good He's given you. Then you'll be able to trust Him in the darkest times.

And be devoted to the Author of life! Give Him thanks continually for His good gifts.

Now's the time to get on with it—with life! Enjoy life by *doing the significant*—by doing what's important with your life. Work hard at it! As Jim Elliot said, "Wherever you are, be all there!"

This is what Jesus was referring to in John 9:4—"We must work the works of Him who sent Me, as long as it is day; night is coming, when no man can work."

Life means doing the significant; another way to say it is *doing the ministry*—serving God by ministering to others. (It's not just a job.)

The time to do the significant for God is *now*—on this side of the grave. For when death comes, the days of opportunity will have passed.

The grief you endure, the mysteries of the presence of evil, the common fate of death for all—let none of these be obstacles to dedicating yourself to the significant work of God.

If you're elderly, I urge you especially to think about this. Of all people, you should be the first to be working for the Lord, not the last. If your days on earth are coming to an end, don't go on vacation now.

THE POWER OF FRIENDSHIP

Two are better than one because they have a good return for
their labor. For if either of them falls, the one will lift up his
companion... If two lie down together they keep warm... And if
one can overpower him who is alone, two can resist him.
—Ecclesiastes 4:9-12

Commitment to relationships is a fast fading concept among us. One observer has called us "a nation of strangers."

Of course, there's a down side to relationships, a cost to friendship: the loss of independence, the cost of listening, the cost of adjusting to another's lifestyle and having to consult another's feelings, the cost of keeping faith with another's trust.

But the foundational truth is that it's better not to be alone. It's better to have a friend. Solomon has much to say about this friend in Proverbs: He'll be committed to you (18:24, 27:10); he'll be honest with you (27:6,17); he'll have counsel for you (27:9); he'll protect your feelings, not trading on your affection (27:14). When you are and have this kind of friend, you'll enjoy three great blessings from God which Solomon outlines in Ecclesiastes 4: assistance in time of failure, comfort in time of need, defense in time of danger. And if the companionship of two is better than one, the addition of another is even better: "A cord of three strands is not quickly torn apart" (4:12). The sum of the whole is greater than its parts. From this comes great strength against attack, and that's why marriage is based upon covenants made to a third party—to God.

In this life, you're going to need a little help from your friends. Do you have them in place?

FOSSILIZED

*A poor yet wise lad is better than an old and foolish king
who no longer knows how to receive instruction.
For even though he was born poor in his kingdom,
he has come out of prison to become king.*
—Ecclesiastes 4:13-14

Age and position are not guaranteed advantages. This poor lad is claimed to be wise, and the aged king is foolish. Why is he foolish? He "no longer knows how to receive instruction."

Sometimes having age and position only fossilizes one's self-will. There's more prestige to protect. By not receiving instruction, you no longer have the protection that comes from the counsel of others who have gone before...

"A wise man will *hear* and *increase* in learning" (Proverbs 1:5).

"A man of knowledge increases power. For by wise guidance you will wage war, and in abundance of counselors there is victory" (24:5-6).

"Do you see a man wise in his own eyes? There is more hope for a fool than for him" (26:12).

Age and position are the last excuses for not growing and changing. The natural course of things, if history repeats itself, is that you reach the pinnacle of human glory, only to be stranded there alone.

As we grow older, the danger is to grow less teachable. The mind grows narrow and the waistline broader, instead of the other way around.

The reason it's hard to remain teachable is that it becomes harder to say you were wrong.

Are you a student? Do you seek counsel? Do you have good counselors in your life?

TO WIN THE LOST TO CHRIST

The tongue of the wise makes knowledge acceptable.
—Proverbs 15:1

Some of us have more zeal about soul-winning than others. And some of us have more zeal than tact. As the old saying goes, "If we don't use tact, we'll lose contact."

Do you have a plan, a strategy for winning people around you to Christ? Or does even the thought of it run cold water through your veins?

How do we witness? Is there a plan of wisdom that makes the knowledge of the gospel acceptable?

The apostle Paul had one. How do we communicate the gospel to people to whom it seems so alien? Part of Paul's plan, as he says in 1 Corinthians 9, was communicating the gospel *through self-denial.*

"Though I am free from all men," Paul said, "I have made myself a slave to all, that I might win the more" (1 Corinthians 9:19). Paul was free to enjoy what God created to be enjoyed, and to be concerned only about what pleased God, not man. *But,* he says, I have chosen to convert my freedom into slavery—literally, "I enslave myself."

This word speaks of a freely chosen servanthood, as Jesus speaks of in Matthew 20:26—"Whoever wishes to become great among you shall be your servant."

This is a mentality of stewardship, a mindset that says, *I care what others truly think…that is significant to me. Not that I am controlled by the prejudices of some, but rather I view myself as a servant of all.*

TO WIN THE LOST TO CHRIST

I have made myself a slave to all,
that I might win the more..
—1 Corinthians 9:19

Paul said the reason for his chosen servanthood was "that I might win the more"—more people into the kingdom of God than he could have won by acting otherwise.

"To the Jew," Paul said, "I became as a Jew, that I might win Jews; to those who are under the Law, as under the Law" (9:20). Paul knew that Jewish traditions and regulations had nothing to do with his relationship with God—but it had much to do with his relationship with the Jews. For Paul, these legal restraints had become "love restraints"—to win the Jew to Christ.

This was wisdom. This is building bridges without having to compromise. Is it wisdom to attack a man's religious background to win him to Christ? Maybe you will win an argument—but is that what we're after?

The rule in sharing the gospel with nonbelievers: Don't attack what they believe; be sensitive to and respectful of their beliefs.

Paul was also willing to live like a gentile when he worked among gentiles. "To those who are without law I became as one without law...that I might win those who are without law" (9:21). He adds, "though not being without the law of God, but under the law of Christ." Paul did not violate God's moral laws (the Ten Commandments). Compromise was not the issue; personal preference was.

TO WIN THE LOST TO CHRIST

I have become all things to all men, that I may by all means
save some. I do all things for the sake of the gospel,
that I may become a fellow partaker of it.
—1 Corinthians 9:22-23

How far do you go in order to win someone to
Christ? At times the line must be drawn, but too often
we draw the line too soon—and win no one to Christ.
Where is the line? A good guideline is this: When do I
destroy my credibility with others by trying to relate?
Paul says he wants to be "a servant of all," not just a
servant of one kind of people.

How adaptable are you? "To the weak I became
weak," Paul said, "that I might win the weak" (9:22).
These were those whose conscience still could not be
freed to enjoy the full gospel, the freedom in Christ to
receive all things from God to enjoy, without the en-
tanglements of manmade religiosity. Paul's commitment was to curb his own freedom—to not do certain
things around certain people. Even if his own conscience was free and grateful to God for everything,
he would not cause others to go against theirs.

Are you interested in what's important to others?
Do you care about the fact that *they care* about these
things? We must be sensitive to and respectful of the
conscience of others. Some call this work of establishing relationships with nonbelievers "pre-evange-
lism." Some call it "building bridges" to carry truth
over later. If a person is offended by God's Word or
biblical principles as they are carried out in the
church, that's his problem. But if he is offended by
me, it is my problem—a problem of my love.

TO WIN THE LOST TO CHRIST

I run in such a way, as not without aim.
—1 Corinthians 9:26

It's easy to say we ought to do these things Paul speaks of. But are we serious enough for some *self-control?*

Our sinfulness resents restrictions. It is one thing to know what needs to be done, and another to do it, to live it out. Paul could be successful because he *wanted* to be successful. "Those who run in a race all run, but only one receives the prize" (9:24).

For Paul, the race is *winning people to Christ*, and every Christian who will pay the price of personal discipline will run and win. We do not compete against each other, but against common obstacles. "Run in such a way that you may win," Paul says (9:24). Be serious about this.

The committed athlete "exercises self-control in all things," Paul said (9:25). This self-control is mastery over yourself—the ability to do exactly what you deeply desire to do, to make choices that move you toward your goal of winning others to Christ.

Paul changes the picture from racing to boxing: "I box in such a way as not beating the air; but I buffet my body and make it my slave" (9:26-27). Paul knew that his biggest obstacle was himself. Thus he buffeted himself. He made his body do what he wanted it to do: Win people to Christ.

For most of us, our bodies reign over us. We are their slaves. Our bodies decide when we eat, when we sleep, when we get up. But for the athlete in training, and the effective Christian soul-winner, he leads his body, rather than the other way around.

DRAW NEAR TO HEAR

Guard your steps as you go
to the house of God, and draw near to listen
rather than to offer the sacrifice of fools;
for they do not know they are doing evil.
—*Ecclesiastes 5:1*

When you come into God's house, "guard your steps," Solomon says. Be aware of what it is you are going to do and why you are going to do it.

The purpose of the house of God (the temple, in Solomon's case) is to be a place of worship. And the first priority in coming to worship is to come with the intent to listen. We draw near to hear. You go to the house of the Lord to listen, not to tell God what He ought to be doing.

The Hebrew word for *listen* has a double force—it means to pay attention, and thus *to obey*. The alternative is to offer up "the sacrifice of fools," Solomon says: empty worship; rituals without meaning.

What was the purpose of offering a sacrifice, anyway? It was to bring you into communion with your God. The offering was to remove whatever it was that blocked that communion. The offering brought forgiveness, because it was accompanied with a contrite heart expressing thanksgiving.

Worship begins with our mouths closed and hearts and ears open to listen, with the anticipation of obeying.

Samuel asks, "Has the Lord as much delight in burnt offerings and sacrifices as in obeying the voice of the Lord? Behold, to obey is better than sacrifice, and to heed than the fat of rams" (1 Samuel 15:22).

KNOW THE QUESTION

*Do not be hasty in word or impulsive in thought to bring up
a matter in the presence of God. For God is in heaven
and you are on the earth; therefore let your words be few.*
—Ecclesiastes 5:2

As we come before God to start asking for things, Solomon says, "Don't be hasty in word, and don't be impulsive in thought." The Hebrew rendering is, "Don't rush to open your mouth, nor hurry your heart."

Before you speak…think! What is it you really desire to bring before your God?

"God is in heaven and you are on the earth." That doesn't mean God is millions of miles away. It means that God is God and you are not. You are not his peer. Remember what humility is all about.

Here's a riddle: What is it that God has never seen, but you and I and other people see it every day? (A clue: " 'To whom then will you liken Me that I should be his equal?' says the Holy One"—Isaiah 40:25).

Therefore, Solomon says, "Let your words be few." Jesus also warned about "many words" in prayer (Matthew 6:7).

What is it you really want to express to God? What is the one thing you are most concerned about? If you aren't sure about the exact request—how can you listen for the answer? Listen for the answer by first knowing the question.

"And in the same way the Spirit also helps our weakness; for we do not know how to pray as we should, but the Spirit Himself intercedes for us with groanings too deep for words" (Romans 8:26).

TIME AND CHANCE

I again saw under the sun that the race is not to the swift, and the battle is not to the warriors, and neither is bread to the wise, nor wealth to the discerning, nor favor to men of ability; for time and chance overtake them all.
—Ecclesiastes 9:11

The path to success is not always the way we think. These five assets appear to be everything you would need to guarantee success: "the swift" are those who are quick to see and grab opportunities; "the warriors" are the strong, the tough, the competitive; "the wise" have good sense; "the discerning" are the shrewd, the meticulous; and "men of ability" are those trained and educated. But these human abilities do not guarantee success. Ultimately, success or failure depends on something else.

"Time and chance overtake them," Solomon says. *Time* is the same word used by Solomon in Ecclesiastes 3:1—"There is an appointed time for everything. And there is a time for every event under heaven." *Chance* here means "an occurrence," something that happens, an event. But this context gives it an interesting twist. Time and chance are paired because they both have a way of taking matters suddenly out of our hands. God permits the good and bad to happen in our lives—but He is is more interested in our responses to them than He is in the events themselves. He knows He can take *any* event that occurs and still produce good out of it.

The issue, then, is this: When you fall down, what do you fall back on? When you've done all you can do, followed every success formula, and it still doesn't come off—what do you do?

TEST THE SPIRITS

Test the spirits to see whether they are from God.
—1 John 4:1

"Discerning" is another way of saying you are careful of what you believe to be true. "Deceived" is another way of saying you haven't been. Faith without discernment can be like driving a race car without a steering wheel; you don't know where you're going, but you're headed there fast.

The Bible is filled with warnings about the deception and confusion caused by false teachers. Satan from the beginning has attacked God's truth ... and does it through those who claim to be teachers of God's truth.

"Stop believing every spirit," John is saying. Stop placing your confidence, your trust, in anyone and everyone. Our tendency is to believe what someone says if we like him. Faith naturally moves to being in people rather than in truth. John didn't say "people" in this verse, but "spirits." People are influenced by spirits, and John says not everything out there in the spirit world is good. Just because something appears to be supernatural does not at all mean it's good. "Test them," John says.

How do we test them? It comes down to what they say about Jesus Christ. "Every spirit that does not confess Jesus is not from God; and this is the spirit of the antichrist" (4:3). The attack of evil spirits is always against the One whom Satan fears more than any other, the One who will cast Satan and all his angels into the lake of fire. If the spirits fail on this one issue — Who is Jesus Christ, and what did He do on the cross — they are influenced by antichrist spirits.

BETWEEN THE EARS

BLESSED ARE...
the poor in spirit... those who mourn... the gentle...
those who hunger and thirst for righteousness...
—Matthew 5:3-6

What happens when we get between a rock and a hard place has a lot to do with what's happening between our ears. Our reactions to life come from the way we really *think* inside. Let's not talk about values, about practices, about behaviors, until first we talk about *thinking* — our attitude.

In His teaching in the Sermon on the Mount, our Lord wants to help us think right, because He knows we have to think right to be able to *do* right. Thinking is basically our self-talk, what we tell ourselves. And we believe what we tell ourselves. Even if we lie to ourselves we believe it. If you keep saying, "You're dumb, you're dumb, you're dumb," you'll soon start thinking you're really dumb.

That's why we must tell ourselves truth, because our thinking—what we tell ourselves—is the source of our attitudes about things. And from our attitudes come our actions and all the different activities we fill our lives with. The whole thing begins with, "How do you think?"

We're a holy people. God says so. That means we're set apart from the rest of the world to be used by God. Therefore we must think distinctively. That's why in these blessings called the Beatitudes, Jesus wants to make sure we're *thinking right* about what it is that makes life worth living.

What are you telling yourself? What's your self-talk like these days? *What are you thinking?*

ON SEXUAL INTIMACY

This is the will of God, your sanctification;
that is, that you abstain from sexual immorality.
—1 Thessalonians 4:3

Remember God's design for sexual intimacy? "For this cause a man shall leave his father and his mother, and shall *cleave to his wife;* and they shall become one flesh" (Genesis 2:24). Sexual intercourse is to come only when the two have become one in God's sight, in marriage.

In speaking to this issue, I want to follow the pattern of 1 Thessalonians 5:14—"Admonish the unruly, encourage the fainthearted, help the weak."

If you are *unruly* — if you know what God says about sexual purity but don't care, because your desire for pleasure is more powerful than your desire to follow Christ—I want to admonish you from Scripture: "Cleanse your hands, you sinners; and purify your hearts, you double-minded.... Humble yourselves in the presence of the Lord, and He will exalt you" (James 4:8-10).

If you are *weak*—you want to do what is pleasing to God, but don't know how—I want to help you: How do you abstain from sexual immorality? What qualities will keep you from stumbling? Look carefully at the list in 2 Peter 1:5-11, and the guarantee there against stumbling.

And if you are *fainthearted*—the temptations to fall are great, but you're hanging in there—I want to encourage you: Keep remembering what motivates us to purity: the resurrection of Jesus Christ. He is very much alive, and we will see Him face to face concerning all of this. Speak to Him now, and ask for His help.

COMING CLEAN

Therefore, having these promises, beloved,
let us cleanse ourselves from all defilement of flesh and spirit,
perfecting holiness in the fear of God.
—*2 Corinthians 7:1*

We have God's attention, His focus, upon us: He has promised, "I will be a Father to you, and you shall be sons and daughters to Me" (2 Corinthians 6:18). He says of His people, "I will dwell in them and walk among them; and I will be their God" (6:16). As His children, we listen to what He desires for His own: "Do not touch what is unclean" (6:17). "Like the Holy One who called you, be holy yourselves also in all your behavior; because it is written, 'You shall be holy, for I am holy'" (1 Peter 1:15-6).

"Therefore," Paul says, "let us cleanse ourselves from all defilement of flesh and spirit" (2 Corinthians 7:1). The Greek word here for "cleanse" is where we get our word *catheter*. It means to draw out damaging fluids. "Defilement" comes from the root meaning "to smear something with filth." The defilement of flesh represents the drives for immediate pleasure that leave only smears of filth and scars of pain; the defilement of spirit represents the doubts begging to become unbelief as they gnaw at our faith.

We cleanse ourselves from these defilements by "perfecting *holiness* in the fear of God" (7:1). To be holy—set apart for God's use—does not mean being better than anyone else; the goal rather is being better able to be used by God to *serve* anyone else. We do it "in the fear of God," realizing He is bigger than our capacity to understand, letting Him be God, and not shaming Him by our constant doubting.

THE INTEGRITY OF GIVING

This is to your advantage…
—2 Corinthians 8:10

Giving is an issue of integrity.

Paul told the Corinthians, "I give my opinion in this matter" (2 Corinthians 8:10). If it's just his opinion, does that mean we ignore it? Is his opinion credible? It is inspired, as much as anything Paul said. Paul calls it his "opinion" because he wasn't giving the Corinthians a command; rather, this is wisdom, good counsel—"this is to your advantage," he added. If you do it, he was saying, it should be because you *want* to, not because you *have* to.

And his counsel was this: A year earlier the Corinthians had begun their collection for the saints; because they felt the Lord led them to do it. And if God had led them into it back then, why would God change His mind now? "Finish doing it also," he said (8:11). Complete what you committed to, "that just as there was the readiness…so there may be also the completion of it" (8:11).

Good intentions that go unmatched by the deed are hurtful to people, and are dishonored by God because they demonstrate an unfaithful steward. "Little children, let us not love with word or with tongue, but in *deed* and in *truth*" (1 John 3:18).

If we say "Jesus is Lord," then He possesses everything we own, everything we are, everything we can produce—for He possesses us. We're not in bondage to anything. In giving, we simply administer what He has given us.

It comes down to *integrity*: Are we who and what we claim to be?

A DEBT IS OWED

See that you abound in this gracious work also.
—2 *Corinthians 8:7*

Your giving, Paul said, "is not for the ease of others and for your affliction, but by way of equality" (2 Corinthians 8:13). It is not to ease the suffering of others by adding to yours. It's not giving it all away and leaving yourself destitute. Rather, it's an issue of equality. Giving is not a one-sided matter. Equality means "two sides even, alike, balanced." It means, "your abundance being a supply for their want, that their abundance also may become a supply for your want, that there may be equality" (8:14). Does that mean "Scratch my back and someday I'll scratch yours"? Is it a form of financial insurance? Or is it "Christian communism"—everything shared equally?

In our Lord's parable of the talents in Matthew 25, the master didn't give equal amounts to each of his servants. Paul says the whole point of stewardship is *free will*, not command or law. The point is this: A debt is owed. The material possessions which God has given directly to you—this is your abundance; the spiritual possessions which God needs to give to you through others—this is your deficiency. We need each other. An exchange can be made, and that's the communion of the saints.

God is the great equalizer. Paul quotes Exodus 16:18—"He who gathered much did not have too much, and he who gathered little had no lack." Manna gathered by someone who had more than he needed had a strange way of shrinking; manna gathered by one who didn't get enough had a strange way of expanding. So it is with our stewardship.

IN THE SIGHT OF ALL

*We have regard for what is honorable, not only in the sight of
the Lord, but also in the sight of men.*
—2 Corinthians 8:21

Paul was very concerned about ministers and ministries being above reproach. It was not an encumbrance to him; he wanted to remove any opportunity for anyone to call his integrity into question, and taught this standard to the churches. He told Titus that an elder in the church "must be above reproach as God's steward" (1:7). The word translated "above reproach" is *anegkletos*, "one not called into question." In a similar instruction in 1 Timothy 3:2 ("An overseer... must be above reproach"), the word is *anepilempton*, meaning "one not to be taken hold upon."

Paul's personal practice was one of "taking precaution" to avoid accusations of evil (2 Corinthians 8:20). It was not enough to just do right "in the sight of the Lord"; he also recognized the importance of the *appearance* of doing right—"also in the sight of men" (8:21). As Charles Hodge put it, "It is a foolish pride which leads to a disregard of public opinion." God sees our hearts; men must see that we are honest.

Paul demonstrated his precaution for the sake of integrity in the matter of the collection for the saints. For this work in Corinth he sent his trusted partner, Titus, along with two unnamed men. One had "fame in the things of the gospel" (8:18); the churches had confidence that his zeal was to bring glory to God, not himself. The other man was one "whom we have often tested and found diligent in many things"—in other words, whatever he committed himself to, he did.

Are these your standards as well?

THE PRINCIPLE OF INCREASE

He who sows sparingly shall also reap sparingly;
and he who sows bountifully shall also reap bountifully.
—2 Corinthians 9:6

Why do you think the issue of money and giving is so sensitive to most of us? One reason is the abuse we feel from people begging for our bucks. We get bombarded with every kind of gimmick under heaven to try loosening our money from our pockets. "Give a dollar a day and keep the devil away."

Another reason: We want a certain quality of life—and by giving something away, aren't we giving up a portion of that quality? If I always focus on others' needs, will I have enough for my own? Our fear is that we won't be able to pay for the things that bring us the quality of life we want. In the words of C. S. Lewis, "For many of us the obstacle to charity lies not in our luxurious living or desire for more money, but in our fear—a fear of insecurity." That's why money is so important to us—and why we're threatened by anyone or anything that might be after it.

Paul reminded the Corinthians that they had slacked off in their giving. The reason: "covetousness" (2 Corinthians 9:5). They wanted to help, all right—to help themselves. Their desire was "more and more for me." Paul reminded them of the Principle of Increase, which is how giving becomes a great blessing to the giver. God designed grain to be sown and to yield its return; He designed the same with money. Money is not to be thrown away, but invested where there will be a return—to you and to Him!

Little investment, little increase; larger investment, larger increase.

THE PRINCIPLE OF INTENT

Let each one do just as he has purposed in his heart;
not grudgingly or under compulsion;
for God loves a cheerful giver.
—2 Corinthians 9:7

The Principle of Increase reminds us that faithful stewardship brings more abilities, more influence, more resources. *But can't this be abused? What if I give just to get more for myself?*

That's why there's a second principle: the Principle of Intent. We're not to give "grudgingly"—which means "from grief," being sorry about letting it pass out of our hands. And we're not to give "under compulsion"—from feeling the pressure to give. Giving is not to be legalistic. Paul says, "God loves a cheerful giver"—the Greek word is *hilaros*, from which we get "hilarious." We're give with joyful *freedom*, expressing our love and faithfulness.

God loves for my giving to be of faith. The intention is not "I want more for me," but "I want more responsibility of stewardship so I can communicate more of my love and faith in Him."

Paul continues: "And God is able to make all grace abound to you" (9:8). God will give you "all sufficiency in everything"—that is, He'll give everything you need. Is this so you can burn it up on yourself? No, Paul says it's so "you may have an abundance for *every good deed*" (9:8). God gives the increase of your stewardship so you can see Him use you in the lives of others—to help, to encourage, to strengthen, to enlighten in the faith. God will put these gifts in our hands *if He can trust us to use them!*

Can He trust you?

THE PRINCIPLE OF INVESTING

He scattered abroad, he gave to the poor,
his righteousness abides forever.
—2 Corinthians 9:9

Paul quotes this passage from the Psalms to tell about the godly giver: the person who scatters the seed of his resources because he is concerned about what concerns God. And what concerns God is the suffering of people, both physically and spiritually. The godly person gives to help relieve that pain. The picture is of scattering seed—sowing. Sowing is not throwing money away. Sowing is investing in a harvest, investing in what God is doing in people's lives.

How do we know how much of our money should be scattered, and how much is God's provision for our own household? Paul says, "He who supplies seed to the sower and bread for food, will supply and multiply your seed for sowing and increase the harvest of your righteousness" (2 Corinthians 9:10). God supplies both the "bread for food"—the food for you —and the "seed for sowing" for others. And note which one is increased!

How can you know which is which? You must first know what you need for bread to live on. That includes long-range planning for retirement, life insurance, your children's schooling, future planned purchases, even vacations—in other words, a budget. How else can you know what God has increased for seed money to invest?

And what is this "harvest of your righteousness" (9:10)? Jesus said, "By this is My Father glorified, that you bear much fruit" (John 15:8). It is to see the grace of God *in* you and *through* you—for His glory.

THE REAL ISSUE

God loves a cheerful giver.
—*2 Corinthians 9:7*

In the Old Testament we find both required giving and freewill giving. God commanded Israel to "bring the whole tithe into the storehouse" (Malachi 3:10)—to withhold it was to "rob God" (3:8). This was the tithe—*ma aser* in Hebrew, meaning "one-tenth part"—and not the freewill offering. According to Mosaic law, a tenth was required to be given to support Levites and priests, those who ministered for God over Israel. The Jews also understood a second tithe (a tenth of the remaining nine-tenths) to be set apart for the religious festivals as described in Deuteronomy 12. It didn't stop there; Deuteronomy 14 tells of a third tithe every third year to provide for the poor, the fatherless, and widows. These tithes were clearly specified for every Israelite, whether believer or nonbeliever. All were obligated to give a total of about twenty-two percent of their income. This was Israel's national tax. Above this was their freewill giving—whatever they desired to give the Lord as an expression of thanksgiving.

In the New Testament, Paul tells us to pay our taxes (Romans 13), but he and all the apostles shun any mention of tithing. Not one word of Jesus favored it—His only references to the tithe were derogatory (Luke 11:42, 18:12; the only other New Testament reference is a purely historical one in Hebrews 7).

In the New Testament—and for us—the real issue is *stewardship*, not tithing. It is not, "One-tenth is God's and the rest is mine." No, *it all belongs to God*—and is entrusted to me for faithful stewardship.

FOR THE SERIOUS INVESTOR

Do not lay up for yourselves treasures upon earth...
but lay up for yourselves treasures in heaven.
—Matthew 6:19-20

We invest to get a return, and few things burn us more than being ripped off.

Our investments affect everything about us. What you value is what you think about, and what you think about is what you become. If you want to know what you're becoming, take a look at your checkbook. Take a look at your career. What's important to you?

Jesus says, If you're going to do some serious investing, I have a few warnings: Beware of moths, beware of rust, beware of thieves.

The security of your investments is His point. Investments on earth can wear out, be eaten away, be stolen from you. Investments here, no matter how profitable, are transitory, perishable.

What are the best investments for the greatest returns? *Investments in the lives of people.*

However God leads you to do so, investing in people creates a treasure that will not wear out, be eaten away, or ever be stolen from you. It's an investment that will be converted to praise from the lips of those who have been given the peace with God stored up in heaven for you to reap in eternity.

"Where your treasure is," Jesus says, "there will your heart be also" (6:21). That's another way of saying, "Choose to treat something precious, and it will become precious to you." Where I invest my time, energy, money—to this I will be drawn! It will affect my passion and attitude toward everything in life.

ONLY ONE MASTER

The lamp of the body is the eye;
if therefore your eye is clear, your whole body
will be full of light. But if your eye is bad,
your whole body will be full of darkness.
—Matthew 6:22-23

Jesus takes a part of the body and shows how one thing affects the whole thing.

Through your eye, light enters the body. Just about everything you do has to do with being able to see. People who have lost their sight understand this; they have to develop other faculties to compensate.

Jesus is saying, When your eye is right, your heart is right. But if "the light that is in you is darkness, how great is the darkness!" (6:23).

What you deeply desire, what you have a passion for, will be directly tied to what you are investing in. It will affect the way you look at the world. When you sacrifice for something, that something becomes special.

You can't be cross-eyed about this. Jesus says, "No one can serve two masters; for either he will hate the one and love the other, or he will hold to one and despise the other. You cannot serve God and mammon" (6:24). You can't be equally devoted to both. One will be used to serve the other. Either we use "mammon" (money) to serve God, or we use God to try to get blessed with money. (Do you remember Satan's question: "Does Job fear God *for nothing?*")

A good description of a man's god is the power in whom he will trust. "In God We Trust" is still on our money. Or should it read, "In Money We Trust"?

GOOD FATHER, GOOD GIFTS

Ask, and it shall be given to you; seek, and you shall find;
knock, and it shall be opened to you.
—Matthew 7:7

Do you believe God is good, and that He desires your good? If so, don't be afraid to *ask* Him for what is good. Then don't get discouraged when the goodness doesn't seem to flow your way; *seek* and *knock* for the good you asked for. *Asking* is your response to a need or desire. *Seeking* is asking plus acting—you look for what you're asking for. *Knocking* is asking plus acting plus persevering. (Notice the increase in intensity: We value what we seek more highly than what we ask for; and we value most what we've sacrificed for.)

God knows the best time to answer. There are times when the waiting and the trusting bring about a greater good for you than merely the answer to your request.

And when the answer does come, accept the gift of that good from the hand of God.

Accept the gifts that come from God as *Creator*—harvest, babies, food, life—things we receive whether we pray or not, whether we believe or not. He sends the rain from heaven upon all, He sends His sun to rise on the evil and good alike.

But the gifts from God as our *Father* are different. God does not give salvation to all alike, but only to those who call on Him. For "everyone who calls upon the name of the Lord will be saved" (Acts 2:21). The same applies to the other "good things" which Jesus says the Father gives His children. For these gifts we must ask, seek, and knock.

O TASTE AND SEE

The Lord is gracious and merciful...
The Lord is good to all.
—*Psalm 145:8-9*

God is good, and as David reminds us, God's goodness means the giving of *mercy* and the giving of *grace*.

Mercy is His protection—He does not give us the bad which we deserve.

Grace is the giving of the good which we do not deserve.

God is good. "Good and upright is the Lord" (Psalm 25:8). "O taste and see that the Lord is good" (Psalm 34:8). "For the Lord is good; His lovingkindness is everlasting, and His faithfulness to all generations" (Psalm 100:5).

God is good means *God is for you!* "If God is for us, who is against us? He who did not spare His own Son, but delivered Him up for us all, how will He not also with Him freely give us all things?" (Romans 8:31-32).

God is good, and God is the source of all that is good. "Every good thing ... is from above, coming down from the Father of lights" (James 1:17).

God's goodness is *benevolence* as opposed to *violence* — He secures the good for us, not the bad.

God's desire is to secure for you your happiness and well-being. And if you trust Him that this is true *...it will affect the way you pray!* When we begin to understand that a good God is going to respond to our prayers with goodness—with the best gifts for our well-being—we begin to understand prayer.

We begin to be *not afraid to ask.*

RECEIVING, RESPONDING

What man is there among you, when his son
shall ask him for a loaf, will give him a stone?
—Matthew 7:9

Part of understanding how to pray is to understand how to receive.

Jesus paints a picture: A father asks his son for
bread; will the man give him one of those limestone
rocks on the shore that looks like a loaf of bread? "Or
if he shall ask for a fish, he will not give him a snake,
will he?" This would be to violate him spiritually:
Under Jewish law, snakes were to be abhorred
(Leviticus 11:12).

Instead of listing all the kinds of things God is
going to give us, Jesus does the reverse and tells us
what God is *not* going to give us: anything that would
harm us physically or spiritually. "If you then, being
evil, know how to give good gifts to your children,
how much more shall your Father who is in heaven
give what is good to those who ask Him!" (7:11).

God gives "what is good," and only that which is
good, no matter how much we beg for otherwise.
This word "good" here is *agatha,* meaning the things
which evoke a state of well-being and happiness.

If we believe this—then the goodness we receive
from our heavenly Father will be seen in our responses to the requests that others make of us.
"Therefore," Jesus says, "however you want people to
treat you, so treat them" (7:12). Jesus says, Let what
constitutes well-being for you be the standard you
use for the well-being of others who ask of you. "For
this," Jesus says, "is the Law and the Prophets"—as
in Matthew 22:37-40: Love God, and love people.

THE TURNSTILE

The gate is wide, and the way is broad that leads
to destruction, and many are those who enter by it....
The gate is small and the way is narrow that leads
to life, and few are those who find it.
—Matthew 7:13-14

Here is piercing truth: There are not hundreds of options. There are only two. Two gates. Two ways. Two destinies. One gate is wide, and "many"—most —go through it; the other is narrow, and few will find it. We all reach a crossroads, and must choose which of the gates we will enter.

All religions of this world are "in order to" faiths —individuals gaining enough merit "in order to" go to some heavenly experience. For these faiths, one word describes their essence: *Do!* But the Christian faith is a *therefore* faith. Jesus has already finished the work of providing a way to God by paying the debt for our sin on that cross...*therefore* we are accepted by and in Jesus. The word is not *Do*, but *Done!* That's what makes the way narrow, the gate small. The gate is like a turnstile—only one at a time, responding in personal faith. This is no groupie deal. And no baggage is allowed. The wide gate lets you bring all the baggage you want: selfishness, self-indulgence, self-righteousness. There is no self-denial. That's why so many will always go after the self-made religions.

Are you still stuck in the turnstile? Or do you know you have committed your life to following Christ? Did you hear the gospel—that Jesus paid the debt for your sin? Did you enter the narrow gate, leaving all baggage behind, trusting only what He did for you on that cross?

SIMPLE, BUT NOT EASY

If anyone wishes to come after Me,
let him deny himself, and take up his cross,
and follow Me. For whoever wishes
to save his life shall lose it; but whoever
loses his life for My sake shall find it.
—Matthew 16:24-25

Jesus said, "The gate is small, and the way is narrow that leads to life" (Matthew 7:14).

Few will find the narrow gate...because who's into self-denial? There isn't a cheap-and-easy way to ensure entry into heaven. God's way into heaven is remarkably *simple,* but it's not *easy*—it's never easy to trust someone else more than you do yourself. Salvation comes only by trusting Jesus alone, and what He has done.

To trust self is eternal suicide, for it leads "to destruction" (Matthew 7:13). The word is *apoleia,* "total ruin and loss."

In one city's daily newspaper, a reader wrote this in a letter after hearing Billy Graham preach the gospel: "I am heartily sick of the type of religion that insists my soul (and everyone else's) needs saving—whatever that means. I have never felt that I was lost. Nor do I feel that I daily wallow in the mire of sin, although repetitive preaching insists that I do. Give me a practical religion that teaches gentleness and tolerance, that acknowledges no barriers of color or creed, that remembers the aged and teaches children of goodness and not sin. If in order to save my soul I must accept a philosophy as I have recently heard preached, I prefer to remain forever damned."

So be it.

FRUIT

*They will not endure sound doctrine; but wanting to have
their ears tickled, they will accumulate for themselves
teachers in accordance to their own desires,
and will turn their ears away from the truth.*
—2 Timothy 4:3-4

Jesus said, "Beware of the false prophets, who come to you in sheep's clothing, but inwardly are ravenous wolves" (Matthew 7:15). What is a false prophet? Anyone who lies about what God has said. There will always be a market for them, because people know what they want to hear.

They come "in sheep's clothing," Jesus says. They aren't trying to impersonate sheep; they're trying to impersonate the shepherd, who wore woolen clothing. They want to lead, not follow. They want to appear as caring and warm as a shepherd. "Such men," Paul says, "are false prophets, deceitful workers, disguising themselves as apostles of Christ" (2 Corinthians 11:13). And they're *sincere*, of course. "Evil men and impostors will proceed from bad to worse, deceiving and being deceived" (2 Timothy 3:13).

How do you spot them? Jesus says (in Matthew 7:16), "You will know them by their fruit"—by the outward expression of the life within. "Every good tree bears good fruit; but the bad tree bears bad fruit" (Matthew 7:17).

Look at your own life: Do you see good fruit— "The fruit of the Spirit is love, joy, peace, patience, kindness, goodness, faithfulness, gentleness, self-control" (Galatians 2:20)? Do you see evidence of a change, evidence of growth?

MAKE IT CERTAIN

I never knew you. Depart from Me.
—Matthew 7:23

If someone claimed to be a Christian and later bags the whole thing, did he lose his salvation, or is he still saved? Has he got "fire insurance"? Is he protected by his past confession of faith, or has this guy lost it? The answer is neither: The guy is lost not because he lost anything, but because he never had anything. John writes about people like that: "They went out from us, but they were not really of us; for if they had been of us, they would have remained with us; but they went out, in order that it might be shown that they all are not of us" (1 John 2:18).

A Gallup poll reported that more than half of all Americans claim to be Christians. Does our culture around us give evidence of that? In the end, many who claim to be Christians will hear Jesus say that He *never knew* them, for they never knew Him as their Lord.

"I never knew you," He will say. "Depart from Me, you who practice lawlessness" (Matthew 7:23). *Lawlessness* is the habit of indifference to the law, the commands of Jesus. A disciple who has a relationship with Jesus as Lord cares about and attempts to carry out the wishes of His Lord.

You say, *Are you questioning my salvation?* No, I'm not—but *you* should. Paul says, "Test yourselves to see if you are in the faith; examine yourselves!" Peter said, "Be all the more diligent to make certain about His calling and choosing you" (1 Peter 1:10).

Does He know you as His disciple…because you know Him as your Lord?

THE DILEMMA OF TRUTH

*And there is salvation in no one else; for there
is no other name under heaven that has been given among men
by which we must be saved.*
—Acts 4:12

The favorite question of most antagonists to Christianity — on a talk show or on the street — is this: "How can you say Jesus is the only way?"

It's such an emotional powder keg because Christians are perceived as thinking we're better than others, more spiritual than the Muslim, the Hindu, the Buddhist, or anyone else. Are we a glorified bigot club, some kind of private fraternity with a spiritual racial clause? Why is *Jesus* such an issue? Why can't we just agree with believing in God?

Because it isn't what we think, or even desire to think, that's the issue; the issue is, What do the Scriptures say? "For there is one God, and *one mediator between God and men,* the man Christ Jesus" (1 Timothy 2:5). "Truly, truly, I say to you, I am the door... if anyone enters through Me, he shall be saved" (John 10:7-9).

If we have integrity of faith, we can't say we follow Jesus and then affirm anything and everything else. We are faced with the dilemma of truth. If Jesus is the Son of God and says there is no other way to God, we can't change what He said with a popularity vote. (How often in history have the masses been right when it comes to spiritual truth?)

Now as always, it comes down to this: What do you believe about Jesus Christ?

THE GIFT OF PARENTS

Every one of you shall reverence his mother and his father.
—Leviticus 19:3

Honor your father and your mother.
—Exodus 20:12

To *reverence* is to fear to shame in any way the one revered, and to have as an ambition to please the one revered.

To *honor* is to weigh heavily, to consider something of great worth to you.

This attitude of reverence and honor for parents has some practical ramifications. For example, the instruction in Proverbs 1:8—"Hear, my son, your father's instruction, and do not forsake your mother's teaching."

Remember Proverbs 22:6? "Train up a child in the way he should go." Part of our blessing from parents —something only our parents can give in their unique way—is a deep understanding of who the child is and what he or she is really like. Their insight into their children's character can have a lot to do with their future success—or lack of it. This is why a son or daughter should listen to them speak, especially when they give counsel on the choice of a future mate.

Many people can pray for us and advise us, but I believe God has entrusted parents with special privileges and responsibilities to bless their son, their daughter.

Paul notes that the command to honor parents was the first of the Ten Commandments with a promise: "That it may be well with you, and that you may live long on the earth" (Ephesians 6:3).

A BLESSING FOR YOUR CHILD

They were bringing children to Him
so that He might touch them...
And He took them in His arms
and began blessing them,
laying His hands upon them.
—Mark 10:13-16

Here's a blessing you can give to the children in your life...

The careless abandon, the love of liberty, and the joy of life are the blessings of youth. May God add to you that discipline by which a successful life is lived, and by which character is achieved.

May you learn that just as steam is effective when contained in a cylinder, so will your youthful energies be effective when they are controlled.

May God protect you physically. May He throw around you the golden aura of His protecting presence.

May God be your Teacher and your Guide. May God send into your life the specially chosen companions and friends He wants you to have.

May God save you from any costly blunder that would haunt you down through the years.

Be filled now with God's joy — for that will enable you to meet life and find the satisfaction which only He can bestow.

PUT IT IN GEAR

Everyone who hears these words of Mine
and acts upon them, may be compared to a wise man
who built his house upon the rock....
Every one who hears these words of Mine
and does not act upon them, will be like a foolish man
who built his house upon the sand.
—Matthew 7:24-26

Jesus here is not contrasting professing Christians with those who do not profess Christ. On the contrary, this is family business.

Both the wise man and the foolish man have heard "these words of Mine." Both are reading their Bible. Both hear the sermons. Both buy Christian books. They profess to know Him. For now, you can't really tell the difference between them, for the deep foundations of their lives are hidden from view.

But later, when the storm comes...

This word *wise* in 7:24 depicts one who is thoughtful, cautious in character, thinking things through. To lay the foundation for his house (his life!), he dug down deep to the rock—the "rock" is who Jesus is and what He has said. The foolish man, one who is "unthinking," built his life on sand. He was like those whom Paul described as "always learning, and never able to come to the knowledge of the truth" (2 Timothy 3:7).

The difference between the two is made up of four words: "and acts upon them" (Matthew 7:24). There is no substitute for obedience in the formula for following Christ:

Discipleship = Hearing + Doing

Hearing alone keeps truth in neutral. You have to put it in gear for it to have any effect in your life.

WORK'S REWARD

Here is what I have seen to be good and fitting:
to eat, to drink and enjoy oneself in all one's labor
in which he toils under the sun.
—Ecclesiastes 5:18

This is *not* the Epicurean philosophy of "eat, drink, and be merry, for tomorrow we die." Our enjoyment includes our *labor*, even our "toils under the sun"— hard work. Of all the things you've thought to be grateful for, hard work probably isn't one of them.

Can hard work be enjoyable? Absolutely, when you know you're creating something good, as when your Father in heaven created, and later looked back and said, "It is good!" God enjoys what He worked to create.

To not work hard is a canker that brings misery to a life. The biblical term for such a person is "sluggard." The sluggard, Solomon says in Proverbs, is hinged to his bed (26:14); he will not begin things (6:9-11) or finish things (19:24); his excuses are ridiculous: "There's a lion outside" (22:13). And "all day long he is craving" (21:26). The sluggard hasn't learned that labor is a gift from God's hand. God has designed us to work—and to feel good about our work.

"For this" continues Solomon in Ecclesiastes 5:18, "is his reward"—his share or portion. Most of us run right by it and miss the whole thing every time. The rewards are in the blessings of the labor and the fruit of our work. "For every man to whom God has given riches and wealth, He has also empowered him to eat from them and to receive his reward and rejoice in his labor; this is the gift of God" (5:19).

LIFE IS NOT A THREAT

God keeps him occupied with the gladness of his heart.
—Ecclesiastes 5:20

To be grateful is not natural for us. If it were, the apostle Paul would never have written, "In everything give thanks, for this is God's will for you in Christ Jesus" (1 Thessalonians 5:18).

Our mindset is that we have the "right" to just about everything. At the core of us is this simple, observable attitude: If I have a need for something, I expect to have the need met. So we get angry or depressed when it isn't met.

Solomon says, "Here is what I have seen to be good and fitting: to eat, to drink and enjoy oneself in all one's labor" (Ecclesiastes 5:18). Our pursuit in life is not the accumulation of wealth and possessions, but rather the capacity to be able to enjoy them, no matter how great or small. It is of God for us to be joyful by enjoying what He has given. We may not have as much as others have, but we can learn to enjoy all of what we do have. And the key to enjoying it is to learn what gratefulness is all about.

"This is the gift of God," Solomon says (5:19). When we begin to see everything as a gift—and not as a prize we have won or a need we expect to have met—there will be gratefulness. And where there is gratefulness, there will be joy. Jesus commanded us not to be anxious for tomorrow (Matthew 6:34). Have we learned that life is not a threat, but a joy?

We need times of reflection to know what we're grateful for. Slow down today and think about it. You may find yourself with a wave of gratefulness flowing over you.

THE MOTIVATING FORCE

*Let us continually offer up a sacrifice of praise to God,
that is, the fruit of lips that give thanks to His name.*
—*Hebrews 13:15*

The writer of Hebrews says that gratefulness is the motivating force behind our worship.

It isn't that God is insecure without it. It has something to do with *something about us.*

Thanksgiving, Paul says in 1 Thessalonians 5:18, is God's will for us. Why?

Thanksgiving in everything is the key to joy. The experience of joy is all about well-being, a sense of security, a deep rest, the absence of fear. It's enjoyment! The absence of thanksgiving is what makes joy fade. It's God's design for us to give thanks lest any of our joy slip away.

Solomon speaks of one who "will not often consider the years of his life, because God keeps him occupied with the gladness of his heart" (Ecclesiastes 5:20). The man who has learned to enjoy his life is not wrapped up with how many days he has left. God makes him sensitive to the goodness of his life, and fills him with the satisfaction of contentment. Have you asked for that contentment lately?

The fear of death belongs to those who have not learned to delight in today, as they worry about how much time they have left.

Have you ever been asked the question, "If you knew you had only one week to live, what would you do?" Luther was quoted as saying, "If I knew Jesus was to return tomorrow, I would still plant an apple tree today." God wants us to be happy about what He has given us to do.

YOUR ÉCLAIRS

You are the salt of the earth…
You are the light of the world.
—*Matthew 5:13-14*

We are God's salt to retard corruption, and His light to reveal truth. Others watch the way we live…

as salt— They see what we *don't do,* and they figure there must be a good reason. They just may take the warning unto themselves.

as light— They see what we *do,* and they figure there's a good reason. They just may follow our leading.

The issue, then, is *credibility.* Without it, the salt is tasteless and the light is dim. There is no influence. With it, you have *that unique difference that affects!*

The issue in credibility is *no compromise.*

What is compromise? *Impurity.* What is impurity? *Being double-minded.* What is being double-minded?

To borrow an illustration from a friend, being double-minded is "éclairs in the refrigerator"—being on a diet and putting them there until later, when you can justify eating them.

What are the "éclairs" in your life—your compromises with what God has commanded you?

Can God trust you?

The issue is to have a saltiness in my life and an effervescent shine. Because of who I am and what I do and don't do, I will influence others. They'll see I am different, and though they may attack that difference, *it's the very thing that will draw them to Jesus Christ.*

THE ONLY SALT

You are the salt of the earth; but if the salt
has become tasteless…it is good for nothing anymore,
except to be thrown out and trampled under foot.
—Matthew 5:13

It is impossible to follow the norms of the kingdom of God in a purely private way. We can't live our lives in splendid isolation. In Matthew 5:13-16, Jesus unfolds this truth by using two metaphors, two pictures—of salt and light—to show how His disciples leave their prints on the world around them. In both illustrations, the *you* is emphatic and plural: "You, the children of the kingdom, are the only salt of the earth"; "You, the children of the kingdom, are the only light of the world."

In ancient times, salt was primarily a preservative. We are to be salt—adding preservative, flavor—by influencing the world. What keeps this from happening? Why does salt lose its saltiness? Salt, by its nature, cannot become anything other than salt. It can lose its saltiness only when something else is mixed with it. When Jesus spoke of salt, He might have glanced southward. Most of Palestine's salt came from the shores of the Dead Sea, but it was often contaminated with gypsum and other minerals, leaving the taste flat or even repulsive. At that point it became no more than road dust.

We are uniquely different from the world, and it's this difference that both preserves and flavors the life of those around us. Contamination is compromise which wipes out that influence, making us ineffective, useless. Our impurity negates our effect on others.

A CERTAIN WINSOMENESS

You are the light of the world.
A city set on a hill cannot be hidden…
A lamp…gives light to all who are in the house.
—Matthew 5:14-15

Jesus said He was "the light of the world" (John 9:5). Here He says that we are too. Paul adds, "You are light in the Lord; walk as children of light" (Ephesians 5:8).

Jesus says, "Let your light shine before men in such a way that they may see your good works" (Matthew 5:16). "Good works" in Greek is formed from the two words *agathos*, defining a thing as good in quality, and *kalos*, meaning something not only good, but attractive. There must be a certain winsomeness in Christian goodness.

There is something attractive when you see men and women who will not rob their employers by being lazy on the job. There is something winsome when you see a person who is the first to help a colleague in difficulty, and the last to barb a criticism. It's a beauty recognized by all when people help others to be successful, and do it with transparent integrity.

The light is *truth in action*. "For with Thee is the fountain of life," David prayed; "in Thy light we see light" (Psalm 36:9). "Thy word is a lamp to my feet and a light to my path" (Psalm 119:105). "For God, who said, 'Light shall shine out of darkness,' is the One who has shone in our hearts" (2 Corinthians 4:6).

When the world sees the children of the kingdom living lives of obedience—the world sees light.

THE GREAT TRADE-OFF

> *Beware of practicing your righteousness before men*
> *to be noticed by them; otherwise you have no reward*
> *with your Father who is in heaven.*
> —Matthew 6:1

Imagine what it would be like to be out on a golf course on a beautiful day, and to hit a hole in one… *and no one was around!*

When we finally do something right we want the world to know. We want a pat on the back, a good word of encouragement—anything, as long as it's now. Postponed encouragement seems like no encouragement at all. Is it wrong to want reward?

Jesus doesn't condemn the idea of receiving rewards. In fact, He guarantees it. (We need to be careful about "pseudo-spirituality": making something more spiritual than what Jesus taught.) Jesus' warning is: Don't blow the reward from the Father. From whom do you want to receive your reward? Who'll give you the greater blessing: God later, or man now?

Seeking it from man is what I call "The Great Trade-Off," which ultimately becomes "The Great Rip-Off."

Take our giving, for example. With a little satirical humor, Jesus spoke of those who would "sound a trumpet" when they gave. We may not be that blatant. But isn't it interesting how we accidentally let it be known what we've done? "Yes, God led me to help so-and-so…" Jesus says we have forfeited receiving anything from God, for we have been paid in full.

When we're tempted to seek notice…what can temper it? *An act of murder!* Kill the flesh! Purposely do that which antagonizes the flesh. *Do something you know is right … and do it in secret.*

PREPARE FOR AGING

Even to your old age, I shall be the same…
I shall bear you, and I shall deliver you.
—Isaiah 46:4

Throughout Ecclesiastes, Solomon has honestly laid out reality, not pulling any punches. As the last chapter opens, he writes about getting old. He tells us aging is not fun, so don't expect it to be.

"Remember also your Creator in the days of your youth" (12:1). This *remembering* is not just taking note of God, but acknowledging His presence. To make it through your aged years, start now by getting your perspective straight on who God is and who you are. Youth is the time to prepare for aging. Do it "before the evil days come and the years draw near when you will say, 'I have no delight in them'" (12:1).

Solomon speaks of the cloudy skies of winter, and a great household in decline (12:2-5). The picture is a sad one of gradual dissolution, every part in decay, hastening to ruin, of failing desire and fading pleasures, and the imminence of death. We have come to the final struggle: "The silver cord is broken and the golden bowl is crushed, the pitcher by the well is shattered and the wheel at the cistern is crushed" (12:6). Here is the moment of death: "The dust will return to the earth as it was, and the spirit will return to God who gave it" (12:7). Solomon repeats his theme: Life is vaporous, and passes so quickly. At times it appears senseless, but there is One who makes sense out of it all: "Remember…your Creator…"

Aging can be horrible. We must be prepared for it, and there are things *to learn now:* Where is your worth? Where is your hope?

PEACE...OR THE PIECES

Be at peace with all men.
—Romans 12:18

Murder can be with the hands or with the lips. Both can equally kill the sacredness of the life God has given. From our mouths come either the spirit of death or the spirit of life. Either we recognize the image of God in others out of reverence for God, or we attempt to destroy it all, to the pleasure of the adversary.

Taking a dim view of the image of God affects *every relationship we have!* Life is relational. Everything in life was created to be enjoyed, but not as a solo. You see the beauty of a sunset...then go running around trying to find someone else to enjoy it with you. People—and relationships with people—can be a taste of heaven. They can also be a taste of anything but heaven. They can become one crisis after another. It takes much wisdom to know how to be at peace with others, be it your brother or your enemy.

At times there's something invigorating about getting angry. It's a catharsis to blow off steam, release some stress, show others you're not a wimp: *I can get mad just like the other guy.* It *just feels good* to rip—until you turn around and see the pieces of people left on the floor. When you go back to heal the damage caused by your fit of ego, you begin to understand something Paul was saying, something that otherwise seems like weakness: "If possible, so far as it depends on you, be at peace with all men. Never take your own revenge..." (Romans 12:18-19).

How important is it to you to "hang in there" with people—in peace?

CHANGES

And now, little children, abide in Him,
so that when He appears, we may have confidence…
—1 John 2:28

Life changes.

And you'd better be changing with it!

Life does not get easier. Life changes gets more complicated with every passing year. Things just don't fall into place for us all the time. Like it or not, we tend to move through identity crises from time to time, and that's when we start filling up our frustration tanks in a hurry.

You really can't make good sense out of everything you do unless you can make some good sense out of *you*. There's nothing wrong with asking yourself again, when everything is said, some basic tires-on-the-road questions:

Who am I? I am a child of God. I want to carry out His righteousness. (Are these *your* answers?)

Where am I going? I am going to the kingdom of God in glory.

What am I doing here? I am being prepared to be a servant in His kingdom, and that is why I do what I do.

We know we exist—and we ask the deep questions about our existence—because there is a God who made us and has placed that knowledge of Himself within us. "That which is known is evident…for God made it evident" (Romans 1:19).

My point of reference in all this is my Creator. If anyone is going to identify who I am and what I'm all about, so I can know if the things I am doing make any sense at all, it will be the God who created me.

THIS IS THE PROMISE

*And this is the promise which He Himself
made to us: eternal life.*
—1 John 2:25

When did Jesus make that promise? "For God so loved the world, that He gave His only begotten Son, that whoever believes in Him should not perish, but have eternal life" (John 3:16). "Truly, truly, I say to you, he who hears My word, and believes Him who sent Me, has eternal life" (John 5:24).

If we're going to ask the question *Who am I?*—we can't limit it to a life span on earth, if indeed there's more to it than that. The Bible says existence does not end at the grave for *anyone.* There is an eternal life and an eternal death. "For the wages of sin is *death*" (Romans 6:23). This word for death, *thanatos*, does not mean the end of existence, but only the end of life. What is life? "This is eternal life," we read in John 17:3, "that they may know Thee, the only true God, and Jesus Christ whom Thou hast sent." *Thanatos* is to be separated from that life...to exist in separation from the One who made you. We are born spiritually dead (Ephesians 2:1), and when this body dies we will be confirmed in that separation from God (Hebrews 9:27).

But the promise of Jesus is eternal life. Life is relational, and it begins with a relationship with God. Eternal life is to spend eternity, the rest of your existence, with Him. And He wants you to be with Him! "Let not your heart be troubled...for I go to prepare a place for you...that where I am, there you may be also" (John 14:1-3).

FUTURE CONFIDENCE

The anointing which you received from Him abides in you,
and you have no need for anyone to teach you…
His anointing teaches you about all things.
—1 John 2:27

John is not saying we don't need teachers (he is teaching us here himself). What he's saying is that we need no one to clarify for us who Jesus is, no one to add to or take away from the fact that He is the Messiah and God the Son. The "anointing" we have received is the Holy Spirit, and the Spirit is the One who causes us to recognize this truth about Jesus.

"And now, little children, abide in Him" (2:28). "Abide" is to "remain"—remain in that which you know to be true. (You can know something is true and still rebel against it.) Since you know, because of the anointing of the Holy Spirit upon you, that Jesus is the Christ, the Son of God, then continue in the fact that He is your Savior and Lord; you are *forgiven*, and you have *submitted*. In so doing you can "have confidence and not shrink away from Him in shame at His coming" (2:28).

In the next verse, John bottom-lines it: "If you know that He is righteous, you know that everyone also who practices righteousness is born of Him." We know God is righteous. He knows and does that which is right; He is the One who establishes what is right. We can then come to recognize His children *by the way they respond to Him.* Those who are born of Him—those who have gone from death to life, from no relationship with God to God as their heavenly Father — will carry out His righteousness, His will.

THIS MAKES SENSE

See how great a love the Father has bestowed upon us,
that we should be called children of God; and such we are.
—*1 John 3:1*

"See how great"—the word means "how foreign."
Behold how foreign a love this is—that God would
identify *us* as His children.

Yet we *are* His children, and thus carry out His
righteousness. We do things *his* way, not the world's
way. Therefore the world—people who bought into
the world system—can never quite figure us out.
They do not understand us because they *cannot* understand us—because they do not know Him. "For
this reason the world does not know us, because it
did not know Him" (3:1).

John continues, "Beloved, now we are children of
God, and it has not appeared as yet what we shall
be." He doesn't know what eternity for us will entail.
As Paul said, "Things which eye has not seen and ear
has not heard, and which have not entered the heart
of man, all that God has prepared for those who love
Him" (1 Corinthians 2:9). *BUT*, John says, this I do
know: "When He appears, we shall be like Him, because we shall see Him just as He is" (3:2). We will
have glorified bodies like His glorified body. He will
"transform the body of our humble state into conformity with the body of His glory" (Philippians 3:20).

This hope of the future motivates me for the present. "Everyone who has this hope fixed on Him purifies himself, just as He is pure" (1 John 3:3). This
"hope," this expectation of our future, puts things
into perspective as to what I ought to be doing, and
what I'm really all about. *This is what makes sense.*

TOTALLY INCOMPATIBLE

No one who abides in Him sins…
No one who is born of God practices sin.
—1 John 3:6,9

I know I can't ignore God, but I still struggle with sin.
What should I do?

It begins with the lust to do it. "Each one is tempted when he is carried away and enticed by his own lust. Then when lust has conceived, it gives birth to sin…" (James 1:14-15.

Confess it, don't defend it.

Why does it sometimes take us so long to confess sin? For when we do, God "is faithful and just to forgive…and to cleanse" (1 John 1:9).

It comes down now to choices you make. You have no excuse to sin. For a Christian, it's downright rebellion. It's an attitude you have, a habit you've fallen into, a response you haven't addressed.

Sin and saints don't mix well. Without dealing with it, sin will cause you to slide back. Sin will stop your spiritual growth.

What are you going to do about it?

The point John makes in 1 John 3 is that *sin is totally incompatible with the Christian faith.*

John brings sin down to its basis: "Sin is lawlessness" (3:4). Lawlessness is not breaking the law (that's "transgression"), but rather total indifference to the law; in this context, to God's Law. Sin is incompatible with the Law of God.

The saint will not be indifferent to who God is, nor to what God said.

WALKING RIGHTEOUS

And you know that He appeared in order to take away sins;
and in Him there is no sin.
—1 John 3:5

The first coming of Jesus was to provide a way for us to come into the kingdom of God. His second coming will be to bring the kingdom of God to this earth. John says Jesus came the first time "to take away sins" (John 1:29). *But it didn't work. Look around you. Sin is still all over the place.*

Go back to the word John uses for "take away." It's *airo*, "to lift up and carry away." It wasn't sin itself that was lifted away, but *the consequences of sin* for those who believe in Jesus Christ. We are released from the domination of sin and the judgment of sin. We are "justified as a gift by His grace through the redemption which is in Christ Jesus, whom God displayed publicly as a propitiation in His blood through faith" (Romans 3:24-25). Jesus could be the propitiation for our sin because, as John tells us, "in Him there is no sin" (1 John 3:5).

Here's the logical deduction that follows: "No one who abides in Him sins; no one who sins has seen Him or knows Him" (3:6). The one who habitually practices indifference to God and to what He has said has not seen or come to know who God is.

John continues, "The one who practices righteousness is righteous, just as He is righteous" (3:7). Jesus is the model, and He has removed all excuses for us not to follow His example. He walked righteously in an earthly body—so that we can also.

THE END OF ALIENATION

The one who practices sin is of the devil.
—1 John 3:8

The one who is indifferent to what God says is not a child of God, but still a child of the devil. To ignore God is to give deference to the devil.

"The Son of God appeared for this purpose: that He might destroy the works of the devil" (1 John 3:8). Jesus, the Son of God, came to destroy, to "dissolve," the devil's works. What are they? In Ephesians 6:11 Paul calls them the "schemes of the devil." These are the devil's plans to alienate us from God, to make sure we never worship the One who created us. Jesus destroyed that alienation by providing a way back to God. He made alienation from God now *a choice to be made*, no longer *a bondage to remain in.*

"No one who is born of God practices sin, because His seed abides in him; and he cannot sin, because he is born of God" (3:9). It is impossible for a child of God to be able to continue in sin, in indifference to God, because of the Holy Spirit implanted within us (3:24). His Holy Spirit convicts us of sin (John 16:8), and "bears witness with our spirit that we are children of God" (Romans 8:16). There is *communication* going on here within me.

John summarizes what he is saying in 3:10—"By this the children of God and the children of the devil are obvious: Anyone who does not practice righteousness is not of God, nor the one who does not love his brother." Here's how we know who's who. It comes down to your *walk*—is it worthy, or not? Now that you know what is right, there are really no excuses for you not to live it right!

BATS, ANTS, FROGS, WORMS

Consider your calling, brethren, that there were not many of
wise according to the flesh, not many mighty, not many noble;
but God has chosen the foolish things of the world to shame the
wise, and God has chosen the weak things of the world to shame
the things which are strong.
—1 Corinthians 1:26-27

This is a command: "Consider your calling." Paul's admonishment is to open your eyes to the fact that God didn't accept you as His child because you were brilliant or wealthy, intelligent or powerful. If you are any of these, you were saved in spite of them, not because of them. For these things tend to keep people from the sense of need in their lives. It's the feeling of inadequacy that makes people aware that they have a need, and they are drawn to the truth of the gospel.

In A.D. 178 the philosopher Celsus bitterly attacked Christians with these words: "We see them in their own houses, wool dresses, cobblers, the worst, the vulgarest, the most uneducated persons... They are like a swarm of bats or ants creeping out of their nest, or frogs holding a symposium around a swamp, or worms convening in the mud." (If they were such nothings, it's interesting to me why they bothered him so.)

God's wisdom is a paradox. In human thinking, strength is strength, weakness is weakness, intelligence is intelligence. But in God's thinking, some of the seemingly strongest things are the weakest, the seemingly weakest are the strongest, the wisest are the most foolish. The paradox is not by accident, but by God's design. Christianity was, and still is, the most uplifting thing in the whole universe.

NO STRUTTING

God has chosen the things that are not,
that He might nullify the the things that are,
that no man should boast before God.
—1 Corinthians 1:28-29

So often we think, *If only so-and-so great athlete or popular entertainer or world leader would just become a Christian, what an impact it would have!* But Jesus didn't seem to think that way. He said the greatest man who had ever lived was one who had no formal education, no money or rank or political position, no social pedigree or prestige or impressive appearance; and yet, Jesus said, "there has not arisen anyone greater than John the Baptist" (Matthew 11:11).

God chose "the things that are not"—literally, "the things not existing"—which to the Greeks was the deepest of insults. These nothings would "nullify" the brilliant, the influential, the socially in — attributes which in the sight of God mean absolutely nothing.

God has done it all! The weak cannot claim the glory, for they know better—and if they don't, everyone else does. They will not rob God of what is rightfully His: "I am the Lord, that is My name; I will not give My glory to another" (Isaiah 42:8).

"That no man should boast," Paul said. There will be no strutting before God, no taking the credit, no absorbing the praise, no stealing the glory. We're insecure people inside; we boast because we seek credit, glory, and acceptance; yet inwardly we're ashamed of our shallowness.

"Let him who boasts, boast in the Lord" (1 Corinthians 1:31).

WISE, MIGHTY, AND NOBLE

By His doing you are in Christ Jesus, who became to us wisdom from God, and righteousness, and sanctification, and redemption.
—*1 Corinthians 1:30*

"By His doing..." Our salvation is "not of ourselves" (Ephesians 2:8). God initiated it, accomplished it, provided an opportunity for you to hear about it, then drew you to it. All *you* had to do was respond to love!

"You are in Christ Jesus..." You're in union with Him. In the sight of God we are tied to His Son; and thus, we're His children. Christ was the firstborn; we are adopted into the family. *We have a relationship with God because of our relationship with His Son.* And here is what the world sees in us:

We're right with life—Jesus has "become to us wisdom from God." We're given God's wisdom to replace our own. We know exactly what to do: "If you abide in My word, you are truly disciples of Mine; and you shall know the truth, and the truth shall make you free" (John 8:31-32). In Christ we are *wise*.

We're right with God—Jesus has become for us "righteousness and sanctification." We need not keep trying to get right with Him, or earn His favor. In Christ we're in a right relationship, as He desired: a father/child relationship. We're set apart and made holy, to be used by God in His plans *to do the significant.* He is changing us to be like His Son, so we can effectively do what He did. In Christ we are *mighty*.

We're right with ourselves—Jesus has become our "redemption." We have been purchased, and therefore we walk worthy. In Christ we are *noble*. We shall reign with Jesus!

Amen!

SIGNS OF LIFE

Such confidence we have through Christ toward God.
—2 Corinthians 3:4

When a doctor examines an injured man, he does not look for signs of death, but for signs of life. If he doesn't find them, he knows the patient is dead.

Life produces its own distinctive marks: purpose, worth, fulfillment, joy, peace, love, friendships, power.

Death is the absence of those marks. Instead of love there is hate. Look for joy and you'll see misery and fear. Fulfillment and worth are rather frustration and boredom. There is worry, hostility, jealousy, malice, loneliness, depression, and self-pity.

That, Paul says, is where the old covenant of the law leaves you. It's therefore a tutor to lead us to Christ and the new covenant, which gives *life*.

Jesus died in order that He might live within us. It's *His* life in us, in the presence of the Holy Spirit, that is the power by which we live a true Christian life. He places within us the deep desire and attitude to do His will.

The change in us is simply this: We begin to do the will of God because we are given the deep desire to do so! And it is not a passing "religious experience."

The presence of God will surely be seen in you, as others see the change within you.

The change is permanent. As Paul said, "He who began a good work in you will perfect it until the day of Christ Jesus" (Philippians 1:6).

Is this your confidence today?

WHY WE DO WHAT WE DO

Do all to the glory of God.
—1 Corinthians 10:31

Blind purpose is no purpose at all. How can there be significance to what we do unless we know *why we are doing it?*

Man's "chief end," according to the Westminster Shorter Catechism, is "to glorify God and enjoy Him forever." If life is designed to glorify God, what is *life?* When Jesus was praying to the Father in John 17, He said eternal life is a *relationship* with God and with Himself. Life is relational, and life is to glorify God—it all has something to do with how we relate to Him and to each other. It comes down to some basic sensitivities to each other.

"All things are lawful," Paul said, "but not all things are profitable. All things are lawful, but not all things edify" (1 Corinthians 10:23-24). This "all things" includes those practices not specifically identified in Scripture as sin. They are lawful, but not all of them are profitable, and not all edify. We have freedom in Christ, but with that freedom comes responsibility. We have to ask questions like, Is this profitable? Does this edify?

Edify means "to build." It's to build something into your life or into the life of another. What are we to build? *God's glory.* To become the kind of person God created us to be in the first place. This is at the core of spiritual maturity and the discipleship of others. "Therefore encourage one another, and build up one another, just as you also are doing" (1 Thessalonians 5:11).

WHY WE DO WHAT WE DO

Let no one seek his own good, but that of his neighbor.
—1 Corinthians 10:26

Self-interest scars your spirit; that's not how we were created to live. As Howard Hendricks says, "A life wrapped up in itself makes a very small package."

We are to seek the good of our neighbor, Paul says. And who is my neighbor? Jesus told the story of the Good Samaritan (Luke 10:29-37) to answer that question. The issue isn't so much *Who is my neighbor,* but *Whose neighbor am I?* I'm to be a neighbor to anyone in need of mercy.

This basic sensitivity to others is kindness in its purest form. "With humility of mind let each of you regard one another as more important than himself; do not merely look out for your own personal interests, but also for the interests of others" (Philippians 2:3-4). God is glorified by a basic sensitivity to others and a merciful interest in their interests.

It includes being sensitive to others' liberty. "If one of the unbelievers invites you, and you wish to go, eat anything set before you without asking questions for conscience' sake" (1 Corinthians 10:27). Don't put your personal convictions on others, especially upon unbelievers.

There is also sensitivity to others' legalism.

"If anyone should say to you, 'This is meat sacrificed to idols,' do not eat it, for the sake of the one who informed you" (10:28). Why would anyone say that to you unless he was struggling with it? Let his feelings and welfare be an issue with you. A weak conscience can have very strong feelings.

WHY WE DO WHAT WE DO

*Give no offense either to Jews or to Greeks
or to the church of God
—1 Corinthians 10:32.*

"Do all to the glory of God," Paul said. *Glory* means something worthy of praise and exaltation, something brilliant and beautiful. God's glory is everything He is—His person and personality. And it is all so good, so worthy of exaltation and praise! We can't really *give* glory to Him, but as Psalm 29 says, we can *ascribe* it to Him—to recognize and acclaim it. That is glorifying God, reflecting all that is good about Him through the way we live. Our lives either *honor* God, or *dishonor* God.

We glorify God, we honor God, by treating others as God would. With every person I meet I have an opportunity to glorify God. How? One way is *by not offending anyone*, Paul says in 1 Corinthians 10:32. The word is literally "become an offense." It means not giving others any just cause to stumble in regard to God and the gospel.

"Take care lest this liberty of yours somehow become a stumbling block to the weak" (1 Corinthians 8:9). "Determine this—not to put an obstacle or a stumbling block in a brother's way" (Romans 14:13). With obstacles and stumbling blocks we move others away from God.

Instead of being profitable, we harm unbelievers when we seem more concerned with our own interests and convictions than with theirs. And when we're insensitive to the weaker conscience of other believers, we help to sear it, teaching them to ignore the very instrument God uses to warn of harm.

THE ART OF GOOD SENSE

Wisdom is better than weapons of war.
—Ecclesiastes 9:18

It's easy to point out all the frustrations and problems of life, but there's a management maxim that says, "Don't bring me the problems, bring me the solutions." In Ecclesiastes, Solomon puts his focus on the practical solutions, the things that will help bring some sense to life.

Use good sense when it comes to…

your reputation— "Dead flies make a perfumer's oil stink, so a little foolishness is weightier than wisdom and honor" (Ecclesiastes 10:1). Something as little as an insect can foul up the whole bottle. It only takes something relatively small to spoil something relatively big — like your name.

your composure— "If the ruler's temper rises against you, do not abandon your position, because composure allays great offenses" (10:4). Don't "abandon your position" — don't run from the situation when someone's mad at you. Exercise your composure: calmness, self-possession. A calm, conciliatory spirit, not prone to take offense, goes a long way. Discretion is a virtue. Don't keep giving "a piece of your mind" to those who upset you; you'll soon run out of mind.

your success— "If the axe is dull and he does not sharpen its edge, then he must exert more strength." Have the good sense to take the time and prepare to do the job right.

"Wisdom has the advantage," Solomon continues, "of giving success." Wisdom prevents mistakes.

THE ART OF GOOD SENSE

Wisdom is better than strength.
—*Ecclesiastes 9:16*

Use good sense also when it comes to...

your mouth— "Words from the mouth of a wise man are gracious, while the lips of a fool consume him" (Ecclesiastes 10:12). Our mouth is a direct link to our wisdom, because it's a direct expression of our hearts. What we say is the acid test of wisdom. Words are the pegs by which our thoughts hang. Using good sense with your mouth means speaking words that give grace to others. That's why you were given a mouth in the first place. Jesus sets the example: "And all were speaking well of Him, and wondering at the gracious words which were falling from His lips" (Luke 4:22).

your thinking— "The toil of a fool so wearies him that he does not even know how to go to a city" (10:15). The fool may work *hard*, but not *smart*. This "not knowing the way to the city" is a proverbial saying for not understanding the most obvious of things. When you can't figure out the road map, ask for help. The issue is: How teachable are you?

your discretion— "In your bedchamber do not curse a king, and in your sleeping rooms do not curse a rich man, for a bird of the heavens will carry the sound, and the winged creature will make the matter known" (10:20). The saying "A little birdie told me" comes from this Scripture. Be careful in telling someone about your frustrations with others. Once spoken, they have a way of returning to them—and to you. It's a question of judgment.

THE VERY AIR OF HEAVEN

Love never fails.
—1 Corinthians 13:8

This word *fail* has the basic meaning of "falling," such as a flower or leaf that falls to the ground to wither and decay. The true nature of love is that it will never fall, wither, or decay. By its very nature it is eternal, permanent. Love cannot fail, for it is from the nature of God. "God is love" (1 John 4:8) — and God is eternal.

In heaven we will have no more need for faith and hope, and no more need for spiritual gifts. None of the gifts will have a purpose or place in heaven. Yet love is, and forever will be, the very air of heaven!

Love will always be there, that great worth God has placed upon us, reflected in the dimensions of love listed in 1 Corinthians 13:4-7.

Paul strengthens his emphasis by comparing love's permanence to the impermanence of the three spiritual gifts most sought after by the Corinthians. As with all Greeks, who worshiped knowledge and oration, the Corinthians loved to know and to speak of what they knew. That's why the gifts of prophecy, tongues, and knowledge were so popular among them. Paul says all three will some day cease to exist (13:8): prophecy and knowledge will each "be done away with," while tongues will "cease," literally, "cease of themselves." (Not only are these gifts temporary, Paul says, but they're also partial: "We know in part, and we prophesy in part" — 13:9).

Love, however, never fails.

I CAN LOVE NOW

But now abide faith, hope, love, these three;
but the greatest of these is love.
—1 Corinthians 13:13

Paul mentions the three greatest virtues (and notice the gifts are not mentioned): faith, hope, love. This triad comes up in Scripture again and again — in Romans 5, Galatians 5, Ephesians 4, 1 Thessalonians 1, Hebrews 6 and 10...

Faith is the heart of life. Faith is believing what God says, simply because it is God who says it. It was Kierkegaard who said the reason we find it difficult to believe is because it is difficult for us at times to obey. But our faith is what we believe to be fact, not feeling.

Hope is that which makes us live today as if tomorrow were yesterday. Others see only a hopeless end, but the Christian rejoices in an endless hope!

And so—why is *love* the greatest? It is because love encompasses faith and hope. (Remember verse 7 in this chapter: Love *believes* all things...love *hopes* all things.)

Faith and hope will be completed and have no further purpose in heaven, but love will still be there. Love is eternal...and yet it can be touched, seen, and enjoyed *now, in this life!*

Love is the one thing we will have for eternity. Therefore: What is love's significance in your life now?

As C. S. Lewis put it, "All that is not eternal is eternally out of date."

I can love *now* as I'll be loved...and this will not stop at the grave.

HE DIED, ALL DIED

*For the love of Christ controls us, having concluded this, that
one died for all, therefore all died.*
—2 Corinthians 5:14

You can't dismiss the truth … because it's not dismissable.

Paul is saying, "Our love for Christ is kindled and constantly fed by His love for us—our worth to Him." We know we have that kind of worth to Him because we've come to the conclusion that He died for *all*—you and I and everyone else are part of that "all."

Jesus agonized on the cross to His death. He died not for one man, or a few, or even several, but for *all men and women.*

"One died for all," Paul says, "therefore all died." All men died in His death. He was their substitute. Jesus Christ was God, and that is why His death replaced all others.

"Behold the Lamb of God who takes away the sin of the world!" (John 1:29).

This has got to be the hardest thing for people to understand, or to believe it could be true: He died so that they who live may live!—"that they who live should no longer live for themselves, but for Him who died and rose again on their behalf" (2 Corinthians 5:15). He died that they might no longer be self-servants, which gets empty very quickly, but that they would live as servants of Christ—and thus of others.

The point is this: Why should we become a servant of others? Because Jesus died for them. That is the perspective of the worth of people to God.

THIS TIME GOD'S WAY

From now on we recognize no man according to the flesh.
—2 Corinthians 5:16

As Christians, we have a new view of humanity. Our whole way of looking at people has undergone a change. "We recognize no man according to the flesh"—No longer are we interested only in what we can see from the outward appearance of others—their race, social status, wealth, title, opinions. We don't respond to people according to the rules the world sets up for us.

Paul said he had formerly "known Christ according to the flesh" (5:16). He had once done what he here condemns. He had formed his opinions about Him entirely according to the outward appearance of things. Paul had despised and hated Him because he judged Him as a poor, suffering man claiming to be the Messiah, the Son of the living God. "Yet now," Paul says, "we know Him thus no longer."

He continues: "Therefore if any man is in Christ, he is a new creature; the old things passed away; behold new things have come" (5:17). "In Christ" is to be in union with Jesus by the covenant of the indwelling of His Spirit. We have become "new creations." The old desires, the old plans for our lives, have passed away. New things have come: new desires, new plans, a new purpose. It's like coming out of the womb again with a new chance at life, *this time doing it God's way*.

The point: We have a new view of people, a new perspective of their worth. We know them by what God says about them—that they can be a new creation, because Jesus died for them.

MAKING THEM GREAT

He died for all, that they who live
should no longer live for themselves,
but for Him who died and rose again on their behalf.
—*2 Corinthians 5:15*

Because we believe in God, we believe in people.

We no longer live for ourselves; we live for others, to serve others, to make others great. Why make someone else great?

Because people are that significant to God. He sent His Son to die as their substitute; He gives us a whole new view of humanity and of what they can be in a new creation. And He has called us, as our higher authority, to tell people of their worth to Him.

If people are that significant to God, they had better be that significant to us—significant enough that we want to serve them and help them become great in the kingdom of God.

I call upon you now to prayerfully consider how you will serve those whom God has brought into your life. Who have you snubbed rather than served?

Begin by treating your family with that kind of respect. What can you do to make your husband or wife great? What can you do to make each of your children great? What can you do to make the people you work for and with great? (If any of these are non-Christians, believing the gospel is the first step in their path toward greatness.)

Will you make the commitment to try?

Build a bridge into each person's life by making this inner affirmation: "I am committed to your success!"

PEACE ON EARTH

We are ambassadors for Christ.
—*2 Corinthians 5:20*

"All these things," Paul says, "are from God." The entire change, the full new creation experienced by those in Christ—all this is "from God, who reconciled us to Himself through Christ" (5:18). God has removed enmity between people who were at variance with each other. God is the Reconciler (the stronger always initiates the peace in a relationship). God took responsibility to remove the problem, doing it "through Christ"—through His death as a substitute sacrifice. Until God's wrath and curse were removed, there was no possibility for change; we were aliens, enemies, cut off from God's favor and fellowship.

But now: God has given us "the ministry of reconciliation" (5:19). We are to announce to others that God is not charging our sins to us because of what Jesus Christ did on the cross. This is the gospel, the preaching of the cross. This is the greatest service to another human being—to call him or her to be reconciled to God. Anything with that purpose gives meaning to serving.

Because He has deposited with us this commission, "we are ambassadors for Christ"! As His messengers, His representatives on earth, we do not act on our own authority; what we communicate is not our own opinions or demands, but simply what we have been told to say, what we have been commissioned to say. It is God speaking through us, and we are careful to speak only what God has told us to say: that Christ bore the guilt of our sin, that we might be in a right relationship with God, our Creator.

WHY JESUS CAME

You have an anointing from the Holy One, and you all know.
—*1 John 2:20*

This "anointing" is a form of the word for *Christ*, "the Anointed One." To be anointed is to have something (usually oil) rubbed into you. We have been anointed, John says, by "the Holy One"—the Holy Spirit, "the Spirit of truth," as Jesus calls Him, who "abides with you, and will be in you" (John 14:17). Therefore, John says, because you have the Spirit, "you all know" (1 John 2:20). Know what?

We know *who Jesus is.* There's no way we on our own could recognize that Jesus is the Christ, the Son of the living God (which is why we can't convince others of that on our own). When Peter said, "Thou art the Christ," Jesus answered him, *"Flesh and blood did not reveal this to you,* but My Father who is in heaven." Recognizing Christ is not an I.Q. thing, but rather a supernatural thing revealed to you by the Holy Spirit of God.

To the world, Jesus is simply another great moral teacher. But as Napoleon Bonaparte put it, "If Socrates would enter the room we should rise and do him honor. If Jesus Christ came into the room we should fall down on our knees and worship Him."

The genuine Christian believes that—and will always believe it.

"As for you," John says, "let that abide in you which you heard from the beginning." What the church has heard from the beginning is the true gospel of Jesus Christ—who He really was, *and why He came to this earth.*

If you believe what is true, then *you are true.*

THE WORTHY WALK

Be on the alert,
stand firm in the faith,
act like men...
—1 Corinthians 16:13

Paul's closing exhortations in 1 Corinthians tell us what we are to *be*—and they simplify the worthy walk for all of us. Don't get lost in religious platitudes!

Be alert. Don't be careless, easily deceived. Watch. Be awake—spiritually awake. Be alert to the "schemes of the devil." "Your adversary, the devil, prowls about like a roaring lion, seeking someone to devour" (1 Peter 5:7). How does Satan influence a believer? To get an idea, look at his basic character (in John 8:44). Be aware of his deceptions. Paul makes it clear that spiritual beings can and will instill thoughts within us (Romans 8:16). *Don't believe everything that comes into your mind.* Test those thoughts with what the Scriptures say.

Be firm. "Stand firm in the faith"—*the* faith (it doesn't say "your" faith). Have you made up your mind about what you believe? Are you still trying to rework the Bible to fit with your way of thinking? Many do not like simple truth because it's harder to twist. Because of social pressure, we want to at least make it appear that we're Christians because we're brilliant. Paul says to decide who you want to believe and who you want to please—and be firm in it.

Be mature. "Act like men." The word speaks of courage as opposed to cowardice—the courage of conviction, the courage to obey what you've made up your mind to obey.

THE WORTHY WALK

Be strong.
Let all that you do be done in love…
be in subjection…
—1 Corinthians 16:13-16

Be strong. This word is *kratos,* "strength in action."
Where does our strength come from? God always empowers obedience. Strength comes from prayer…
faith…*doing it!* Move out with confidence, and do it!

Be loving. "Let all that you do be done in love." Behind all this alertness, firmness, maturity, and
strength, let there always be a deep respect for God's
creation. "If we love one another, God abides in us,
and His love is perfected in us" (1 John 4:12). "God is
love" (1 John 4:8). But how will the creation know
that unless God's children touch them with that respect and value? Peter said we are to always be ready
"to give an account for the hope that is in you, *yet
with gentleness and reverence*" (1 Peter 3:15).

Be submissive. Paul told the Corinthians to "be in
subjection to such men" as Stephanas and his household, who were among the first believers in the entire
province, and who had "devoted themselves for ministry to the saints" (16:15). They had served on their
own initiative. They hadn't waited to be appointed or
asked—they just served.

How are we to be submissive? A submissive spirit
is humility replacing self-preservation. Do you want
to do God's will, or to preserve your pride? Can God
use others to speak to you? Does He? Then trust Him
to do so. Give godly people who work and labor in
ministry the right to be used of God to speak to you.

THE CONCLUSION

The conclusion, when all has been heard, is:
Fear God and keep His commandments,
because this applies to every person.
For God will bring every act to judgment,
everything which is hidden,
whether it is good or evil.
—Ecclesiastes 12:13-14

Do you take God seriously?

When you can't figure Him out, you still fear Him. For either you will fear the Creator or fear the creation; it takes the greater fear to dispel the lesser fear.

God is God, and we are not. Fear Him without terror; fear Him with honor and reverence. Fear Him— and do what He says.

As it is with fear, so it is with faith: "Faith, if it has no works, is dead" (James 1:17).

We will give an account for our lives, whether or not we believe that, like it, or agree with it. Our feelings will not change the fact that we shall give an account. He "will bring to light the things hidden in the darkness, and disclose the motives of men's hearts" (1 Corinthians 4:5).

Do you take God seriously?

If you do, you'll keep His commandments.

And you'll take seriously what He said about Jesus. God Himself declared from heaven: "This is My beloved Son, with whom I am well-pleased; *listen to Him!*" (Matthew 17:5).

As I live the "now" of my life, forgetting neither what I've learned from my past nor the hope of my future, I want to understand what I can so I can know what I need to know—and do it right.

A MIND MADE UP

Daniel made up his mind
that he would not defile himself
with the king's choice food.
—Daniel 1:8

Daniel "made up his mind" to submit his will to God rather than to man.

Have you made up your mind to do the same? Have you yielded your will to God?

Most of us want to grow as we live on, for our aim is to mature. Yet change can be painful because it calls for an honest look at ourselves and an honest answer to the question, "What needs changing in me?"

We freely admit we need to exercise our bodies, educate our brains, and do anything we can to try figuring out our passions. But there's another dimension to us: our spirits. We can't continue to pretend it isn't there. If I'm thinking of growing as a whole person, aiming for maturity, there are questions I need to ask about my spiritual self.

Paul closed 2 Corinthians with a warning: "Test yourselves to see if you are in the faith; examine yourselves!" (13:5). It's a good test to take today.

Christian, if you pass the test, Paul's prayer for you is that "you do no wrong." Be strong and complete. Rejoice and don't fear. Be aiming for complete maturity. Be a whole person, a got-my-act-together person; remove the confusion, contention, and evil from your life. Be comforted. Be committed to what's important, and tolerant over what isn't. Be at rest deep within.

"The grace of the Lord Jesus Christ, and the love of God, and the fellowship of the Holy Spirit, be with you" (13:14).

YES OR NO?

When Jesus had finished these words,
the multitudes were amazed at His teaching;
for He was teaching them as one having authority.
—Matthew 7:28-29

Twelve times in "these words" which Jesus "had finished"—the Sermon on the Mount—Jesus said things like, *I say to you… But I say to you… Truly I say to you…* But never, *Possibly…* or *I think…* or *My opinion is….* The people were amazed—literally, "dumbfounded."

Jesus didn't *suggest.* He spoke with authority. He didn't use weasel words. He wasn't tentative, hesitant. Nor did He use confusing "double-speak."

The Sermon on the Mount was really a synopsis of everything Jesus taught. Here is the essence of what it means to be a believer in Jesus, a follower of Jesus. This is "the mind of Christ." He began with the Beatitudes—how people of the kingdom should think—then moved into how to demonstrate that holy thinking with holy living. He gave us God's laws as they read when written on a heart—for God is interested in your heart, what you really believe. And at the end of the sermon, Jesus had only one question: "Will you be My disciple? Yes or no?" *Yes?* "Everyone who hears these words of Mine, and acts upon them, may be compared to a wise man who built his house upon the rock." *No?* "Every one who hears these words of Mine, and does not act upon them, will be like a foolish man who built his house upon the sand."

This is not a suggestion, but a call: a clear call to be His disciple.

Will you be His disciple? Yes or no?

THE END OF THIS DANCE

Thy kingdom come…
—Luke 11:2

If there's going to be a kingdom, the first person who needs to be there is the king. Who's the king in the coming kingdom mentioned in the Bible?

He's the One coming "with the clouds of heaven" in Daniel's vision: "To Him was given dominion, glory, and a kingdom, that all the peoples, nations, and men of every language might serve Him. His dominion is an everlasting dominion which will not pass away; and His kingdom is one which will not be destroyed" (7:14). The apostle John also saw Him coming from heaven in a vision: "His name is called The Word of God…and on His robe and on His thigh He has a name written, 'KING OF KINGS AND LORD OF LORDS" (Revelation 19:11-16).

He is the resurrected Christ, the firstborn from the dead. Because of the resurrection of Jesus the King, as Paul explains in 1 Corinthians 15, there will be the resurrection of the kingdom people, and the restoration of the kingdom of God. "The earth will be filled with the knowledge of the glory of the Lord" (Habakkuk 2:14).

To pray "Thy kingdom come" is more than reciting a wishful thought, more than saying the words without real expectation that you'll ever see it happen. Most people want to believe that life as it is now will just dance on. But the Bible makes it clear: This age will come to an end, snapping shut with the coming of Jesus Christ.

The King is coming again…are you ready today?

TOPICAL INDEX

TOPICAL INDEX

TOPICAL INDEX

TOPICAL INDEX

TOPICAL INDEX

TOPICAL INDEX

TOPICAL INDEX